Morristown

MORRISTOWN

The Darkest Winter of the Revolutionary War
and the Plot to Kidnap George Washington

WILLIAM HAZELGROVE

Guilford, Connecticut

An imprint of Globe Pequot, the trade division of
The Rowman & Littlefield Publishing Group, Inc.
4501 Forbes Blvd., Ste. 200
Lanham, MD 20706
LyonsPress.com

Distributed by NATIONAL BOOK NETWORK

British Library Cataloguing in Publication Information available

Library of Congress Cataloging-in-Publication Data

Names: Hazelgrove, William, 1959– author.
Title: Morristown : the darkest winter of the Revolutionary War and the
  plot to kidnap George Washington / [William Hazelgrove].
Description: Guilford, Connecticut : Lyons Press, [2021] | Includes
  bibliographical references and index. | Summary: "The winter of 1779 to
  1780 would mark Washington's darkest hour where he contemplated the army
  coming apart from lack of food, money, six years of war, desertions,
  mutiny, the threat of a devastating attack by the British, and
  incredibly, a plot to kidnap him. Yet Morristown would mark a turning
  point"— Provided by publisher.
Identifiers: LCCN 2021010904 (print) | LCCN 2021010905 (ebook) | ISBN
  9781493056620 (hardcover) | ISBN 9781493063451 (epub)
Subjects: LCSH: Washington, George, 1732–1799. | Arnold, Benedict,
  1741–1801. | Political kidnapping—United States—History—18th century.
  | Morristown (N.J.) —History—Revolution, 1775-1783. | United
  States—History—Revolution, 1775-1783—Secret service. | United
  States—History—Revolution, 1775-1783—Campaigns.
Classification: LCC E236 .H39 2021 (print) | LCC E236 (ebook) | DDC
  973.3/3—dc23
LC record available at https://lccn.loc.gov/2021010904
LC ebook record available at https://lccn.loc.gov/2021010905

For Kitty, Clay, Callie, and Careen

The oldest people now living in the Country do not remember so hard a winter as the one we are now emerging from.
—GEORGE WASHINGTON, IN A LETTER TO THE
MARQUIS DE LAFAYETTE, MARCH 18, 1780

Unless some expedient can be instantly adopted, a dissolution of the army for want of subsistence is unavoidable.
—GEORGE WASHINGTON, IN A LETTER
TO CONGRESS, WINTER 1779

Contents

Prologue

The Road to Morristown

Like two punch-drunk fighters in the tenth round, the two countries had been battling it out for five years. The British and the Americans had seen victory vanish into the cannon smoke of sieges, offensives, retreats, and then finally the entry into the war of another power, France, that would have seemed to have tipped the scales toward the Americans. The British had begun the war with the Battles of Lexington and Concord followed by a surprising stand by the Americans at Bunker Hill, which, while technically a British victory, had shown that the Americans could fight. General William Howe took his bruised army into Boston and waited for reinforcements while the disparate colonial militias began to slowly erode from expiring enlistments, disease, and a lack of artillery to dislodge the British.

The new leader, George Washington, who arrived in May 1775 to take the reins of power, had no experience at all with laying siege and forcing an occupying army to abandon a barricaded city. Washington had been a country squire for the last fifteen years and found he was now the commandeer of an army made up of local militias and backwoodsmen, hardly an army at all. He also found out he had little gunpowder and, more importantly, no artillery with which to force the British to abandon Boston. It is here that Henry Knox, a twenty-five-year-old bookseller, would step in and, using oxen and sleds, drag 60 tons of cannons from the recently taken Fort Ticonderoga 300 miles back to Cambridge. Washington placed the cannons on the Heights of Dorchester and shocked the British with a morning bombardment that forced them to abandon the city, giving the Americans their first victory.

But General Howe struck back at New York, bringing in a mighty armada of ships and reinforcements along with Hessian mercenaries that chased Washington and his young army from Manhattan and almost trapped them on Staten Island. It was only through a masterful overnight retreat that Washington was able to keep the Continental Army alive and brought to fruition a strategy he would pursue the rest of the war, and which would become the standard for every guerilla force from the Revolution to Vietnam: hit and run. The Americans would wear the British down by never taking on the full power of the British army at any one spot, by weaving and striking back at parts of the army, winning by survival and a slow withering attrition that would bleed the British of money and men and force a reconsideration of the price they were willing to pay to hold on to their overseas colonies.

Then there was the bold strike that also became a hallmark if not a personal trait of George Washington. Crossing the Delaware River on Christmas Eve in 1776 during a terrible storm while the Hessian mercenaries were in winter camp at Trenton and Princeton, Washington scored a dramatic victory that gave the American cause a much-needed jolt in the arm and became a rallying cry for the nation. Washington's crossing of the Delaware gave the world notice that the most powerful nation on earth might not be able to quash the American rebellion so handily and a protracted war might be in the offing.

Still the British came on, and Valley Forge proved that even a renegade insurgent strategy had its limits. The American army in the winter of 1777 had no food or money with which to continue the war and took refuge in the hills of Valley Forge and what would become a Dante's hell of frozen suffering that set the bar even lower for desertions, disease, and the price men were willing to pay for freedom and liberty.

This was followed by disastrous defeats at Germantown and Brandywine, leading many to doubt Washington's abilities as a leader of the American Revolution. The Conway Cabal, led by General Horatio Gates, came close to becoming a coup to replace Washington as his own generals turned against him. The coup would fizzle when Washington became aware of the machinations, but it was telling that the forces against the revolution came from not only outside but inside Washington's inner circle as well.

The only bright spot during the dark winter of 1777–1778 was the entry of France into the war on the side of the Americans. To many, including Washington, this would seem to tip the balance in favor of the Americans. But a year and a half later the much-needed French support had not materialized, and in the fall of 1779, George Washington took his 10,000 men into winter camp at Morristown, New Jersey, after five long years of fighting. In fact, Washington had been to Morristown before. He had survived a smallpox epidemic there in 1777; then he made it through the winter of 1778–1779 in nearby Middlebrook, New Jersey, and the most brutal winter, which was 1779–1780. A final winter would be spent by troops there in 1781 even though Washington was not present.

The reason Washington preferred Morristown was the Watchung Mountains. The mountains are a thirty-mile-long, 600-foot-high range of volcanic ridges halfway between New York City and Morristown. This natural barrier was the perfect refuge for Washington's army and close enough to keep an eye on the British movements in New York.

The winter of 1779–1780 would be different from all others. It would be a brutal winter of suffering, depression, starvation, betrayal, mutiny, treason, and, incredibly, a British attempt to kidnap George Washington. As amazing as this sounds, it was part of military strategy on both sides. This did not entail killing the intended victim; there was a code of honor between officers in the Revolution by which taking a general or another officer was almost like a game of chess, with the nabbing of a top leader a real checkmate. Washington had been in support of kidnapping British general Henry Clinton in New York in 1778 and wrote, "I think it one of the . . . most desirable and honorable things imaginable taking him prisoner."[1] The British never recognized the nationalist cause of the Americans for liberty and freedom and saw it as a rogue rebellion inspired by a few inspirational leaders, George Washington being at the top of the pyramid. So, to take George Washington was to win the war.

All during the winter Washington was certain the British would attack. "Clinton is not ignorant of the smallness of our numbers,"[2] he told New Jersey governor William Livingston. "He cannot be insensible of the evils he would bring upon us by dislodging us from our winter quarters."[3] In fact, if the British had attacked, they would have destroyed the Continental Army. They did not attack, but instead enacted the bold plan to kidnap George Washington and strip the Revolution of its leader.

We are told that the worst winter of the American Revolution was spent at Valley Forge. This has been held up by history as the American Revolution's finest hour, where men suffered in silence, leaving bloody footprints in the snow, and survived to fight again in the spring. Valley Forge was a turning point if not a poster for American endurance, tenacity, and toughness, where a German general trained the soldiers and George Washington shared the awful conditions with his men and everyone emerged tougher, more determined, more American than at the start of the winter.

Books have cemented Valley Forge as one with Omaha Beach, the Death March of Bataan, and Washington crossing the Delaware. But the winter of Valley Forge was mild in comparison to other winters. Temperatures did not plummet to unheard-of levels and snowfall was normal. Indeed, it was the once-in-a-century freezing of the Hudson River two years later that brought on the plot to kidnap George Washington. But because the Revolution needed inspirational moments, Valley Forge made the cut and was handed to history to mythologize and prove once again that the American Revolution was a series of inspirational moments.

By the same token, the less inspirational moments, the true stories of survival and human failings, were pushed down and ignored by history. Morristown was one of those moments. The winter of 1779–1780 was the worst in a century and would mark Washington's darkest hour, where he contemplated the army coming apart from the combined pressure of lack of food, lack of money, five years of war, desertions, mutiny, the threat of a devastating attack by the British, and an attempt to kidnap him. When Washington and the Continental Army decided to winter in Morristown, New Jersey, there was already a foot of snow on the ground. Even Washington noted after the winter that "the oldest people now living in this Country do not remember so hard a winter as the one we are now emerging from. In a word the severity of the frost exceeded anything of the kind that had ever been experienced in this climate before."[4]

This came from the man who had suffered the terrible winter of 1776–1777, when his army had to cross an ice-choked Delaware River, and who had witnessed thousands of his men die in the freezing winter of 1777–1778 at Valley Forge. From late November to June 22, 1780, this would be home for the Continental Army. Things had not been going well. Patriots under French commander Count d'Estaing had failed to recapture Savannah or make any progress on the east coast. The British had hunkered down in New York after evacuating Philadelphia, with a stalemate developing between Washington's army and the redcoats. In 1779 the main theater of operations was in the southern United States.

Morristown was between New York and Philadelphia, with farming, mining, and timber centered in the area. Washington wrote to Congress that Morristown would provide a place "compatible with our security which could also supply water and food for covering and fuel."[5] The army settled in a mountainous area, Jockey Hollow, and soldiers went to work cutting down thousands of acres to build a virtual log house city consisting of over a thousand cabins, which each held twelve men. Washington and his staff established headquarters in the mansion of the late Colonel Jacob Ford Jr., along with his wife, Theodosia, family servants, and the Ford children. It was a full house.

The ten thousand men and Washington were in for six months of the worst suffering imaginable. As twenty-one-year-old James Thacher, an army surgeon, wrote, "We experienced one of the most tremendous snowstorms ever remembered; no man could endure its violence many minutes without danger to his life. . . . When the storm subsided, the snow was from four to six feet deep, obscuring the very traces of the roads by covering fences that lined them."[6] Morristown would be hallmarked by tremendous suffering because of the cold, but more than that, because of starvation and then, finally, a mutiny.

A soldier in the Connecticut Line, Joseph Plumb Martin, remembered, "We were absolutely literally starved;—I do solemnly declare that I did not put a single morsel of victuals into my mouth for four days and as many nights, except for a little black birch bark which I gnawed off a stick of wood, if that can be called victuals."[7]

This starvation along with the absolute brutality of the winter combined to incite a mutiny that threatened to spin out of control. As if to foreshadow this breakdown, Benedict Arnold would be tried in Morristown and found guilty of bad judgment while ruling Philadelphia and planning his much larger crime of treason. It was a time of extreme uncertainty. The narrative of men willing to endure any hardship for the cause broke down here as the army declared it had had enough, and not from the cold, but primarily from the lack of food and the failure of Washington and others to do anything about it.

Private Martin remembered how he and his fellow soldiers were "venting our spleen at our country and government, then at our officers, and then at ourselves for our imbecility in staying there and starving in detail for an ungrateful people who did not care what became of us, so they could enjoy themselves while we were keeping a cruel enemy from them."[8]

This does not fit into the Valley Forge motif of gallant suffering by stolid men who would emerge as even better soldiers at winter's end. More men perished in Valley Forge from disease, but Morristown is the real story of the American Revolution's winter of discontent for George Washington, the army, and the American Revolution itself. After a cold clear day on the 1st of January, an immense blizzard began that lasted from the 2nd to the 4th, dropping temperatures into the low 20s (though it felt colder with the high winds) and dumping four feet of snow (with drifts over six feet) on the encampment. This storm and over a dozen more over the coming months immobilized the army and stopped all supplies and information from moving along the roads. With no help from the surrounding communities in New Jersey, the army was in danger of starving and dispersing, effectively ending any resistance to the British in the northern theater of the war.

Morristown is an inspirational story, but it is also a true story of suffering in which George Washington and his soldiers in the winter of 1779–1780 reached their breaking point and the army of the fledgling republic nearly disbanded. For the British, Morristown would give them an opportunity to end the war with a knockout blow. They needed something audacious that would bring the Americans to their knees before France could enter the war in a meaningful way. The once-in-a-century cold had made life hell for the British, but the freezing of the Hudson River provided just the opportunity to end the American Revolution once and for all.

Part I

Winter

CHAPTER ONE

On the Frozen Hudson River

February 11, 1780

BRITISH GENERAL JOHN SIMCOE LOOKED ACROSS THE LONG PLAIN OF ice that tunneled into the far trees of New Jersey. The light snow on the ice was beautiful under the full moon. How amazing that the mighty Hudson River had frozen. There was no memory of this happening before. Men said that ice would form along the shore, but never had the river effectively become an ice bridge that would allow men, horses, and artillery to travel from Staten Island to New Jersey as if someone had laid out a perfect path for the invasion of George Washington's winter camp in Morristown.

The mighty Hudson was now a frozen, snow-covered expanse bisecting the heart of the young nation. There were no transportation systems except for the rivers and the rough roads hacked out of the forests. So this made a river like the Hudson a vital artery for the Americans, and for George Washington it was a buffer between his army in Morristown and the British in New York. No one would dare to cross it in winter; that is, until the worst winter in a century descended and changed what had been a moat into a bridge. And Lieutenant Colonel John Graves Simcoe saw his chance for a knockout blow.

He had lost his father at an early age; John Simcoe was the commander of the British ship *Pembroke* and lost his life in an expedition in Canada in 1759. To the son, twenty years later, looking across the Hudson River, it was one of the coldest nights he had ever experienced. The breath of the men and the horses steamed in the air like small ghosts. The horses defecated. The men swore in English and German. The blue ice of the Hudson River spread out before him and his men, with the shores of New Jersey frosted white under the full moon.

It was a clear, cold night where the temperatures saw no abatement and had already fallen to zero. The cold planet smoked with this cold. Where did it come from? The inlets and bays had frozen and the horses didn't like it, snorting blasts of steam and chafing under the men waiting for the signal to cross. But it was this cold that gave Simcoe the once-in-a-lifetime opportunity to end the American Revolution by kidnapping George Washington.

Lieutenant Colonel Simcoe looked at the other regiment of 17th Light Dragoons along with the Black Hussars. The German soldiers, wearing their distinctive uniforms of a "red jacket with white facings, buckskin breeches, blacktop boots,"[1] talked not at all. Their leather helmets glowed eerily under the lunar light, emblazoned with the skull and crossbones and the words OR GLORY beneath the death's-head. They held straight sabers and the light carbines they were trained to fire from the saddle.

The 17th Dragoons along with the Black Hussars would do the actual capturing of George Washington. The Hussars were former German prisoners known for their brutality and their distinctive uniforms of "a hussar cap and black coat with white trousers and boots of the hussar style."[2] Simcoe's own regiment of Queen's Rangers, a lightning force of elite British soldiers specializing in speed and cunning, were dressed more closely to the Hussars, with their own "hussar style cap with the crescent or half-moon insignia of the Rangers mounted on front, a green wool jacket, green trousers tucked into short boots and a sword belt over the right shoulder."[3]

The American Revolution showed how Britain depended on Hessian soldiers. The German soldiers had no love affair with Britain, but King George III had several treaties with Germany that allowed him to rent soldiers. "Hessians" has become the blanket term for German soldiers in the American Revolution, but only half of them came from the province of Hesse-Cassell. The real reason Britain needed the German soldiers was that there were only 20,000 soldiers in the British army in 1776 and they were about to invade a country 3,000 miles to the west that was massive in comparison to European countries.

Being in the British army was not an appealing proposition for most German soldiers, with poor pay and brutality from noncommissioned officers along with miserable living conditions and no chance for advancement. It gets worse. The German princes with whom England had treaties were paid by the head, much like trade in animals. The Hessians were paid the same as British soldiers, but if a Hessian was killed, then the prince received a lump sum, with the family receiving nothing. There was also a stipend for wounded men, with two wounded men equal in pay to one man killed. During the war, the brutality of the Hessians was well-known, with many blamed for raping and pillaging, but in fairness they had been promised by British officers that America was rich in plunder for the taking. In all, 30,000 Germans would serve in the Revolution.

Simcoe's plan to kidnap Washington was simple in the beginning: "March by very secret ways made more so by inclement season and to arrive near General Washington's quarters by daybreak, to tie up his horses in a swamp, and to storm the quarters and attack his guard on foot, for this purpose, his party were to carry muskets as well as swords, and he meant it to consist of eighty men."[4]

This was Simcoe's original plan, but that had quickly changed when General Wilhelm von Knyphausen and Captain George Beckwith became involved. Simcoe didn't want to think about it now, but it still rankled him that the Queen's Rangers had been relegated to a diversionary attack so that the Hussars and the 17th Light Dragoons could do the actual work of kidnapping Washington and then get back to New York before the Americans knew what hit them. But there was little he could do. Lieutenant Colonel Samuel Birch and Captain Beckwith were to be the commanders of the expedition, and to that end Simcoe comforted himself that the result would be the same, the capture of General George Washington and maybe the end of the war.

The glittering blue ice that had been cleared creaked under the combined weight of the 500 troops. Another snowstorm had delayed the kidnapping expedition by a day and Simcoe was worried the weather might still be their undoing. It had snowed so much and been so brutally cold that horses had suffocated from ice in their nostrils and men on guard had expired after just thirty minutes of exposure to the elements. This historic cold had given them a once-in-a-lifetime opportunity, but it also killed men by the dozens. After the snowstorm, Knyphausen had finally given his consent for the mission to proceed on February 8 and Simcoe felt a measure of secret satisfaction that he would finally get revenge for the dishonorable treatment at the hands of the Americans when he was imprisoned, even if he wasn't leading the men who would actually rouse Washington from his sleep and spirit him away into the night.

Simcoe envisioned George Washington asleep in the Ford Mansion with his Life Guard soldiers on patrol in front and back. Stealth was everything, along with its cousin, surprise. There must be no alerting of the main army or the main unit of Washington's personal bodyguards in the log huts nearby. Simcoe had even recommended leaving the horses in a nearby swamp and coming in more like the Indians, creeping in and silencing the sentinels, grabbing Washington while he slept, clapping a gag on him, and then taking him to a waiting horse and riding like the wind back toward the Hudson River. Of course, this was a plan he had devised for the Queen's Rangers and would have all the hallmarks of speed, surprise, agility, and cunning execution that the Rangers were known for. But once General Knyphausen had endorsed Captain Beckwith's plan over his, he had lost all control.

Lieutenant Birch raised his sword and the German mercenaries, with their painted and greased black mustaches and the copper bands around their leather helmets, straightened the line. Simcoe saw the glowing death's-heads clearly now with the words jumping out at him as General Birch pointed to the New Jersey shore. The Black Hussars, the 17th Light Dragoons, and Simcoe's Queen's Rangers exploded across the ice. The snow dust rose up behind the galloping cavalry and Simcoe's eyes watered as he hunched down and felt the sword belt slapping against his back, staring toward the Jersey shore and, further beyond, Morristown.

Yes, they were on their way now, and Simcoe believed in the Black Hussars' motto in this mission to snatch the supreme leader of this disgusting rebellion that had dragged on for five years. The war should have ended years ago. The intent was not to kill Washington, but if he resisted, then death might become a reality. Simcoe himself had been faced with the same decision in the American prison. Death or Glory. That is what George Washington would be faced with as the blade touched his throat in the darkness of the Ford Mansion. Death or Glory. Death or Glory.

Chapter Two

General in Winter

December 29, 1779

OUTSIDE THE FORD MANSION, THE SNOW BLEW DOWN FROM THE ROOF and then caught the crosswind and streaked into the sky before falling with the constant white of the blizzard that had not ceased for days. From outside the window, one could see a man hunched over close to a fire with a powdered white wig, leggings, and buckled shoes. The quill in his hand was bright against the tawny wood more golden in the firelight. The man would be instantly recognizable to anyone in the young republic as the leader of the American Revolution.

George Washington's father was not a rich man, and his mother and he did not get along. Most of his life had been one of climbing up the big hill of his background that he hid with books on elocution that taught him not to spit when he spoke. He had contracted smallpox in Barbados, and that left him with pockmarks on his nose, and his teeth were rotting out and gave him so much pain he sometimes had to stay in bed. He had been bold in his youth and fought with the British against the French and was responsible for the catalytic battle of the French and Indian War. When he took over the reins of commanding the Continental Army, he had no idea how to pry the British out of Boston. In fact, he had been living on his wife's money for fifteen years and had to educate himself on the latest military strategy.

But George Washington was bold and at the same time plodding. He was an anal man who measured his own progress every day in life by inches and was fond of the Scottish idiom "Many a mickle makes a muckle,"[1] meaning that small things add up. His boldness at times bordered on a sort of Evel Knievel daring that courted disaster. When he sent Henry Knox to retrieve artillery from Fort Ticonderoga in the dead of winter in 1775, everyone said it was foolish and Knox would never make it back with the 120,000 pounds of cannons. But Henry Knox did return, and Washington forced the British out of Boston.

Then he repeated his bold move by crossing the Delaware on Christmas Eve 1776 and surprising the Hessians at Trenton and Princeton, keeping the fledgling country in the war and waking up France to the possibilities of an alliance with the Americans. And on top of that, he was often just plain lucky. The one thing George Washington was not good at was waiting, and that was what he had to do now. He had to wait for the worst winter in a century to pass and essentially do nothing.

The clock ticked in the study in the Ford Mansion. The fire crackled. The white glare from the snow burnished the floors with a dull gleam. Washington sipped his tea and moved his neck. He had lately developed excruciating headaches from being bent over paperwork. Even his aides could not keep up with the flow of paper between his headquarters and all the branches of the army, including Congress. He was irritated and hungry, but he dared not go to the kitchen where Mrs. Ford and her children roosted close to the stove. It was the warmest room in the house, and in the winter of 1779, this mattered, as the mercury seemed to have been adhered to zero on the thermometers.

Mrs. Ford was not thrilled to have the commander in chief in her stately white mansion. A letter from New Jersey governor Livingston written on December 10 reveals that Mrs. Ford had complained to him about Washington moving into her home. Livingston lamented that "General Washington could have been as well accommodated without taking up his quarters at Mrs. Fords . . . but his amiable disposition and the pleasure he takes in making everybody about him happy will, I am persuaded, induce him to make it as easy for her not to resent that her house has entertained such a general, nor the Neighborhood regret that a disproportionate quantity of their wood was sacrificed in such a cause."[2]

Washington stood up and picked up another log and placed it into the licking flames. The fireplaces of eighteenth-century homes were horribly inefficient, and most of the heat went up the chimney. Washington warmed his hands and the quill by the fire for several minutes before going back to his writing desk. The snow was falling outside the window in large tufts, more the kind one would see in March than December, but of course the snow had been incessant since November when they had arrived outside Morristown and set up camp in Jockey Hollow.

George Washington moved the desk closer to the fire. The Ford Mansion had many fireplaces, but the near-zero temperature and brutal wind that even now rattled the windows had penetrated Washington's headquarters situated three miles from the main body of his troops. The snow fell as it had been doing since before November. It was astounding. The heavens seemed full of an infinite amount of snow and Washington could not help but think it was all being directed against his encampment.

Even when his men first arrived in late November, they had immediately been exposed to the unseasonable snowstorms. Army surgeon James Thacher, who kept a journal, wrote, "The snow on the ground is about two feet deep and the weather extremely cold; the soldiers are destitute of both tents and blankets and some of them are actually barefooted and almost naked. Our only defense against the inclemency of the weather consists of brush wood thrown together. Our lodging the last night was on the frozen ground."[3]

The scratch of Washington's quill on the parchment irritated him. It irritated the commander almost as much as when he had received the news in November that the French fleet under Vice Admiral Charles Henry Hector, Count d'Estaing had left the coast of Savannah and headed down to the West Indies for the winter. Washington had hoped that the French would sail north from Savannah and join him in an attack on General Clinton's British forces occupying New York. But then he received the news on November 15 that not only had a combined attack of French men-of-war and American forces failed in Savannah but that the French had turned and sailed off in search of warmer weather to ride out the ungodly winter that had clapped down on the east coast of

America. Realizing the fall campaigns were over, he had put into effect his wintering plan of taking his army into Morristown, where he had spent the cold months two years before.

In the 1776–1777 winter operation, Washington had come to Morristown with 3,500 rank-and-file soldiers. Now he was heading into the frigid months with 8,433 soldiers, who would camp in and around the town of Morristown. The problem was that the town could nowhere near provide for an army the size of Washington's. Morristown was not a big town. In 1780 the town consisted of only "sixty or eighty houses around the meeting house. This would suggest a total village population of 200 to 300 people. The village was the county seat of Morris County and the courthouse and country jail stood on the town green around which was centered most of the towns activity."[4] Close around the town within the radius of a mile there were several churches, schools, sawmills, grist mills, five ironworks, and one powder mill. A large store in Morristown advertised "alum and awls to watch chains and wool cards."[5] Farm goods could be exchanged for merchandise, and a circular dated March 14, 1780, stated, "We give the highest prices for bees-wax and hog bristles."[6]

Other towns nearby were even smaller: Parsippany, Troy, Hanover, Whippany, Bottle Hill, and Mendham dotted the countryside with small farms every half mile. But these farmers grew only enough food for their own consumption and had only enough cattle to make it through the winter, and if they did have surplus, they held it in reserve for the British buyers who paid in hard currency. Washington's real problem was that not one of these farms could come even close to feeding an army. "Probably not over one acre in a hundred within ten miles of Morristown was under cultivation: the balance was swamp and timber land."[7] The land could provide Washington with the timber for the soldier's huts, but there was no food for any foraging by the commissary. In this way Morristown was a terrible wintering headquarters.

But Washington had chosen it for its location which provided security and an ability to keep an eye on the British in New York. The general noted that a range of mountains will "preserve us from the insults of the collected force of the enemy."[8] Washington conceded that food would be a problem, noting, "I very well know that a supply of Forage will be difficult at this post and so it will be wherever the Bulk of the Army shall sit down"[9] for the winter.

To make matters worse, there was a grain shortage in 1779–1780 in the mid-Atlantic states that forced Washington to have his army come to Morristown over different routes in hopes that foraging might provide some grain or cattle to their diminished stockpiles. This lack of food for his army was just one of many problems he'd had to confront since arriving at Morristown. There were personal bothers as well. He was cold. Alone. His wife, Martha, had yet to arrive. The small hearth fire did little against the subzero temperatures. And when he had arrived on November 29, the British were about to sail out of New York harbor and there were reports that "the enemy are making or preparing for a pretty considerable embarkation of troops from New York."[10] Washington feared they were heading for Georgia or South Carolina and put the Virginia troops in motion. This had forced the Virginia troops to stop building their winter huts and head out to intercept the British, who ultimately were headed for Charleston to open a new front. Word came that the eighty-eight ships of the British fleet had set sail and left behind in New York 6,613 British and 6,427 German auxiliaries under General Wilhelm von Knyphausen. This combined force of 13,040 regulars dwarfed Washington's 8,433 in Morristown. Still, after Clinton had set sail, Washington ordered his troops to stand down and return to camp.

Washington put down his quill and stood up and walked to the window. The white contagion swirled outside. He rubbed his forehead and thought of the letter he had received from Silas Condict, a member of New Jersey's executive council. "I take the liberty to suggest my apprehension respecting Your Excellency's situation, which I do not think so secure as I would wish, while the frost [ice] makes firm passing into Jersey from every part of the enemy's lines."[11] The prescient councilman advised Washington that the solid ice could make possible a "bold" attempt to surprise him and allow a party of cavalry to reach Morristown undetected. "The importance of the object may induce them to hazard an attempt," Condit warned, "and it will fully justify every means to be ready to receive them."[12]

Kidnapping. It was always a danger, and Washington was well aware of the checkmate that would be set up by trying to take the king off the board of chess which was war. There had even been an effort to kidnap his wife Martha in 1775. John Murray, 4th Earl of Dunmore, the last royal governor of Virginia, had hatched a plot involving ships around Norfolk that could reach his home, Mount Vernon. The ships conceivably could go up the Potomac and anchor, whereupon men would stealthily make their way up to his home, take his sleeping wife, and then hold her until Washington capitulated to British demands. It was a dastardly plot and one Washington could hardly believe as he had socialized at one time with Murray. "I can hardly think that Lord Dunmore can act so low and unmanly a part as to think of seizing Mrs. Washington by way of revenge upon me."[13] Washington made arrangements for Martha to be moved from Mount Vernon at a moment's notice. One thing was for certain: Nothing was off the table in trying to win the war.

In fact, Washington had supported kidnapping efforts by the Americans against various leaders in and outside the British army. A plan to kidnap the British commander in chief Henry Clinton at his headquarters in New York in 1778 had won his early support: "I think it is one of the . . . most desirable and honorable things imaginable taking him prisoner."[14] There was never any attempt to kill the intended victim, yet kidnapping was another strategy in winning a war. This was a war of innovation, as the submarine *Turtle* had proved, and each side was willing to entertain the unconventional to win the day.

The *Turtle* was used by the Americans with Washington's approval. It was a crude submersible with a single keg of gunpowder that would be attached to a ship. The Yale graduate David Bushnell had invented the submersible with the explosive, which he called a "torpedo," to sink the British ships off the coast of Boston. The operator propelled it by hand while looking forward through a crude glass tower that allowed navigation to the target. The plan was to sink the flagship *Eagle* with British general William Howe aboard. The plan was no less than an assassination approved by General Washington.

Things did not go right. A Sergeant Ezra Lee maneuvered the submersible to the back of the *Eagle* and began to drill with a corkscrew mounted on the front. The metal plating along the rudder foiled Lee's attempt to penetrate the hull, and the effort proved unsuccessful. By the time he gave up, dawn was slanting across the harbor and Sergeant Lee began cranking the propeller to get back to shore. The British spotted the *Turtle* and took off in a boat in pursuit. Sergeant Lee flooded his vessel, submerged, and released his timer-rigged explosive. The resulting funnel of water blew up close to the British, giving him time to escape to an American whaling boat.

Submarines, espionage, and kidnapping were all levers at the disposal of the British and the Americans to break what each side now saw as a war of slow attrition. The weariness and the years of war had worn down both armies and their leaders. At forty-seven, Washington was still the physical specimen who walked with "the unmistakable heel to toe gait of a native warrior . . . his grandson attributed to his long service on the frontier."[15] At six feet two, with the long, powerful legs of a superb horseman, pockmarked cheeks from a smallpox infection when he was a boy, pale blue eyes, and the fair sunburnt complexion of a redhead, Washington was still very much the man who had ridden off into the wilderness and survived a bloody confrontation with the French in his twenties, setting off the French and Indian War. The book he had published about his exploits made him famous.

George Washington was otherworldly. There was something about the man beyond his ability to survive battles, defeats, intrigue, and assassination plots and then to deliver the bold stroke just when the British and even his own generals and Congress had written him off. He not only acted the part of a deified leader, but he looked it as well. As Dr. James Thacher had written years before when he first saw Washington at Concord, he was not a man to be forgotten. "His excellency was on horseback, in company with several military gentlemen. It was not difficult to distinguish him from all others. His personal appearance is truly noble and majestic, being tall and well proportioned. His dress is a blue coat with buff colored facings, a rich epaulet on each shoulder, buff underdress, and an elegant small sword, a black cockade in his hair."[16]

Benjamin Rush, a physician in Philadelphia, wrote that Washington had "so much martial dignity in his deportment that you could distinguish him to a be a general and a soldier among ten thousand people. There is not a king in Europe that would not look like a valet de chamber by his side."[17] A man of habits, Washington always rose at dawn and padded about in his nightshirt and slippers doing paperwork before going to inspect his farms in Virginia. He was not above throwing off his coat and working alongside his men. A nitpicker of details, he ate the same breakfast of biscuits, honey, and tea every day and dined on fish with ample amounts of madeira with his meals.

Washington was never far from Mount Vernon in his mind. Even during the war, on the eve of battles Washington would write letters home directing the work on Mount Vernon. "I wish most ardently you could get the north end of the house covered in this fall, if you should be obliged to send all over Virginia, Maryland and Pennsylvania for nails to do it with. Unless this is done it will throw everything exceedingly backward—retard the design of the planting trees . . . besides keeping the house in a disagreeable littered situation. It is equally my wish to have the chimneys run up. In short I would wish to have the whole closed in."[18]

His wife's money had allowed him to be a planter with a custom carriage, an expanding estate (Mount Vernon), and plenty of foxhunts to fill his time. A common quote of the time certainly applied to Washington: "he liked his glass, his lass, his game of cards."[19] It was only the "glorious cause" and "honor" that had propelled him from Mount Vernon to take the reins of the ragtag colonial army outside of Boston in 1775. Many would wonder later why such a man would risk being hanged to take on the most powerful army on the planet, but Washington believed he was destined for greater things than just being a successful planter, and that was nothing less than creating a new nation out of whole cloth.

So, the threat of being kidnapped, when compared with the close scrapes he had endured over the last four years, where death was literally a musket ball away, was nothing to get concerned about. Still, the Ford Mansion was separated from the main body of his troops, and this had done in General Charles Lee the year before. A gifted general who had been a thorn in Washington's side throughout the war with his belief he knew better (and many times, he did), Lee was known by the Indians as "Boiling Water," referring to the profane rants that bubbled out of the grizzled sixty-year-old general like a smoldering volcano capable of erupting at the slightest provocation. He had been part of the Conway Cabal, the schemers and political Machiavellian players led by General Gates who wanted to oust Washington and replace him with himself. General Lee had decided a night with a prostitute was warranted during the second week of December in 1778. He left his army and went to a home in Basking Ridge, New Jersey, a few miles away from the main body of his troops. After his romp with the prostitute, Lee sat down to write a letter critical of his commander, noting that "a certain great man is the most damnably deficient,"[20] believing he should lead the American army, not Gates, when a knock was heard at the door. Lee, still in his nightshirt and slippers, found himself surrounded by British dragoons and had the ignominious fortune of being whisked away on horseback still essentially in his pajamas.

So, the salient point here is that both men, Washington and Lee, were miles from their own armies and in that way vulnerable. Still, Washington regarded this warning as spurious. He believed the snow would thwart any attempt, and besides, he had his "Life Guard" unit that was always with him. He had established the unit in 1776 at Cambridge. Preceding the Secret Service by a hundred years, these handpicked soldiers had one primary job, and that was to protect the life of George Washington. Other duties included handling the papers and money of the moving headquarters and in some cases filling in on domestic duties. This had happened in the Ford Mansion, where the Life Guard unit had already shrunk from 150 men to 115 in 1778 and then was further diminished by other duties. The unit, led by Major Caleb Gibbs, had lost 28 more men who went on leave, and 6 others worked as servants and 3 others worked as stable hands or served as messengers. Even with this diminished force, the commander saw no real threat coming from New York to snatch him away. Washington had picked Morristown for winter camp because it was situated between Philadelphia and New York, where he could keep an eye on the British, but the army was also protected from attack by the Watchung Mountains and swamplands to the east and the Ramapo Hills, which ran north to the Hudson Highlands. The countryside was densely wooded, and Washington could defend the few passes;

still, he also knew the British could overwhelm any frontline troops and he questioned his decision to be so close to New York where the British could easily reach him.

Washington turned from the window and walked back to his desk. He rubbed his eyes. He had just realized that his personal fortune along with the buying power of the army was slowly being whittled away as a result of the debased Continental currency. "A wagon load of money will scarcely purchase a wagon load of provisions," he wrote to John Jay. "A rat in the shape of a horse, is not to be bought at this time for less than $200."[21] He was at the end of five long years of war, and now he had to wear spectacles for any kind of paperwork. He pulled out another piece of paper and began writing Congress, imploring them for food and supplies. "The situation of the Army with respect to supplies is beyond description alarming, it has been five- or six-Weeks passed on half allowance, and we have not three days Bread or a third allowance on hand nor anywhere within reach."[22] Washington voiced his concerns regarding the shortages of food, supplies, and pay for the army, detailing the absence of adequate rations and funds for acquiring necessary provisions. According to Washington, the army had "never experienced a like extremity at any period of the War,"[23] signifying his distress over the conditions his troops faced. He expressed his fears that without relief, "the Army will infallibly disband in a fortnight."[24]

What he wanted to tell Congress was this. The Continental Army had been fighting for five years. Congress had used up all monetary sources including loans from France. The army was in deplorable shape, with shortages of equipment, gunpowder, ammunition, shoes, uniforms, and, most importantly, food. Continental currency had depreciated to 3,000 to 1 and was virtually worthless. "Not worth a Continental"[25] was a common phrase of the time. The army had not been paid for years, and when it was paid, the scrip was worthless.

As the wind howled outside his window, Washington filed a dreary summation. "Many of the men have been four or five days without meat entirely and short of bread and none but on very scanty supplies."[26] Washington continued, reporting that "his men were eating every kind of horse food but hay"[27] and that the army "never experienced a like extremity at any period of the War."[28]

In the thousand huts of the log house city that the men had erected, there was acute hunger, and what made it worse was that outside Jockey Hollow, the area a few miles from Morristown where the camp was located, there was abundance. As Washington later wrote, "A country now overflowing with plenty are now suffering an army, employed for the defense of everything that is dear and valuable, to perish for want of food."[29] The farmers who had food didn't want the worthless scrip of Continental currency, but preferred the hard currency of silver the British buyers offered. As early as 1778, Washington had seen the disparity between those living in luxury and the sacrifices made by his men in the army. After spending time in Philadelphia, Washington had written Benjamin Harrison V:

> *If I were called upon to draw a picture of the times and of men that I have seen, heard, and in part know, I should say in word that idleness, dissipation, and extravagance seems to have laid fast hold to most of them. Speculation peculation and an insatiable thirst for riches seem to have got the better of every other consideration and almost of every order of men. After drawing this picture which from my soul I believe to be a true one, I need not repeat to you that I am alarmed and wish to see my countrymen aroused.[30]*

Washington could only plead his case to Congress that while there were cities and towns with plenty of food, the Continental Army was starving.

Washington finished his letter and turned and looked out the window toward the snow-covered log huts of his Life Guard, where his men were slowly freezing. The snow was so thick he saw only a great blanket of white wool pulled across the window. If the British attacked now, it would be all over. Desertions were at an all-time high, and over a third of his men were too weak or sick to fight. Wisps of blue smoke puffed from the chimneys. His men. His cherished men. What hardships they had suffered, and yet the winter had just begun. Washington turned back to his desk and stared at his quill. He blew on his fingers, then stopped. The ink had frozen solid.

CHAPTER THREE

General Simcoe's Affront

October 28, 1778

THE BRITISH OFFICER BREATHED IN THE SOUR SCENT OF URINE AND the more rancid, disgusting smell of human feces. He kept his eyes shut, trying to will away the smell, which was so strong he felt he might pass out. The wooden bench he lay upon was cold and rough and his head still throbbed from the recent concussion he had suffered upon his capture. The hacking cough of the man who lay on the floor grated on his frayed nerves. The man was a common thief who lay next to his own excrement. The indignity of his treatment, his situation, produced a rage that only made his head throb more.

Lieutenant Colonel Simcoe stared at the man in his jail cell. His long hair and bushy, unkempt beard gave him the appearance of a creature from the lowest depths of human depravity. Yes, he was a common thief who lay upon the floor of the Burlington jail. It was an insult of the gravest order. He was an officer in the Queen's service and he was being treated as a criminal by the Americans, for whom he had only contempt. No torture could have been worse. An affront to honor was untenable. And to not be regarded as a prisoner of war but to be placed in the foul-smelling confines of a municipal jail was worse than death with honor. Colonel Simcoe had let Governor Livingston know about it and then a letter to Sir Henry Clinton.

Lieutenant Colonel Simcoe thought the entire American Revolution was an affront to the idea of the British soldier. British officers expected to be treated with the utmost respect by fellow officers of the opposing side, and that he was treated so badly by the Americans confirmed his original assumption that the rebels were nothing more than a motley crew of backwoodsmen who deserved neither respect nor quarter. And their leader George Washington was just as bad.

Simcoe had been taken prisoner by the Americans in an ambush, and after a severe concussion when he fell from his horse had been nearly killed by a boy who wanted to run him through with a bayonet. He had been hustled around and ended up in a foul-smelling, dank, dark, crumbling jail cell that he would not put a dog into. The Americans had no respect for his rank as an officer; otherwise, why would he be incarcerated with common thieves?

In a letter to General Clinton, he wrote:

I was removed to Bordentown on my parole until the 9th, when I was taken from it and closely confined to a Burlington jail. As my commitment expressed no reason for this treatment, I wrote to Governor Livingston on the subject and enclose to your excellency the correspondence. I look upon the present situation as most particularly unfortunate. My private affairs called for my greatest attention . . . my fair fame has been struck at and cruelty, the attribute of fear, has been imputed to me in the public prints and industriously propagated by ignorant, designing and cowardly people. My honest ambition has been the most severely disappointed and I am doomed to pass the flower of my youth in a goal with criminals, when my state of health, affected by my fall, leads to an imbecility of mind that will not permit to me the consolations resulting from my liberal education.[1]

Lieutenant Colonel Simcoe's capture by the Americans began when the Queen's Rangers had been directed by General Clinton to "march into the Jerseys and over awe the rebels who were giving countenance and support to General Washington's army."[2] Not unlike the American army in Vietnam, the British army was faced with the unenviable task of ferreting out sympathizers to the Continental Army and then taking appropriate measures, destroying means of support, munitions, garrisons, and even towns if they were deemed material to the rebel army.

But Simcoe believed there were fifty flatboats Washington had been using that should immediately be put to the torch.

With this in mind, Simcoe's Queen's Rangers headed for Van Vactor's bridge, where the boats were said to be located. Simcoe found quickly that only eighteen boats were at the bridge, and after locating and pressing rebel sympathizers for information and learning that his own movements were being monitored, he tried to burn some huts belonging to Washington's army but found they did not readily burn. Again, the frustration of any occupying army is ferreting out the third column, which is the supporting civilian population.

At the bridge the eighteen boats were located, and they were already full of water. Still, a mission was a mission, and Simcoe ordered the boats destroyed with hand grenades, hatchets, and combustibles. This took time, and the countryside had now been alerted to the British intruders, with militias taking shots at the Rangers. This was the worst of all scenarios, the shaking of the hornets' nest of rebels who lived in the area and, what's more, knew very well how to pick off the British with deadeye shots.

Colonel Simcoe proceeded on and freed several Loyalist prisoners, some of whom had been chained to the floor and starved. This enraged Simcoe, who didn't believe in any aspect of the American war for independence.

> *Lieutenant Colonel Simcoe was one of those officers desperately in love with the service; he entered the Provincial Royalist force because of the strong belief he entertained that the Continentals had rebelled without cause, and that they never would succeed in their revolution. . . . He was not alone in the belief of the Royalists of the day, that the Americans would not obtain their independence as a Republican nation, or if they did that they could not maintain their autonomy.*[3]

More shots were fired at Simcoe and his men as alarm bells were heard. The hornets' nest had been disturbed, and more shots came from the rear of the Queen's Rangers, a strategy the Americans had adapted of picking off the enemy one soldier at a time. Simcoe told some women they passed "that if they fired another shot, he would burn every house he passed."[4]

Then a shot rang out in front of the Rangers. Simcoe saw a rail fence very high on both sides between a wooded pass with two men by the fence. He broke his horse into a gallop, realizing the trap of the narrow pass, and put his head down, seeing men in the woods and by the rails of the fence. The shots crackled around him as Colonel Simcoe dug his heels into the horse, which took five bullets in the side. He heard shouts of "Now, now!"[5] Simcoe hit the ground and saw no more until he woke in an American prison cell.

Lieutenant Colonel Simcoe had barely escaped with his life. As he lay unconscious, a boy wanted to bayonet him but was held back by a soldier, who said, "Let him alone, the rascal is dead enough."[6] The Americans did not realize their prize until later, and a man lamented that had he known, he would have shot him through the head. Captain Peter Voorhees of the Jersey Continental Troops was killed with a bullet during the ambuscade, and the surrounding populace wanted revenge upon the lieutenant colonel, and he might not have survived had the governor not intervened and forbade any such retaliation.

Simcoe's incarceration began at Borden Town, where he was kept in a tavern owned by Colonel Jeronemus Hoogland of the Jersey Militia. He was treated with great civility, but after a visit by Governor Livingston, he was removed to the Burlington jail. He had requested a parole on Staten Island but was denied. The American general Charles Lee had taken an interest, and letters were passed regarding a prisoner exchange, but the difficulty arose when men of lower rank were offered, and Simcoe felt insulted once again. His letter from his jail cell to Sir Henry Clinton expressed a deepening wound to his honor, if not his pride.

Yet should I even be doomed to obscurely perish in the quicksand of deceit and calumny with which I am now surrounded, it is my duty to expect that no further ungenerous advantage may be presented to the adversary who, trampling on the respect due to his own adherents and presuming on the attention your Excellency may be inclined to pay to my situation, may think to offer some further insult to the British service, the liberal customs of war, and to the honor of my country.[7]

Colonel Simcoe rejected further proposed exchanges by the Americans. Writing once again to the governor, he fairly boiled with recrimination. "When it was proposed that Col [Christopher] Billop and I should be exchanged for Lieutenant Col Reynolds and as many privates make up the difference of rank between a Colonel and a private sentinel that neither did you or the Council seriously imagine it could be accepted of."[8]

Colonel Simcoe felt the insult to his honor had reached such a level that he wrote directly to George Washington.

Sir I am induced to lay myself before you from what I conceive to be a principle of duty and that not merely personal. You may have heard of the uncommon fortune that threw me into the hands of the Jersey Militia. . . . I was allowed my parole, was taken from it on the 9th, and have ever since been confined as a close prisoner in Burlington, with Col. Billop who is in irons and chained to the floor . . . my mittimus has not expressed what I am imprisoned for . . . I apply to you sir either as a prisoner of war or as appealing to you from unjustifiable stretch of power without precedent or generosity. . . . I hope sir you will make use of the power that I conceive enabled you to transfer Col. Billop to the State of New Jersey in extending me the rights allowed by civilized nations and which without a given reason I have been deprived of.[9]

Simcoe then went on to complain about the terms of the proposed prisoner exchange, imploring him to intercede. Washington never replied to Simcoe's letter, another affront he felt deeply. On December 29, 1778, Colonel Billop and Simcoe were finally exchanged. Simcoe returned to Staten Island to take charge of the Queen's Rangers, smarting under the affront by the Americans to his honor and, more than that, the affront of George Washington, who never replied and whom Simcoe suspected of being behind his incarceration as a common criminal. A silent, brooding lust for revenge began to brew in the young colonel.

Chapter Four

Scott and Zelda

September 1778

THE MUSKY SMELL OF SEX. PERFUME. TOBACCO. COGNAC. HAIR POW-
der. Cigars. Candles. Saddle oil. Benedict Arnold and Peggy Shippen
lay in bed, wet with perspiration and exhausted. They lay wrapped in the
sheets in the bedroom not unlike a college couple who know they are
for now safe from the world, but unlike the college couple, Peggy and
Benedict wanted to control that world and they wanted all the riches
they felt they deserved. Like their intertwined legs, they were two people cut from the same cloth.

They were the Scott and Zelda Fitzgerald of their time. Bright, ambitious, excitable, high-strung, young, mercurial to the point of insanity (on
her part), sexy, profligate, but above all else in love and sure each would
fulfill the dreams of the other. Benedict Arnold and Peggy Shippen were,
if not the Fitzgeralds, then at least the Bonnie and Clyde of their era in
their pursuit of a crime that would have far-reaching consequences to
the American Revolution and most certainly themselves. And they were
another contributor to the growing noose that was closing in on Washington and his army in Morristown in the winter of 1779–1780.

If there is any hallmark of Morristown besides the suffering, the
weather, and the deprivations the men endured, then it was the swirling
conspiracies that threatened to envelop George Washington and destroy
the American Revolution. Benedict Arnold was a character. No novelist
could have created him better. If character is action, as F. Scott Fitzgerald

noted many times, then Arnold was perpetual animation. He led men into battle, had his horse shot out from under him, and while pinned down pulled out his pistol as a British regular demanded he ask for quarter, declaring he was now a prisoner. "Not yet," Arnold exclaimed, shooting the man dead. Beginning with his brash taking of Fort Ticonderoga on Lake George, he then led an attack into Quebec, only to be repulsed and wounded in the leg. Not a man to be sidelined, he quickly healed and was instrumental in several key battles that gave him a reputation for being a fighter and believing, like Washington, that he was divinely inspired and protected.

Wounded again in the same leg, this time he was sidelined as the leg was slow to heal and became the military-appointed governor of Philadelphia, where he immediately began to scheme to build a fortune. To us, his fame rests on his treason. But the road to that treason was based on several catalysts that later historians cited to explain why this man, who was regarded as a brilliant general in George Washington's inner circle, would turn on his country.

After his first wife died, Arnold took on raising his three sons while being on call for Washington. His ego was preeminent, and in letters he described himself as a great lover, invoking "scenes of sensual gratification incident to a man of a nervous constitution."[1] High-strung is a term often associated with Benedict Arnold during the years from 1775 to 1777, and we might add libidinous. He was from the start a man of devious means, and during the Conway Cabal, where General Gates made a play for Washington's job, Arnold threw his support to the upstart general who many thought was the man who would replace Washington.

But if we had a test tube with the ingredients that would create the combustion of treachery, a key ingredient was a feeling of not being appreciated, as he was passed over several times for promotions, combined with his penurious situation from a slow draining of his resources while fighting in the Revolution, combined with a growing assumption that the Americans were ultimately going to lose against the British. This was a perfect catalyst for the flame that was produced when he met the eighteen-year-old Peggy Shippen in Philadelphia. For the thirty-seven-year-old Arnold, the vagaries of the circumstances of his life were now rife for ignition and the young heroine was certainly the spark.

Peggy Shippen was of the aristocracy of Philadelphia, and her father, Edward Shippen, was a dyed-in-the-wool royalist. Like Henry Knox, who reached up when marrying into the Loyalist family of his wife, Arnold addressed their differences in station and politics with a letter to Peggy's father: "Our differences in political sentiments, will I hope be no bar to my happiness. I flatter myself the time is at hand when our unhappy contest will be at an end."[2] He also assured the skeptical Edward that he had more than enough money to make his daughter happy, but in fact, all Arnold had at this point was debt.

But love knows no bounds, and Peggy Shippen was beautiful, ambitious, high-strung, and in love with the limping American general who was the appointed governor of Philadelphia, and Arnold played his hand with an ornate carriage and extravagant parties in the mansion that William Howe had once occupied. Arnold always kept two aides at his side and attended the theater and gave passes to Loyalists who wanted to visit family in New York. Peggy, for her part, threw a screaming fit when her father pushed back against the union, declaring her love for the dark-haired, gray-eyed, swaggering general with epaulets and sword, hobbling around in silk stockings, with a volatile temperament that almost matched her own.

They came together over dissatisfaction with the American cause and a feeling they were due compensation for perceived hardships and slights—Peggy being more than annoyed with the upheaval the rebellion had caused in her own family, while Arnold believed he deserved whatever he could get for services rendered that had left him with a bum leg and not enough money to snare the love of his life.

It was not much different from leading an army into battle. Arnold led the assault with a general's zeal, vying for the hand of Peggy Shippen. "Cupid has given our little general . . . a more mortal wound than all the hosts of Britons could,"[3] Mary Morris reported to her financier husband, Robert. Edward Shippen was right to be suspicious of the much older man, who was from a much different background and was already using his position as governor to enrich himself. But no matter. Arnold quickly came up with a way to show he had the resources Edward required by begging a loan of 12,000 pounds from a French shipping agent, Jean Holker, then taking a mortgage on a mansion, Mount Pleasant, that had once been occupied by John Adams. It was to be Peggy's mansion, but the problem was that Arnold needed the rents from the current tenants to make the mortgage payment. Still, Edward Shippen relented, probably because his daughter was capable of fits that would make an insane person look rational.

On April 8, 1779, they were wed, and Arnold, whose own father had gone bankrupt, now had a beautiful wife from a wealthy and respected family who was reported to be good in bed (Arnold reported this in a letter). But no sooner had he surmounted this connubial mountain than he was forced to resign on charges of graft perpetrated as governor of Philadelphia, and charges brought against him in the form of a court-martial that would ultimately be held in the winter headquarters of Washington's army in Morristown. To make matters worse, his twice-wounded leg was not healing the way it should, and he was suffering from gout in his right leg, and now without the financial advantage of his position as governor he was falling victim to crushing debt. He needed a Hail Mary, some bold action that would solve all his problems in one fell swoop.

By the spring of 1779 he no longer believed in "the glorious cause," and his demanding new wife never believed in the rebellion against Britain. In truth, the American government still had no ability to raise money, and neither the army nor Arnold had been paid in years, and even though France had entered on the side of the Americans, there still was no tangible evidence of support that would break the stalemate. The two armies were like two teams still on the field but neither able to score the decisive victory.

One can see Arnold and Peggy lying in bed, fogged out from the latest bacchanal, tired out from sex, the vitriolic Peggy giving the now self-doubting Arnold the push he needed to make the jump from grave dissatisfaction with the American cause to treason. The war had ruined her father by forcing them to initially flee the city, and then upon their return, the rebels were in charge and all semblance of the coveted position her family had once occupied was gone with the retreating British. And now she had a husband similarly decimated by "the glorious cause," and by proxy she was in danger of being washed out along with him. Peggy was a woman who got what she wanted and had taken on her father and married the man she desired; now she would get that man to take the action that would give them the life they deserved.

Money. They wanted money, and the first letter to the British in May 1779 offered Benedict Arnold's services to the British for a sum of money. The plan was inchoate in the beginning, but the young couple had energy, intelligence, and the boldness of youth at their disposal. Benedict was a general in the American army, and he had a stock to sell that could be priceless if it turned the tide of the war. All he had to do was get through the court-martial in Morristown and to be exonerated to keep the value of his market share. He was a commodity, and he must make himself look as valuable to the British as possible. He would give the British as much information as he could on Washington's situation in Morristown, which Arnold knew was dire. The British could then attack Washington in his winter camp, and he would be the beneficiary. For Arnold, the road to riches and treason ran through the mountains and into the winter encampment of George Washington's army in Morristown.

CHAPTER FIVE

Log House City

November 1779

SNOW. SNOW. SNOW. WHERE DID IT COME FROM? ALREADY THE DRIFTS were giant frosted cakes that could bury a man. And it was only November! The trees dropped large tufts as the men passed, leaving bloody footprints, equipment, and yellowish urine in the long path through the creamy smooth fields and the blankets of frozen powdery snow that lapped the trees and made the men struggle to keep up. It was early, and yet the wind cut through the trees like a howling blast of frigid arctic air that froze their fingers, toes, cheeks, the tips of their noses. It was miserable, this strange, unrelenting cold.

"We marched to Pompton on the 9th and on the 14th reached this wilderness, about three miles from Morristown, where we are to build log huts for winter quarters,"[1] James Thacher, the young doctor, recorded in his journal. "Having continued to live under cover of canvas tents most of the winter, we have suffered extremely from exposure to cold and storms."[2]

People who saw the men of George Washington's army entering Morristown in 1779 were shocked. If they had expected uniformed, healthy men marching in perfect time, then they had not considered the corrosive effects of five years of battling the British. There never were any uniforms, and now most men wore rags, or worse, they were "naked," which did not mean nude, but rather that they were wrapped in blankets or coverings that were not necessarily clothes. "Shoeless" could be applied to large parts of the army that occupied Log House City.

Shirts did have some uniformity, with hunting shirts being most common: garments that reached to the knees, made of homespun cloth. Pants could be leather or homespun. As Harold L. Peterson wrote in *The Book of the Continental Soldier*, "It was almost impossible to differentiate between ranks. . . . At any given time a review of the Continental Army would produce a truly motley effect with coat colors varying from battalion to battalion and from company to company. Because officers were responsible for buying their own uniforms, they often appeared in attire which differed from the men under their command."[3] Generals rode horses, while officers sported colored sashes across their chests.

James Thacher observed that officers were a little better off than the enlisted men when they first arrived. "Those officers who have the privilege of a horse, can always have a blanket at hand. Having removed the snow, we wrapped ourselves in great coats, spread our blankets on the ground, and lay down by the side of each other five or six together, with large fires at our feet."[4]

There was no shelter until the men built their huts, and many of the men had nothing to cover their heads. Among those who did have hats, the styles were varied, but the traditional cocked hat turned up on the left side seemed to be the most common. But most had no hats at all even in the brutal cold. In a letter to George Washington, General Anthony Wayne wrote, "I must confess that they would make a better appearance had they a sufficiency of hats, but as Congress don't seem to think that an essential part of the uniform, they mean to keep us uniformly bare headed as well as bare footed and if they find we can bare it tolerably well in the two extremes, perhaps they may try it in the center."[5]

These naked men built Log House City in an area called Jockey Hollow, which was a hilly area about three miles from the town. The name came from horse trading that occurred in the area, or "jockeying" for position, in the trade. The name Log House City was given to the congregation of huts by a Connecticut schoolmaster. Log House City went up in two months and had a total of 1,000 structures. The construction of the huts was amazingly uniform. "Log houses are constructed with the trunk of trees cut into various lengths, according to the size intended and are firmly connected by notches cut at their extremities in the manner of dovetailing,"[6] James Thacher wrote. "The vacancies between the logs are filled in with plastering consisting of mud and clay. The roof is formed of similar pieces of timber and covered with hewn slabs. The chimney situated at one end of the house is made of similar but smaller timber, and both the inner and the outer side are covered with clay plaster, to defend the wood against fire. The door and windows are formed by sawing away a part of the logs of a proper size and move on wooden hinges."[7]

The layout had been established at Valley Forge, and the buildings were of a quality exceeding anything most of the men had grown up in. They slept in the snow until their huts were finished. Even the horses were freezing and starving. "We could procure neither shelter nor forage for our horses and the poor animals were tied to trees in the woods for twenty-four hours without food except the bark which they peeled from the trees,"[8] wrote Thacher, who had to build his hut like everyone else. Once they were finished, the men scurried inside and began their long Jack London winter, which could only be compared to the experience of those who went to the Klondike in search of gold and found themselves marooned through a brutal winter.

The flickering flames of George Washington's discontent were in the campfires of the men who were still without shelter in the freezing temperatures and unceasing snow that had come with the first men to reach Morristown on November 28, 1778. Even on December 29 there were still men who were forced to sleep on the ground, becoming buried mummies under snow and ice, even though the men were immediately put to work creating their huts with specific instructions. "Each hut had to be fourteen feet wide, sixteen feet long, and six and a half feet high at the eaves. If clay could be found it was packed between the logs, more usually the caulking was a mixture of mud and clay. The roof shakes were installed without nails, small logs kept them in place. Huts had to be erected in a straight line and set apart from another at exact intervals."[9]

George Washington was a man who demanded his troops keep certain standards even though many were without shoes and were dressed in rags. He was inflexible when it came to robbing local farmers for food, no matter how desperate the men had become. The punishments in an eighteenth-century army for infractions were harsh, and even more so in the Continental Army, which was held together by baling wire and not much else. Chaos was a stressed army's constant companion, and Washington realized he must have order, as mutiny was a dark alley that yawned before his men every day. When men were caught for stealing, the common punishment was lashes. This grisly punishment was described by James Thacher.

> *The culprit being securely tied to a tree or post receives on his naked back the number of lashes assigned to him, by a whip formed of several small knotted cords, which sometimes cut through the skin at every stroke. However strange it may appear, a soldier will often receive the severest stripes without uttering a groan, or once shrinking from the lash, even while the blood flows freely from his lacerated wounds. . . . They have adopted a method which they say mitigates the anguish in some measure, it is by putting between the teeth a leaden bullet on which they chew under the lash until it is quite flat and jagged.*[10]

Most of Log City was on the property of a farmer, Henry Wick, who owned about 1,400 acres. The area was rich in timber if not much else, and Thacher, who arrived on December 14 with a Massachusetts brigade, described Jockey Hollow as a "wilderness, where the snow on the ground is about two feet deep and the weather extremely cold; the soldiers are both destitute of both tents and blankets, and some of them are actually barefooted and almost naked."[11]

Thacher went on to say that the army had been without food for seven or eight days except for some "miserable beef." The food that was scant to the young doctor on December 14 would be viewed as a feast by the dire circumstances of Christmas. Joseph Plumb Martin's Connecticut brigade arrived during the third week of December, and he wrote, "I request the reader to consider what must have been our situation at this time, naked, fatigued, and starved, forced to march many a weary mile in winter, through cold and snow, to seek a situation in some (to us unknown) wood, to build us habitations to starve and suffer in."[12]

Building the huts became a literal race against freezing to death, and until then the men would sleep on the snow using straw as insulation in an attempt to preserve body heat. Few had blankets in Washington's army, and fewer had tents. The problem was lack of tools. Martin's Connecticut brigade did not wait for tools to be issued and procured crosscut saws, handsaws, augers, and other tools on their own. The tools were certainly stolen from surrounding farms, and Martin appealed to readers to remember that a "man in that condition will not be overly scrupulous how he obtains relief."[13]

Martin continued his description of the building of his hut. After a foot of snow was cleared away, the building began. The actual construction was a simple log cabin where the logs were interlocked and then "the last thing was to hew stuff and build up cabins or berths to sleep in and then the buildings were ready for the reception of the gentlemen soldiers."[14] Here then was where twelve men would ride out the worst winter of the century. The men would view the huts as their new world, a smoky, dark void where fireplaces were not well ventilated and the air reeked of dirty men, pine, smoke, sweat, urine, sometimes feces, and the sweet smell of death. The officers were not allowed to build their huts until the soldiers were all "hutted." The officers were four to a hut, but they too had to endure the dark, smoky confines of their winter quarters along with the same problems of cold, starvation, and the general despair of an army in winter.

The huts of George Washington's army conjure up Jack London's short story *In a Far County*, in which two men spend a winter in the darkness of the Yukon, and in the story the two men eventually go mad, fighting over meager supplies and descending to murder and insanity. The men in George Washington's log city would experience the same gradual descent that would lead to violence, mutiny, desertion, and death.

David Ludlum, a weather historian, summed up the winter of 1780 in his book *The Weather Factor*: "During one winter only in recorded American meteorological history have all the statewide inlets, harbors and sounds of the Atlantic coastal plain from North Carolina northeastward, frozen over and remained closed to navigation for a period of a full month or more. This occurred during what has been called 'The Hard Winter of 1780.'"[15]

British general Henry Clinton was nearly iced in when he failed to sail until December 26 as the Hudson River froze. By January 30 the once-in-a-century freezing of the Hudson was recorded by Johann Dohla, a Hessian soldier stationed in New York. "The North Hudson and East Rivers were frozen solid. The ice was checked and found to be 18 feet thick. All ships were frozen in." The ice moved southward until "a bridge of ice connected Staten Island and Essex County in New Jersey. Farther west, the Hackensack, Passaic, and Raritan rivers were almost frozen to their bottoms. The Delaware river was so solidly frozen that horse drawn sleighs could travel on the ice from Trenton to Philadelphia."[16]

Men in Jockey Hollow had to chip away ice from streams for drinking water. Quartermaster General Nathanael Greene called it "the most terrible winter that I ever knew.... Almost all the wild beasts of the fields and the birds of the air have perished with the cold."[17] Washington was in constant fear that the British and Hessians would charge across the Hudson and attack his winter encampment. In this way the unheard-of arctic cold had made the winter quarters of 1779 now horribly vulnerable. But the British now had to worry about the same situation; neither side could have anticipated the ice bridge that changed the strategic equation.

Dr. James Thacher wrote about the constant struggle to keep warm in subzero conditions.

The sufferings of the poor soldiers can scarcely be described, while on duty they are unavoidably exposed to all inclemency of storms. . . . We have contrived a kind of stone chimney outside and an opening at one end of the tents gives us the benefits of the fire within. . . . For the last ten days we have received but two pounds of meat a man and we are frequently for six or eight days entirely destitute of meat and then as long without bread. The consequence is the soldiers are so enfeebled from hunger and cold, as to be almost unable to perform their military duty or labor in constructing their huts.[18]

Freak snowstorms in December brought supply trains to Morristown to a halt. Snowstorms on December 15, 16, and 17 brought drifts over two feet deep, then were followed by three storms in the first week of January that swept over the eastern seaboard. Dohla described the storms of December 28 and 29.

> *An astonishing wind arose, accompanied by rain, which was almost like an earthquake and lasted twenty-four hours. It severely damaged ships in the Hudson Bay and New York Harbor. Many ships, which had put out two or three anchors, broke loose and were wrecked. Many old houses in the city collapsed, and the best and sturdiest buildings suffered noticeable damage. The inhabitants of New York remembered no such storms, and it was believed that the world and the city were sinking and that it would be the day of final judgement.*[19]

Indeed, the men who had yet to complete their huts suffered horribly. But even in the huts the men froze. Dr. Thacher wrote of coping with the continuous storms of January 2 and 3, 1780. "We are greatly favored by having a supply of straw for bedding; over this we spread all out blankets, and with our clothes on and large fires at our feet, while four or five crowded together, preserve ourselves from freezing." Thacher then noted that the snow had reached such levels that no supplies could reach the winter encampment. "The snow is now four to six feet deep, which so obstructs our roads as to prevent our receiving a supply of provisions."[20]

George Washington, up in the Ford Mansion, took note on January 6 that "the snow which in general is eighteen inches deep (new snow) is much drifted—roads almost impassable . . . very boisterous . . . sometimes snowing, which being very dry drifted exceedingly."[21] The new priority became to clear the roads for the army to receive food using little more than their bodies as human plows, by walking back and forth to pack down the snow.

Still, life had to go on even though, as Dr. Thacher wrote in his journal, "the soldiers are so enfeebled from hunger and cold as to be almost unable to perform their military duty."[22] But the army was routine, and so the routine in Morristown began with exercise in the morning. The exercise was performed by each company in front of their huts. It is hard to imagine these skeletal soldiers without shoes and in rags doing jumping jacks, but undoubtedly there was some sort of stretching and some light calisthenics followed by a roll call. This was the moment when the number of deserters would be counted, men who had slipped off in the dead of night after calculating the risk of being hanged for desertion against the prospect of freezing to death or starving.

Undoubtedly this was a sober moment for officers and men alike as each day their ranks shrank. Then men had to make their way through snowdrifts towering over their heads for guard duty and then return at the end of the day, if they had not frozen to death, to strip off their frozen, sodden clothes and sit before the cabin fire, slowly thawing out. And then there were the men who took matters into their own hands and deserted or stole from others or robbed surrounding farms. For repeat offenders the sentence of death was handed down, and many times there were groups of men sentenced to hang.

James Thacher describes one such hanging. "The wretched criminals were brought in carts to the place of execution. Mr. Rodgers the chaplain attended them to the gallows, addressed them in a very pathetic manner impressing on their minds the heinousness of their crimes. . . . The criminals were place side by side with halters around their necks, their coffins before their eyes, their graves open to their view, and thousands of spectators bemoaning their awful doom."[23]

Many times there would be a last-minute reprieve, with an officer bringing a pardon for some but not all the men. The men who were then hanged were the unlucky ones who were singled out as an example, and the rope was stretched. The harsh punishment was given as a reminder to all the soldiers that order above all else would be kept regardless of the conditions. The conditions at Morristown were slowly wearing the army down, but George Washington was not a man to sit and watch his army slowly wither away from expiring enlistments, lack of pay, lack of food, and the general hardship created by the cold.

He decided to go on the offensive and take advantage of the frozen Hudson and launch an attack on the British garrison on Staten Island by crossing the narrows at Arthur Kill that separated the two land masses. Never one to miss a chance for the brilliant, game-changing moment, Washington asked Brigadier General William Irving to make sure

Arthur Kill was sufficiently frozen for a crossing and selected Major General William Alexander of the First New Jersey Regiment to lead the attack, which would require speed, cunning, and stealth.

The 1,000-man operation was slated for January 14. It was at this time, while Washington put the finishing touches on his plan, that a disgruntled British leader of the Queen's Rangers saw the new ice bridge across the Hudson as a launching platform for a very different type of mission.

CHAPTER SIX

The Plot

December 1779

THE HUDSON HAD BEEN SILENCED. THE GREAT RUSHING FORCE OF water that ran through the country was now this airy, bleak plane of ice and snow. How could such force be stopped and made to lie in wait under the cold, frozen moon? The eeriness of the silent river was unsettling to the river people who made their homes along the great waterway. They had never seen it freeze before, and this lonely white walkway that separated New York from New Jersey did not seem of this world. The stars and the moon waited upon the river that had never ceased, never frozen, never been silenced, until now.

Twenty-eight-year-old Lieutenant Colonel John Graves Simcoe stared across the glittering expanse at the far trees of New Jersey. He had walked out some distance and felt the strange sensation of being on a body of water that should have been a gurgling river of ice cakes, but now this frozen white expanse was the bridge to assuaging the wound of his three-month imprisonment by the rebels. And they were rebels. His treatment proved it. Simcoe felt the wind pierce his coat as his eyes watered. The strange silence of deep winter was a balm. In this silence Simcoe felt the gestation of a bold plan, one that lay within the frosted trees of New Jersey and beyond, Morristown.

It was the intelligence of a Loyalist who had let him know George Washington was staying in a mansion several miles from the main army. The serendipitous quality of this information along with the freezing of a river that never froze but now could support armed men on horses along with artillery produced the balm for his still-bruised ego. The man who never bothered to respond to his letters imploring him to intercede was now vulnerable to capture. Cut off the head of the serpent, and the venom is no longer a threat. And George Washington was the head of the men who had dragged Simcoe from the field after he had been knocked insensible and then thrown him into a dirty, disgusting jail with a common criminal. The outrage of it even now made him grit his teeth, but this idea was so simple that it made Simcoe wonder why others had not thought of it.

But they had not. At least not yet. But then his life had been one of opportunities, and he never hesitated to exploit the bold move. After his father's death, Simcoe went to Exeter with his mother, where he attended the free grammar school. His education continued at Eton and then Merton College in Oxford. "He was devoted to the study of ancient and modern literature. He was well versed in modern history and eagerly devoured every tale of war."[1] Just nineteen, he was commissioned an ensign in the 35th Regiment, and it is then that he was sent to America to quell the rebelling colonies.

Landing on the day of the Battle of Bunker Hill, Simcoe took command of the 40th Regiment and led them in the Battle of Brandywine, where General Howe defeated Washington and took control of Philadelphia. Simcoe distinguished himself in battle, and Howe rewarded him by appointing him major and putting the mounted Queen's Rangers under his command. When Washington attempted to retake Philadelphia at the Battle of Germantown, he was repulsed by Simcoe and his Queen's Rangers in the thick of battle.

The Queen's Rangers were a provincial troop that had been assembled in Connecticut by Colonel Robert Rogers to be the light mobile scouts of the British army. The Rangers at one time had 400 mounted soldiers who were all Americans, amazingly, and of course all Loyalists. It was a flying squad of young men who wanted to distinguish themselves and enjoyed privilege the regulars did not. The regiment was "principally composed of light horsemen . . . specially organized for rapid movements and irregular outposts and skirmishing."[2] Today they would be closer to Navy Seals. Simcoe set about reorganizing the Queen's Rangers Hussars, and an advertisement was posted in *Remington Royal Gazette* in New York City.

ALL ASPIRING HEROES have an opportunity of distinguishing themselves by joining THE QUEEN'S RANGERS HUZZARS Commanded by Lieutenant Colonel Simcoe. Any spirited young man will receive every encouragement and be immediately mounted on an elegant horse and furnished with clothing, accoutrements . . . to strike a blow whenever they were most needed against the continental rebels.[3]

The Rangers would not be weighed down with red tape and had full autonomy to execute their mission no matter how hazardous. They were the elite mobile strike force of eighteenth-century warfare. "They were penetrating and observant, skilled in ambuscade and stratagem, just the kind of corps suited to a country of wood and stream."[4] They were just the kind of corps perfectly suited to snatch a commander in chief in the dead of night.

Simcoe stared across the river as the plan coalesced in his head. It was a plan built around the intelligence that Washington "was quartered at a considerable distance from his army, or any corps of it."[5] General Lee had been taken by the British when he had slept in a tavern a mile from his army. The sympathizer, who had lived near Morristown, had already provided Simcoe with "a very minute and perfect map of the country."[6] The man who had just a month before been in an American jail saw the broad outlines of the mission to kidnap George Washington.

Simcoe would pick out eighty of his best cavalrymen along with thirteen officers, and this light force would "march by secret ways, made more so by the inclement season and to arrive near General Washington by daybreak, to tie up his horses in a swamp and to storm the quarters and attack his guard on foot. For this purpose, his party was to carry muskets as well as swords. . . . The party was to halt at two cottages in a wood, they should arrive before the appointed time."[7]

The stealthy quality of the mission had more the feel of a commando raid, where even horses were deemed too noisy to use on the actual approach to the Ford Mansion, where Washington had set up headquarters. They would approach like Indians, overwhelm Washington's vaunted Life Guard with complete surprise, and then vanish into the night with the commander in chief before any alarm could be sounded. It was a daring yet logical plan that might end the war. George Washington had become the army, if not the spirit of the nation, and without the deity, the church of rebellion would close.

Simcoe had walked out quite a way on the Hudson, and he came to a stop. The wind whistled through the valley of the river that was the main artery of the beating heart of the Revolution. Control the Hudson, and that heart would stop beating. In the spring Clinton could move on the American Fort West Point. But if all went to plan, there might be no need to attack any fort. If George Washington was taken, then there would be no spiritual head of the rebellion, and Simcoe along with many others believed that would be the chess piece so needed to box the Americans into surrendering, or at least to work out a peace that would restore the colonies to Great Britain. There would be others who could work out the details after the Americans realized their vaunted leader had been taken from his headquarters.

Simcoe squinted and felt his eyes water as the wind roared through the far trees. The moon made the white tabletop of snow bright as day on the river. The plan was to kidnap Washington and not to kill him, but of course should he personally resist, there would be the risk of a struggle and he might be killed inadvertently. There was risk in any plan, and this one more than most. Part of the risk was just getting there.

Simcoe looked beyond the trees and knew his cavalry would have to ride thirty miles through the Watchung Mountains and then across snowbound roads infested with militias and Washington's own Continental troops. Then once they had Washington, it would be a race against the alarms that would surely be sounded, racing all the way back to New York before the Continentals could block their way.

The plan could not have been entertained at all were it not for the ungodly winter that had descended and frozen waters that had never been frozen before. Simcoe knew it all depended on overwhelming Washington's Life Guard quickly. This 110-man force led by Major

Caleb Gibbs had as its sole purpose guarding Washington, and Simcoe thought the surprise and daring of the mission would be on his side and the main force of the Life Guard would not be able to engage the raiding party. Many of the Life Guard men worked as servants and in the stables and would not be armed. He knew that "two sentinels paraded in front and two [patrolled] in the rear constantly, day and night."[8] What Simcoe didn't know was that "in the course of the winter false alarms were given of the approach of the enemy. . . . Immediately, the Life Guard would rush from their huts into the [Ford] house, barricade the doors, open the windows, and about five men would place themselves at each window, with their muskets brought to a charge, loaded and cocked ready for defense. There they would remain until the troops from camp were seen marching, with music, at quick-step down towards the mansion."[9]

Fifty cabins for the Life Guards' 250 men "stood in a meadow formed by an angle of two roads a few rods southeast of the dwelling (the Ford Mansion)."[10] The hornets' nest could not be stirred, and with the muffled sound of the snow and leaving the horses behind, Simcoe's plan does have the feel of a modern tactical mission where stealth and surprise are the greatest weapons. The fact is that Washington had assumed he was safe in Morristown and was just beginning to reconsider his vulnerability even as he made plans to launch his own attack against the British.

Simcoe turned back and was now walking across the ice toward Staten Island. He was going to move ahead with the first steps, and that involved bringing his plan to Brigadier General Thomas Stirling. Simcoe felt he would be in sympathy with his plan as he had launched his own attempt to kidnap Governor Livingston a year earlier. Kidnapping as a stratagem was not new to either side. In fact, the first attempt to kidnap George Washington in New York in 1777 had come close to success and had involved men of his own Life Guard who were to protect him. It was a more nefarious plan than Simcoe would entertain; it was a plan involving the assassination of George Washington.

CHAPTER SEVEN

Sacricide

New York, 1776

THE LIGHT WAS DIM IN THE ATTIC AND THE ROOF LOW, WITH THE WOODY scent of cedar between the creosote of the chimney snaking up behind the two men. There was a pattering on the roof—a light rain had begun—but no matter, the men were absorbed like artisans upon their trade. Artisans, maybe not, but they had the high fire of men pursuing gold, mammon, money. They were poor but determined to change their station.

In Cold Spring Harbor, Long Island, the two counterfeiters stayed bent over their craft. It was an eighteenth-century economy in America where everyone had to scramble to make a buck legally or illegally. And counterfeiting was a thriving business as Congress itself had cranked up the printing presses and devalued Continental currency by flooding the American economy. Henry Dawkins, Israel Young, and Isaac Young wanted to contribute their paper contraband to the flooded market, and so they were in their wooden house in the cramped, freezing space trying to come up with the perfect Continental bill.

But they hit a snag. They had the right ink, the right press, and they had copied an existing bill into an engraved plate, but they didn't have the right paper. The right paper was only available in Philadelphia, and so they needed someone to go get it for them. Enter Isaac Ketchum. He was a Long Islander in need of money. The economy had been a rollercoaster during the American Revolution, and everyone was scrambling for a little extra cash. Ketchum was a family man whose wife had died recently, and he had six children. He needed money. On April 19, Ketchum left for Philadelphia. When he arrived, he sold two horses, his original reason for going before he took on the role of procurer of counterfeit paper. Then he went looking for the paper that would make the counterfeiters rich.

It did not go well. He had a sample of the paper in his bag and showed it around and was told the paper could only be obtained by those who are "sworn." For the family man, this task was getting difficult and he was afraid he might get caught. He might have lost his nerve, but he returned empty-handed to Long Island. He would later point to several reasons why he could not get the paper. "He thought it dangerous and determined not to bring the paper, even if he could obtain it, that he considered if he got the paper it would not go into his saddle bags and that if he should carry it in a bag it would be discovered."[1]

Isaac told the brothers the bad news, then proceeded about his business of trying to make a living to feed six children. His life changed when the brothers answered the door on the morning of May 12, 1776, and were arrested by soldiers, who immediately went to the attic. Counterfeiting was a serious crime, and more serious during the Revolution. The British were using currency devaluation as a weapon to destroy the colonial economy and had flooded the sputtering financial markets with counterfeit bills that made the Continental even more undervalued. So counterfeiting was not only illegal, but bordered on treason.

The counterfeiting ring of Dawkins, Young, and Ketchum had been under scrutiny for some time, and the New York Congress issued a resolution.

Whereas this congress is informed, on oath, that there is a great cause of suspicion that Henry Dawkins, Israel Young, Isaac Young . . . of Cold Spring on Nassau Island are counterfeiting the paper currency emitted by the Continental and this Congress: Ordered therefore . . . to dispatch Captain Wool with a sufficient guard to Cold Spring on Nassau Island and that the said guard do take all possible means in their power to apprehend and seize the said Henry Dawkins, Israel Young, Isaac Young, Isaac Ketchum . . . and bring them before this Congress without delay.[2]

So, they were clapped in jail, but Isaac Ketchum felt he had been unjustly accused and had a bigger role to play in history than that of a counterfeiter. Nothing less than uncovering the plot to assassinate George Washington.

~ — ~

Kidnapping comes from a deep well. And it is usually sparked by a personal vendetta as well as opportunity. The first attempt to kidnap George Washington and possibly kill him came from the same sort of rage generated by Lieutenant Colonel Simcoe's imprisonment in a common jail cell with common criminals.

British Governor William Tryon was furious as he sat in a small boat while being rowed out into New York Harbor on the night of October 18, 1775. The oarlocks grated on his nerves as the British man-of-war became larger and larger. He was literally being chased from the governor's mansion in fear for his life by angry rebel mobs when no less than the American congress had requested that "prominent enemies of America be seized."[3]

And so, he left and slipped out to the *Halifax*, where he sent a letter to the mayor of New York. "I shall be ready to do such business of the Country as the situation of the times will permit. The citizens, as well as the inhabitants of the Province, may be assured of my inclination to embrace every means in my power to restore the good peace and order and authority of Government."[4]

Tryon was essentially a governor in exile as the full weight of the American Revolution changed the dynamics in all the colonies. He was shuttled to a larger ship in the harbor, the *Duchess of Gordon*, where there was more space for him to set up his office; and more than that, it was next to the British warship, *Asia*, with sixty-four guns to further protect the governor and his staff.

The governor stared from the ship at Manhattan a mile away and knew his mansion would be ransacked by angry mobs. It had all begun when George Washington had marched through the city with his rebel army, and from then on Tryon felt his power slipping away until he was forced to literally flee with the clothes on his back and take refuge on a

British ship in the harbor. It was this hatred for the leader of the American Revolution that was the flint that sparked the plot to assassinate George Washington.

Washington knew that Tryon was a danger and wrote, "A continuance of the intercourse which has hitherto subsisted between the inhabitants of this colony, and the enemy on board the ships of war, is injurious to the common cause. . . . I should be anxious to remove an evil which may contribute not a little to the ruin of the great Cause we are engaged in, and may . . . prove highly detrimental to this colony in particular."[5]

Washington felt something akin to fear or at least a prescience that one strategy for the British would be to eliminate him from the equation of the American rebellion. He already felt as if he was being spied on after a trusted confidant, Benjamin Church, was revealed to be in the employ of the British. "There is one evil I dread and that is their spies,"[6] he wrote soon after Church's treason was revealed, and so on March 11, 1776, Washington acted for self-preservation. He requested handpicked men from each regiment to form a Life Guard unit. "His excellency depends upon the colonials for good men, such as they can recommend for their sobriety, honesty, and good behavior; he wishes them to be from five feet, eight inches high, to five feet ten inches, handsomely, and well made, and as there is nothing in his eyes more desirable than cleanliness in a soldier, he desires that particular attention may be made, in such as are neat and spruce."[7]

The men assembled outside his headquarters, and Washington selected fifty men who met his exacting standards. Obviously a precursor to the Secret Service, these men would have their own uniforms of blue and white and carry a banner that "depicts a revolutionary soldier holding the bridle of a horse; next to the soldier stands Lady Liberty bearing a flag and flanked by an eagle and a shield."[8] The banner was emblazoned with CONQUER OR DIE, which is a modification of the DEATH OR GLORY engraved on the copper bands of the hats of the Hessian Black Hussars.

The Life Guard was there to protect George Washington above all else and would always be with him. This was accomplished in Cambridge, Massachusetts, and soon the victory over the British with Henry Knox's cannons drove the occupying army out of Boston and Washington made plans to head for New York. Governor Tryon on his British ship in the harbor of New York was outraged when he heard of the defeat in Boston, but he soon learned that the British were heading for New York and would make this the seat of their war operations. Tryon's rage had been festering as he heard of attacks by rebels on Loyalists in New York. He knew George Washington would be coming to New York, and he hatched a plan out of a viperous hatred for the man and his cause.

The Committee of Safety in New York knew that Tryon was a menace and tried to limit his interaction with Loyalists by passing a resolution:

> *Resolved and Ordered, that no inhabitant of this colony, upon any pretense, or for any purpose whatsoever, either in person or in writing directly or indirectly, do presume to have or maintain any intercourse whatsoever with any ship or vessel belonging or employed in the service of the King of Great Britain . . . or with any person or persons on board of the same, upon pain of being dealt with in the severest manner, as enemies to the rights and liberties of the United North American Colonies.*[9]

Treason was the penalty for communication with Tryon, but this did nothing to slow down the duplicitous governor. The first thing Tryon did was hire Thomas Vernon, a hatter, who had been smuggling for the governor, to seek out men who would switch to the British side. He quickly found sixty militiamen, who would be bankrolled by the governor. People were still trying to bet on the winning side or at least what they perceived to be the winning side, and for now it was a toss-up, but Tryon's shenanigans alarmed those around Washington, who moved him out of Manhattan to an estate, Mortiers, which was in a secluded wood. His Life Guards never left his side, with two always guarding the front entrance to the estate and two in the back.

Tryon quickly realized that to get to Washington he must get someone on the inside, and to that end he ensnared five members of Washington's vaunted Life Guard: William Green; Thomas Hickey; Michael Lynch; Johnson, a fifer; and a private named Barnes. Now Isaac Ketchum, the counterfeiter, had been in a jail cell desperately pleading with Congress to let him out. His luck changed when two men were arrested for passing counterfeit bills. They had no relation to the Long Island counterfeiters, but a serendipitous moment came when they were all placed in the same cell and the two soldiers begin talking. This is where Ketchum learned of the plot to assassinate George Washington. Washington's Life Guard soldiers Hickey and Lynch were imprisoned for carrying fake bills and shared a cell with Ketchum, where they spoke of a conspiracy to assassinate George Washington, with no less than five members of Washington's Life Guard in on the plot. Ketchum, seeking a lighter sentence for himself, told the New York Congress of the plot, and it was revealed to be an assassination of George Washington the moment the British fleet appeared on the horizon.

George Washington was aware of the many secret plots swirling around New York and put pressure on the New York Provincial Congress to investigate these plots. On May 2, the congress formed a secret committee and acknowledged that there were conspiracies swirling around the commander in chief.

> *Whereas many ill-disposed persons have lately resorted unto and a great number dwell in Queens County . . . and there are also several ill-disposed persons in the City and County of New York, in Kings County, Richmond County, and in sundry other parts of this colony, many of whom will most probably take up arms on the part of our foes . . . it is highly and indispensably necessary to take speedy and effectual measures to prevent the hostile intentions of our foes, to stop the channels of intelligence and communication among the disaffected, and to quell the spirit of opposition which has hitherto prevailed.*[10]

Basically, nothing happened except that Congress recognized that plots were swirling around New York against the government. On June 10, 1776, Washington wrote to John Hancock, frustrated that little had been done to quell Loyalist plotters. "I had no doubt when I left this city for Philadelphia but that some measures would have been taken to secure the suspected and dangerous persons of this Government before now, and left orders for the military to give aid to the civil power, but the subject is delicate and nothing is done in it we may there have internal as well as external enemies to contend with."[11]

The internal enemies were very close to George Washington. On June 22, Washington's aide-de-camp, twenty-three-year-old Lieutenant Colonel Samuel Webb, wrote in his journal a description of the plot against Washington, which he might have learned from Washington himself. "Some days past, the General received information that a most horrid plot was on foot by the vile Tories of this place and the adjacent towns and villages. Having taken the necessary precautions . . . a number of officers and guards went to different places and took up many of their principals, among whom was David Matthews Esq, Mayor of the city."[12]

This revelation that the mayor of New York was in on the plot was shocking. "To our great astonishment we found five or more of the Generals Life Guard to be accomplices in this wicked plan, which was, at the proper time, to assassinate the person of his Excellency and the other General Officers, blow up the magazine and spike the cannon. It was to be put in execution as soon as the enemies fleet appeared, if no proper time offered before."[13]

This is an amazing journal entry, as it shows the blueprint of a plan to assassinate George Washington and discloses that members of his Life Guard were in on the plot. This was a great deviation from the standard plots on both sides to merely kidnap a general or officer and hold them for a swap or to negotiate a peace settlement. This was much more nefarious and almost hard to believe, but it was quickly backed up by Brigadier General William Heath, who wrote in his diary on June 22 a description of the plot that is close to Webb's. "This day a most horrid plot was discovered, in the city and camp. A plan has been laid to massacre the generals of the army on the first approach of the enemy, to blow up the magazines and spike the cannons. A number both of citizens and soldiers are seized and secured among whom are the mayor of the city. One Forbes, a gunsmith, who is said to be one of the principals and several of the Generals Guard . . . are also in the plot."[14]

More details soon came to light, and Heath in his journal described in detail the mechanics of the assassination. It turned out Tryon's plan was to be a sort of first strike to soften up the Continental Army for the invading British. Part of the plan was to blow up the Kings Bridge and then the powder magazine in New York City, and then a Life Guard soldier was to kill Washington. This would have spread chaos and fear and deprived the Americans of the lightning rod that George Washington had become not only for the army but for the inchoate country being born in real time.

Forty arrests were made, and speedy trials were held, with only Thomas Hickey to be hanged for the conspiracy to assassinate George Washington. It is not known exactly why Hickey was made the scapegoat when there were many others in on the conspiracy. It might have been just bad luck, and Washington had a habit of minimizing plots against him and liked to make an example of one soldier versus executing a large group of conspirators, as the latter might show how advanced the plot had become. Then again, Hickey might have been a black sheep. He was from Ireland, and in 1774 deserted the British army and joined the colonial militia in Connecticut. He was among the first group of soldiers selected for Washington's Life Guard unit and was described as a favorite of Washington. It might have been the fact that Hickey was originally a British soldier, and the fact he was an Irishman with a heavy accent might have contributed to a xenophobic component to his selection as the unlucky one to be hanged.

Hickey's statement during the court-martial did not help his cause. The court records read: "The prisoner being here called upon to make his defense, produces no evidence but says, he engaged in the scheme at first for the sake of cheating Tories and getting some money from them and afterwards consented to have his name sent on board the man of war (Tryon's ship) in order that if the enemy should arrive and defeat the army here, and he should be taken prisoner, he might be safe."[15]

It was not a great defense either way: greed or the belief that the British would be victorious and he wanted to make sure he was on the winning side. The order was issued for his execution. "Thomas Hickey belonging to the Generals Guard having been convicted by a General Court Martial . . . of the crimes of sedition and mutiny, and also of holding a treacherous correspondence with the enemy, for the most horrid and detestable purposes, is sentenced to suffer death. The General approves the sentence, and orders that he be hanged tomorrow at Eleven o Clock."[16]

The entire army was ordered to watch the execution. Washington for his part played down the goal of assassinating him in a letter to Congress revealing the plot to the members of the government.

> *Congress I doubt not will have heard of the plot that was form-ing among many disaffected persons in this city and government, for aiding the King's troops upon their arrival . . . several persons have been enlisted and sworn to join them—The matter I hope by a timely discovery will be suppressed and put a stop to. Many citizens and others, among whom is the mayor, are now in confinement—the matter has been traced up to Governor Tryon and the Mayor appears to have been a principal agent or go between him and the persons concerned in it.*[17]

George Washington was undoubtedly the master of understatement, but he did have a purpose to his low-key, laconic style. And that was not to instill panic or to recognize how far the plotters had progressed. The nascent American government would have been dealt a hammer blow if Washington had been assassinated, and to even acknowledge this possi-bility was to acknowledge how fragile the Revolutionary cause, the war, and the new country really were. He gave the members of Congress a rough outline of the plot. "The plot had been communicated to some of the army, and part of my Guard engaged in it—Thomas Hickey one of them, has been tried and by the unanimous opinion of a Court Martial is sentenced to die, having enlisted himself and engaged others—the sentence by the advice of the whole Council of General Officers will be put in execution today at Eleven O'clock."[18]

Twenty thousand people attended Hickey's hanging, where he claimed the ignominious fate of being the first soldier executed for treason in the American Revolution. An enlisted man, William Eustis, later wrote of the hanging: "He appeared unaffected and obstinate to the last, except that when the Chaplain took him by the hand under the Gallows and bade him adieu, a torrent of tears flowed over his face, but with an indignant scornful air he wiped 'em with his hand from his face and assumed the confident look. . . . With his last breath the fellow told the spectators that unless General Greene was very cautious, the Design would yet be executed on him."[19]

The truth is that Tryon's plan never got off the ground. No gun was fired, no cannon detonated, nor any bridges or powder magazines blown up, and no stealthy, seditious Life Guard soldier attacked George Washington with the intent to extinguish his life. It was the greatest unrealized plot of the American Revolution. In this way it does not even qualify as an assassination attempt, rather an elaborate scheme to put in motion a plan that would set up the British for a quick victory and possible end to the war. It was an audacious plan fomented as a knockout blow by a man sequestered in exile on a ship in New York harbor.

For George Washington, he knew how close the plot came to fruition and he wanted everyone to know the penalty for such treason. After Hickey's execution, he issued a general order to every officer and soldier and summed up the aftermath. "The unhappy fate of Thomas Hickey executed this day for Mutiny Sedition and Treachery, the General hopes will be a warning to every soldier in the army to avoid those crimes an all others, so disgraceful to the character of a soldier, and pernicious to his country." And then in a strange segue Washington added another paragraph. "And in order to avoid those crimes the most certain method is to keep out of the temptation of them, and particularly to avoid lewd women, who, by the dying confession of this poor criminal, first led him into practices which ended in untimely and ignominious death."[20]

The lewd women allusion might have been to Washington's own housekeeper, Mary Smith, who was fired by Washington after she was suspected of being in communication with the conspirators. Or it might have just been Washington the prig, who looked down upon anyone who would spend time with a prostitute and lumped assassination plots with sex and drinking. Hard to know. But the point is that the plot to assassinate George Washington was never actualized.

Even though Washington wanted to keep a lid on the plot to assassinate him, it leaked out to the press. The *Constitutional Gazette* ran an article soon after Hickey's execution. "This forenoon, was executed in a field . . . in the presence of near twenty thousand spectators, a soldier belonging to his Excellency George Washington's guards for mutiny and conspiracy; being one of those who formed, and was soon to have put in execution, that horrid plot of assassinating the staff officers, blowing up the magazines . . . on the arrival of the hungry ministerial myrmidons."[21]

A new word came out of the plot to assassinate George Washington: "sacricide." James Thacher, writing about the scheme, first coined it. "Their design was upon the first engagement which took place, to have murdered the best man on earth; George Washington was to have been the subject of the unheard of SACRICIDE."[22]

The word, which is Latin in origin, means "slaughter of the sacred." It was lucky for all that this sacricide did not take place, but the second plot to kidnap George Washington would go forward in every way. Lieutenant Colonel Simcoe was not an inflated public figure grousing about his loss of position and lifestyle and taking his solace in hatching a plan to strike back at his perceived tormentor, George Washington. Simcoe was a warrior and had proved it many times. He was deadly serious in his plan to take the leader of the American Revolution, and his expedition would go forward and would be executed. In this way, it made the first attempt look like a group of comic bunglers who never had any real hope of inflicting any real damage to the Americans or Washington.

After the British landed and took possession of New York, Governor Tryon could leave his ship and once again become governor. He had a hell of a year. Exiled to a ship where he fomented a plot against George Washington and the Continental Army, he then returned to the governor's mansion after the plot failed. He grew restless, and after leading a brigade of British regulars as a major general, he was involved in a series of atrocities along the Connecticut coast where unarmed townspeople were murdered, and their homes burned. He was pardoned for these atrocities, but his days as a leader of soldiers ended and he returned to England in 1779, where nine years later he died. His greatest legacy is his unrealized plot to kill George Washington in 1776, a fantasy knockout blow that would have assuaged his wounded pride and possibly smashed the cradle of liberty just as it was being brought into the New World.

CHAPTER EIGHT

The Pent-Up General

January 1779

THE SNOW OF MORRISTOWN HAD BEEN TRANSFORMED. NO LONGER WAS the snow the prison of the thousand men who huddled in their cabins and looked for salvation with the spring. For the couple, the snow was glorious. The frosted trees and the sparkling, icy wind that took flight like bits of cotton candy over the young man and woman were but the magic dust of love. The darkness of war had given up a rose of love, and Alexander Hamilton was determined to cut the lovely bud and hold it forever.

The aide-de-camp to George Washington was smitten. He was young, brilliant, and had fallen in love during the coldest winter on record in Morristown. The twenty-three-year-old colonel and the twenty-two-year-old Elizabeth Schuyler were the couple of their time. Hamilton was a phenomenon. He was born in the West Indies and lost his parents at age eleven, and then proceeded to teach himself languages, art, economics, and law, migrating to New Jersey and entering King's College in 1772. He was a diminutive man with fine, almost delicate, features, a bit of a dandy who some would later suspect was gay, but no one doubted his mind.

He took a law degree, then enlisted with the New York military, gaining distinction at the battles at Trenton and Princeton before becoming Washington's personal aide-de-camp in 1777. Amazing. The only thing Alexander Hamilton did not have was money and a great family to back him up. Enter "Betsy" Schuyler.

As the daughter of General Philip Schuyler, Elizabeth was born into money and society as a member of one of New York's oldest if not wealthiest Dutch families. She was everything Alexander Hamilton needed as an accomplished man of no means and less family: Elizabeth Schuyler completed the streaking comet that was Hamilton, and it was his luck that Elizabeth was in Morristown visiting her aunt Gertrude Schuyler Cochran and her uncle Dr. John Cochran, who happened to be Washington's personal physician. The family rented a home near the Ford Mansion, where Washington had set up headquarters.

Alexander Hamilton, who had moved up in society at lightning speed, had a criterion for the woman he would marry. As he told a friend, he wanted a woman who was "young, handsome, I lay emphasis upon a good shape, sensible, a little learning will do, chaste and tender."[1] Hamilton was no fool and knew what he really needed if he was to continue to rise was a fortune behind him, and pointed out that his prospective bride must have a "fortune, the larger stock of that the better."[2]

Elizabeth Schuyler shredded Hamilton's expectations. He could do no better. A fellow aide in Washington's headquarters, Tench Tilghman, wrote that Elizabeth Schuyler was "a brunette with the most good natured, lively eyes I ever saw, which threw a beam of good temper and benevolence over her whole countenance."[3] Tilghman noted that Hamilton was smitten after meeting Elizabeth and called him a "gone man." He lost no time in courting the young girl from a family that would elevate his standing in the society of colonial America.

Alexander went over to the Cochrans' home every evening when he could steal away from Washington's headquarters, with Mrs. Cochran chaperoning the young couple. By spring they would be engaged, with the father, Philip Schuyler, welcoming young Hamilton into the family. "You cannot my dear sir, be more happy at the connection than I am. . . . I shall therefore only entreat you to consider me as one who wishes in every way to promote your happiness, and I shall."[4]

So, here was Cupid under George Washington's nose, shooting arrows into young Alexander Hamilton in the Ford Mansion while he entertained his own wife, Martha. The hot romance of Alexander Hamilton was in direct contrast to the wintry situation of Washington's own conjugal relations. Indeed, the weather reflected Washington's own stasis. Increasingly heavy snowstorms during December created a far greater immediate problem, bringing operations in Morristown and Jockey Hollow almost to a standstill. The "very severe storm of hail and snow all day"[5] that welcomed Washington to Morristown on December 1 lasted through a second day. A two-day storm on December 5 and 6 piled up knee-deep snow, and on December 14 the snow reportedly was about two feet deep. More snow fell on December 15, 16, and 18.

During the last week of December and into January no less than three storms broke across the mid-Atlantic states so violently they became a sea change in weather history, with one historian writing that the storms "ranked with the greatest such combinations in our meteorological history."[6] It was during these terrible storms that Martha Washington arrived. Martha had come to the Ford Mansion, but the mansion was crowded with the Fords' four children (ages eight to seventeen), servants, staff, the Life Guard, and the constant stream of people coming to the headquarters of the Continental Army. Mrs. Ford and her family were restricted to the two rooms on the first two floors, and she was not happy about it. She complained to her father about sharing her house with Washington and his staff, who took over the rest of the home. Washington himself felt crowded and had Nathanael Greene begin an addition to the home and an expansion of the kitchen, which Washington was irritated he had to share with the Fords. In a letter to Greene, he wrote that "eighteen belonging to my family (his staff) and all of Mrs. Fords family are crowded together in her kitchen."[7] Even though the mansion was capacious and well-appointed, it suffered like all homes of the eighteenth century from lack of heat. The kitchen was the only place during this severe winter that would have been comfortable, and Washington had to run a war while servants prepared food and cooked. The winter mirrored Washington's frozen situation. The Hudson had begun to freeze by November 15 and the snow soon followed.

Martha Washington had arrived on December 31 along with the connubial bed, and we can only imagine the lack of privacy, with the staff taking all available space including the stable, and the frigid temperatures turning the matrimonial domicile into an icebox. January 1780 produced a two-day blizzard few had ever experienced before, and it was well Martha was not traveling as no roads were passable. So, George Washington was getting no release at all except to focus on a daring attack on the British at Staten Island.

But like John Graves Simcoe, Washington saw a golden opportunity with the freezing of the Hudson River. The glittering expanse now connecting New Jersey to Staten Island was a temporary bridge, and while we know this winter of 1779–1780 was once-in-a-century in its freezing temperatures and record-breaking snow, Washington and Simcoe had no idea if a thaw was right around the corner that might soften the ice and prevent the army from crossing. The first problem, though, was that the army had no sleds, and without sleds to traverse the deep snow on the roads, there could be no offensive.

A call was put out, and amazingly, 500 farmers responded on January 14 with horse-drawn sleds. It was not unlike the situation of Henry Knox, who had had to rely on others to provide him with sleds to transport the artillery from Fort Ticonderoga to Cambridge. In that case the procurement of sleds was problematic and an adventure in itself; here the farmers responded quickly and General William Alexander, Lord Stirling, leading the attack force, loaded his 900 men onto the sleds along with armament that included an eighteen-pounder (5,000 pounds), which eventually had to be left behind as no sled was capable of carrying the weight. The sleds also carried 2,000 planks to provide footing as the sleds and cannon were moved down the ice-covered banks to the Hudson. It was a time when war was still viewed as entertainment, and townspeople followed the expeditionary force to the crossing at Arthur Kill. They reached the frozen river on January 15 and crossed on the planks of the river, a force of 2,700 men who would surprise the British with the audacity of their raid on the lightly defended island.

The day was brilliant, and the surprise did not exist as the army crossed the eye-blinding, snow-covered river. It was worse than that; two days before the attack, Hugh Gaines, the publisher of *The New York Gazette*, wrote that Washington was thinking about an attack on Staten Island. The attacking force spent the first night on the island by fires, trying to stay warm in the subzero temperatures. Stirling heard that British reinforcements had arrived (they would not come for another two days) and decided between the weather and losing the element of surprise to call off the attack and retreat across the ice. The weakened army was skittish, and rumors abounded that they might be trapped, with their only escape a wide-open run across the ice.

James Thacher, the army surgeon, recorded the botched expedition:

A detachment, consisting of about two thousand five hundred men under the command of Major General Lord Stirling was a few days since sent off in about five hundred sleds on a secret expedition. Our party passed over the ice from Elizabethtown in the night, but the enemy having received intelligence of their design, retired into their strong works for safety and the object of the enterprise was unfortunately defeated, they, however, brought off a quantity of blankets and stores. The snow was three or four feet deep and the weather extremely cold, and our troops continued the island twenty-four hours without covering. . . . Six were killed by a party of horse who pursued our rear guard. A number of tents, arms, and a quantity of baggage with several casks of wine and spirits were brought off with seventeen prisoners.[8]

The soldiers, who were suffering from cold and hunger, were frustrated with the decision to cancel the assault on the British, through which they probably thought they might find food and clothes and ammunition. Joseph Plum Martin in his diary, one of the few from the time, voiced their feelings.

We took up our abode for the night on a bare bleak hill, in full rake of the northwest wind, with no other covering of shelter than the canopy of the heavens and no fuel but some old rotten rails that we dug up through the snow, which was about two or three feet deep. The weather was cold enough to cut a man in half. We lay in this accommodating spot till morning, when we began our retreat from the island. The British were quickly in pursuit, they attacked our rear guard and made several of them prisoners, among who was one of my associates. Poor young fellow! I have never seen or heard anything from him since. We arrived at camp after a tedious and cold march of many hours, some with frozen toes, some with frozen fingers and ears, and half-starved in the bargain. That ended our Staten Island expedition.[9]

James Thacher later wrote in a medical report that after the attack "about 500 were slightly frozen."[10] Washington's probing of the British on Staten Island was proving a disaster. Civilians who had accompanied the army had looted homes, and Washington ordered the return of all stolen items valued at more than $10,000. All Washington had done was show the British that crossing the ice was possible and then retreated. Then the British retaliated.

On January 25, a two-pronged attack was launched across the ice from Staten Island and Paulus Hook. The 500 British and Hessian soldiers crossed in darkness and in the morning attacked Newark, burning homes and barns and the Newark Academy with the defenders inside, incinerating many of the colonials, burning the First Presbyterian Church, and capturing 35 soldiers before crossing the ice back to Staten Island. Thacher recorded the event on the 27th. "A party of the enemy made an excursion from Staten Island in the night, surprised our picket guard, and succeeded in taking off a major and forty men. Our offices were censured for their conduct in not being sufficiently alert to guard against a surprise."[11]

The British on the way added insult to injury by rousing Justice of the Peace Joseph Hedden Jr. from his bed and forcing him at bayonet point to walk in his bedclothes to Paulus Hook. A friend passed him a blanket, but he would later die from exposure to the brutal cold that now pushed the two armies into their camps to wait out the worst winter in a century. Private Martin back in his frozen hut wrote that "I have often found that these times not only tried men's souls, but their bodies too, I know that they did mine, and not effectually."[12]

George Washington went back to running the war from Mrs. Ford's kitchen, realizing the real enemy was not the British but the unceasing snow and bitter cold that had turned Morristown into a blasted, isolated tundra. Conspiracy swirled around George Washington like the wind-whipped snow swirling over the Ford Mansion's roof and sparkling down past the windows. The connubial bed of Martha and George Washington was surely a block of ice in the cold, unheated rooms of the Ford manse.

CHAPTER NINE

The Hail Mary General

1777

THE VICTIM BROKE OUT WITH A RASH THAT TURNED INTO PUSTULES OF pus. George Washington lay in his bed in delirium. He was seventeen, but youth was no guarantee one could survive smallpox. His brother nursed him and fretted that the long, lanky young man might go the way of many who had succumbed to the plague of the eighteenth century. He put cool rags on his feverish forehead and tried to keep him covered, and of course the bloodletting of the time did not help, but slowly George Washington got better. He was one of the lucky ones who now had the golden ticket of immunity against the pox.

Even the rich were not spared. The patriarch of the Ford family, in whose house Washington would stay in 1779, had been taken by smallpox. Other diseases were devastating in the eighteenth century, but none as brutal or as feared as the ravages of smallpox. Typhoid, consumption, pneumonia, and dysentery all took their toll, but to the soldier and the civilian, the mass killer of the time was smallpox. The disease took 100,000 people in North America alone between 1775 and 1782. Armies were the perfect incubator for a predator that did its mostly deadly work in close proximity. Even if you survived, you were scarred or possibly maimed.

But if you did survive the fever and the vomiting and the pox, which were fluid-filled pustules that covered the body, then you were immune for life. The Continental Army became infected in Boston in

1775, and the disease began to spread. By winter of 1777, with the army heading into camp, George Washington knew he had a situation on his hands. He wrote of the disease, "We should have more to dread from it than the sword of the enemy."[1] Washington knew firsthand what smallpox could do.

He himself had become infected in 1751 after visiting a British colony in Barbados. He fought off the disease and emerged after a three-week illness with a few pockmarks. What's more, he could no longer get smallpox, and this put him in the advantageous situation of being on the front lines in dealing with the disease.

George Washington did the unexpected, and this went to protecting the health of his troops. He issued an order for Dr. Nathaniel Bond to start inoculating his soldiers, all his soldiers. It was the first mass inoculation in America. He wrote William Shippen, head of the army medical corps, that if the smallpox was not stopped, then the entire army not just in New Jersey, but in all the states, might become infected. Even still, three weeks after the inoculations began, Washington ordered them halted. He feared the men's clothes would transmit the disease, and the army did not have uniforms to replace diseased clothing. A week later, after watching the disease progress, he ordered the inoculations again. "The smallpox has made such head in every quarter that I find it impossible to keep it from spreading through the whole army the natural way."[2]

It wasn't a vaccine. The inoculation of 1777 was a crude attempt to head off the disease's worst effects. A small amount of pox fluid was put in a scratch, and this gave the patient a light case. There was a rising fever and a few poxes, but recovery was rapid. Every inoculation created another sick soldier, so homes, hospitals, and taverns in Morristown were soon filled with thousands of recovering men.

Private Joseph Martin spoke for many soldiers after he received his inoculation and was housed with 400 other Connecticut soldiers in the barracks in the Highlands of New York. "We lost none. I had the smallpox favorable as did the rest."[3] With his soldiers down and recovering from the inoculations, Washington feared an attack if he should immunize too many soldiers at once. "Should we inoculate generally, the Enemy knowing it, will certainly take advantage of the situation."[4] Still others felt they could fight even while recovering. A sixteen-year-old Ashbel Green wrote that "there was not, probably, a day in which the army could not have been marched against the enemy."[5]

All that winter as the men convalesced, the army began to melt away in a foreshadowing of the winter to come in two years. Washington on January 19, 1778 declared that America had reached a point of "scarce having any army at all."[6] Men refused to reenlist when their service expired and simply walked away and headed for home. Many were new soldiers who saw no need to hang around all winter without any fighting. Desertion became rampant, and Washington requested the New Jersey legislature pass a law forbidding harboring deserters, giving the reason that "our new army will scarcely be raised before it will dwindle and waste away."[7] Even the soldiers who remained were looking to leave as they "marched over frosted snow, many without a shoe, stocking or blanket."[8]

Some men surrendered to the British and were then taken prisoner. James Thacher recorded the treatment the "rebel" prisoners then received at the hands of the British.

> *It would seem that the application of the term rebel to our prisoners, is sufficient to reconcile the consciences of their victors to inflict on them the most unprecedented cruelties. . . . They were crowded into the holds of prison-ships where they were almost suffocated for want of air, and into churches and open sugar houses, and without covering or a spark of fire. Their allowance of provisions and water for three days was sufficient for one and in some instances, they were for four days entirely destitute of food. . . . After death had released the sufferers, their bodies were dragged out of the prisons and piled up without doors, till enough were collected for a cartload when they were carted out and tumbled into a ditch and slightly covered with earth.*[9]

Many of the imprisoned men then were made an offer to serve in the Royal Army. Those who took it did not fare much better and were used many times as laborers. The men who had survived the inoculations and the winter at Morristown waited for spring. Among the officers an incident occurred that would have far-reaching implications in the winter of

1779–1780. Five American officers were promoted to the rank of major general. One was not, and he submitted his resignation in disgust at his treatment. George Washington finally convinced the officer to take back his resignation. But the stewing volcano that was Benedict Arnold began to build up the pressure that would one day blow sky-high.

CHAPTER TEN

James Benedict Bond

May 1779

THE LETTERS LOOKED NORMAL. THE PROSE WAS FLOWERY, BUT THIS WAS the eighteenth century, when letters were an event and written on both sides because paper was scarce. If someone opened the letter and read it, there would be talk of ailments, money, relatives, improvements, deaths, births, the normal patois of a colonial family in the late 1700s. And so the letter would be passed on as innocuous until it was opened by the recipient, who would then go to a room and lock the door. He would then take out a vial of acid and apply it to the paper, and between the chatter of familial information would appear as if by magic a very different narrative. It was invisible ink, the cutting edge of spy technology.

Shaken. Not stirred. Peggy and Benedict. It did have a ring to it, maybe even a spy ring. The concentric circle would have Peggy at the center, with Benedict on one spoke, a man named Joseph Stansbury on another, and then Loyalist chaplain and poet Jonathan O'Dell, messenger John Ratoon, and then finally British officer John André. André had just been put in charge of British intelligence operations, and there was no better place to be than the hotbed of intrigue, skullduggery, and espionage that was New York during the years of the Revolution, where the outcome was far from certain and people lay their bets on which horse would eventually cross the line, be it British or American. "Every day a great seething wave of loyalists, patriots, freed slaves, deserters, merchants, and tradespeople washed in and out of the city. It was the perfect environment for espionage."[1]

This gave intelligence a monetary value; there was a market for it, and that market was fluid and ever-changing, but it was there, and Peggy and Benedict were determined to cash in for the best exchange rate they could procure. Peggy pushed Benedict to meet with Stansbury and let him know that he was entertaining the idea of defecting to the British. Stansbury was a crockery merchant, so a meeting at Arnold's residence would bring on no suspicion, and there Benedict got right to the point. Two questions then: Were the British committed to the war with the Americans? And then the more important question: What was it worth to have a man like Arnold passing them information? In short, how much cash could he expect for his treason against George Washington and the American cause.

The spokes of the spy wheel turned, and British officer John André lost no time in responding to Benedict. "No thought is entertained of abandoning the point we have in view. . . . On the contrary, powerful means are expected for accomplishing our end."[2] As far as money went, the sky was limit. If the general should help the British win a major victory and "defeat a numerous body of Continental Soldiers, then would the generosity of a nation exceed even his own most sanguine hopes."[3] So far, so good. And even if things didn't work out, André pointed out that Benedict would be compensated for expenses and time spent, writing that even if "manifest efforts be foiled and after every zealous attempt, flight be at length necessary, the cause in which he suffers will hold itself bound to indemnify him for his losses and receive him with the honor his conduct deserves."[4] In other words, it was a win-win for Peggy and Benedict. Even if the money didn't work out, a new life in London beckoned.

André then got down to business. First there was delineation of tactics: steal dispatches, reveal Washington's strategy, as well as provide the more localized intelligence on location of arms and powder magazines, troop movements. Then came the James Bond moment. How should they communicate? Simple, they would use a large book with numbers designating words that would reveal the message. Arnold used Blackstone's *Commentaries on the Laws of England* first and then eventually Bailey's

Universal Etymological English Dictionary, which had the advantage of being alphabetized. While it wasn't exactly Enigma, it would be a challenge to the eighteenth-century mind that did not have computers, slide rules, or teams of math wizards to crack codes. "Each word was to be keyed to the book with the help of three numbers: the first is the page, the second the line, the third the word."[5]

Then, in keeping with the James Bond motif, there was invisible ink. The ink would transmogrify with the application of either heat or a chemical acid. Children would later use lemon juice, but no lemon juice for these spies, as that would be hard to come by, but it was an acid as well. The method would be designated by a letter at the top of the page: F would be for fire and A for acid. The ruse would be completed by having fake topics, such as an old woman's health, or André suggested that Peggy write to him in chatty, rambling letters where invisible ink could be written between the lines.

André was a go-between for Benedict Arnold and the British general Henry Clinton, and Arnold immediately supplied an example of the kind of intelligence he could provide by letting him know that Washington was planning on moving toward the Hudson in the spring and had been unable to support General Benjamin Lincoln in his defense of Charleston, South Carolina. "They are in want of arms, ammunition and men. . . . Three or four thousand militia is the most that can be mustered to fight on any emergency."[6] George Washington's sense that Morristown provided him some sense of security in its very isolation was now pierced, though he had no idea one of his closest generals was turning on him.

Arnold even supplied information on the French movements, in particular those of Count d'Estaing and the French fleet's location in the West Indies. "The French fleet has conditional orders to return to this continent. . . . They depend on the great part of their provision from hence. A French transport originally a 64 and foreign 28 guns are daily needed here for provision."[7]

This was but a taste, and Arnold knew he had just given the British a leg up with even this general information. He pushed for more information on how much he was to be paid. "I will cooperate when an opportunity offers and as life and everything is at stake, I will expect some certainty. My property here secure and a revenue equivalent to the risk and service done."[8]

The British remained coy, and Arnold immediately got pushy with the commander in chief of the British. "As I esteem the interest of Great Britain and America inseparable . . . Sir Henry may depend on my exertions and intelligence."[9] He then demanded to know more clearly what he could expect for his efforts. "It will be impossible to cooperate unless there is a mutual confidence."[10]

Yes, they wanted what Benedict had to offer, but they needed something big, something that could turn the tide of the war, and then there would be a payday. A big payday. Arnold became obsessed with the get-rich-quick aspect of his treason and pushed for a dollar amount.

Money. Money. Money. Arnold was obsessed with making up for his losses by the perceived damage the American Revolution had caused to his financial standing. The truth was Arnold was always one step ahead of the bank. To coin an old phrase, he had champagne tastes on a beer budget, but more importantly, so did his wife, Peggy. She had been used to the standards of the aristocracy of Philadelphia and demanded Arnold do what it took to improve their station.

That he had turned on George Washington and his country and might be responsible for the Americans losing the war and George Washington ultimately being hanged for treason did not enter his thinking. "Guilt was simply not part of his makeup since everything he did was, to his own mind, at least, justifiable. Where others might have shown, if not remorse, at least hesitation or ambivalence, Arnold projected unwavering certitude. Whatever was best for him was, by definition, best for everyone else."[11]

In Arnold's mind the war was going to be lost. The penurious situation of the Continental Congress, the lack of food for the army, the desertions, the expiring enlistments, the lack of support from the surrounding countryside where cattle and grain were sold on the "London Market" to the British over the Americans because they could pay in hard money rather than worthless Continental currency, made him think the Americans would not prevail. Add to that a population loath to be taxed to support a war that had become tiresome where they resented even the imposition of the army as in Morristown where people had to share their homes or farms with officers and the French had yet to do anything other than sail their ships up and down the coast . . . then this added up to an American defeat and why should he, Arnold, not be compensated for his services that had cost him financially and left him with a permanent limp. His wife thought he should at least, and he did too, but really it was a matter of how much.

Add to all of this the personality of Benedict Arnold, which seemed to trip him up just when he was about to triumph. "For Arnold . . . rules were meant to be broken. He had done it as a pre-Revolutionary merchant, and he had done it as a military governor of Philadelphia. This did not make Arnold unusual. Many prominent Americans before and since have lived in the gray area between selfishness and altruism. What made Arnold unique was the godlike inviolability he attached to his actions. . . . Arnold was in the end the leading personage in the drama that was his life."[12]

To that end, Henry Clinton in the spring of 1779 upped the ante and began to set his sights on the American Fort West Point sixty miles up the Hudson. The control of this series of fortifications on the curve of the river would deny the Continental Army needed supplies and cut the colonies in two. A prize like this would be worth a lot, and Clinton would pay handsomely to anyone who could give him the jewel of the Hudson River. André sent Arnold a message letting him know that Clinton took offense to the tone of his letter demanding to know the amount the British would pay. André went on to say that Clinton "wishes to appraise you that he cannot reveal his intentions as to the present campaign, nor can he find the necessity of such a discovery or that a want of a proper degree of confidence is to be inferred from his not making it."[13]

In other words, the ball was in Arnold's court to wow the British with a master stroke, something that he could give them that was so decisive it would turn the tide of the war. West Point, the Gibraltar on the Hudson, might be just the thing. André pointed out that if Arnold could secure a "conspicuous command" and turn over, say, 5,000 or 6,000 soldiers, then there would be room to talk about how much his treason would engender in financial remuneration. But until then he had no real leverage beyond his promised treason. André did give him a number if things should go his way: "twice as many thousand guineas."[14]

This was the carrot then, and it was now up to Benedict Arnold to get from Washington a command that would be worthy of turning over either a fort or a sizeable part of the army to the British. The truth was the British looked down on all deserters and traitors even as they courted them. Clinton would later write of Arnold, "Whatever merit this officer might have had . . . his situation . . . made him less an object of attention."[15] In other words, Arnold had no real command, and so his value on the open market of treason was low.

Arnold then redoubled his efforts, assuring the British he was committed to giving them what they wanted, but once again he wanted to be sure he was well paid. In the letter that made its way to André he stated that "he wished to serve his country in accelerating the settlement of this unhappy contest . . . yet he should hold himself unjust to his family to hazard his all on the occasion and part with a certainty for an uncertainty."[16] In other words, he would deliver, but to take the risk of treason he wanted a hard number, not a vague promise. The British must have doubted he could deliver, as he was now facing a court-martial in Morristown. But they had underestimated the man who had managed to defy death many times and somehow land on his feet. A lesser man might have realized the folly of turning over thousands of troops or a fort to the enemy, but James Benedict Bond was just the man for such a mission.

But if his court-martial did not go well then, all bets were off. If even one charge stuck, then he might not be given a command, or worse, he might be forced to leave the army. His command had to be significant, and Washington would not award him anything if he was under a cloud of corruption. The trial in Morristown was for the crime of treason, and Benedict Arnold was ready for his benediction . . . and the money.

CHAPTER ELEVEN

The Most Daring Exploit

January 31, 1780

THERE WAS ONLY ONE TRUE ADVENTURE FOR A YOUNG MAN IN THE EIGH-
teenth century, and that was in the military. The service. Young men looked
for glory; they looked for valor. They looked to live the swashbuckling
adventure of the noble officer who stares down death and ends up with
the girl and does it all with the effortlessness of the gentleman. The more
daring the exploit, the better. The more the opportunity to demonstrate
courage unbounded. So it was with Lieutenant Colonel Simcoe.

It is not surprising that Colonel John Graves Simcoe came up with
an audacious plan to snatch George Washington in a targeted night
raid that would depend on speed, cunning, luck, and a ruthlessness that
Simcoe had already demonstrated when he butchered thirty Americans
as they slept in Judge William Hancock's home on March 21, 1778. Simcoe had already had a dry run for the mission he was fomenting against
the leader of the Revolution with a most daring exploit that was already
a legend. It was his amazing night ride on October 27, 1779, where he
terrorized the Millstone River Valley in New Jersey on a fifty-five-mile
spree that eventually led to his capture, but not before he had created
havoc for the Americans.

It was the mission to destroy the boats, but the raid launched
from Elizabethtown by the Queen's Rangers was a rolling assault that
caught the Americans flat-footed. He was headed for the Raritan
River, but along the way he stopped in Quibbletown and impersonated

an American officer, drawing supplies from the quartermaster for him and his men before revealing his identity and taking the unwitting soldier prisoner. Then Simcoe reached the flat-bottomed boats, and after destroying the transports, he galloped and burned a storehouse of ammunitions in an old Dutch church in Van Veghten and then entered the Millstone River Valley and burned the Somerset Court House, the jail, houses, and the church, creating a panic among the populace. It was the ambush at Middlebush where Simcoe was knocked from his horse and captured along with four of his men. The rest of the Rangers reached the safety of New Brunswick.

Except for his own capture, Simcoe had proved that a surprise night raid based on stealth and speed could do great damage before the enemy knew what hit them, and by the time they reacted the raiders would have escaped. The fifty-five-mile ride was a dry run that showed what well-trained men could do when audacity was used to stun the enemy, and suggested that if they had taken George Washington on that night they would have escaped with their quarry. Simcoe regarded his own capture as simply bad luck and gave no credit to the Americans for their ambush.

And with this in mind he approached General Thomas Stirling, the commander of the 42nd Regiment, also known as the Black Watch, and laid out his plan to kidnap George Washington by crossing the Hudson at night and essentially replaying his raid in New Jersey. This time, however, the target was not the destruction of boats but the taking of the leader of the American Revolution. Stirling approved, telling Simcoe, "Your ideas are great and would be of importance if fulfilled; as I am confident of your zeal and capacity, I should be sorry to check them."[1]

Simcoe may well have needed Stirling as well to provide cover for him when recrossing the Hudson at Paulus Hook. It was a bold plan, but the strange winter had presented an opportunity to both sides and Simcoe saw no impediment to the success of his plan. It was on this same day that a prescient Silas Condict of the New Jersey Council wrote George Washington expressing concern for the very type of raid that Simcoe had laid out for Stirling. It might have been a leak of some sort or just the paranoia that had gripped both sides with the vulnerability the ice bridge created. "Respecting your Excellency's situation, which I do not think so secure as I would wish, while the frost makes firm passing into Jersey from every part of the enemy's lines."[2] Conduit went on to predict a "bold attempt" and predicted that a group of cavalrymen could reach Morristown undetected. "The importance of the object may induce them to hazard an attempt and it will fully justify every means to be ready to receive them."[3]

It was an accurate description of Colonel Simcoe's plan and should have given Washington pause. The general wrote back that "he had already taken precautions and that he thought would be effectual in preventing a surprise cavalry raid on the Ford mansion."[4] It would seem Washington had been lulled by his snowed-in fortress and didn't seriously believe anyone would attempt such an audacious plan. He didn't know John Graves Simcoe, who had scouts out, had already ascertained that Washington was still in the Ford Mansion, and was already moving ahead with his plans.

But as luck would have it, others had their own ideas brought about by the Hudson River's sudden accessibility. Like a great idea for a book, Simcoe could not prevent others from coming up with their own plans to shorten the war by kidnapping the man responsible for the British quagmire in America. A Captain George Beckwith had, unbeknownst to Simcoe, come up with his own plan and had already passed it by the interim commander in chief of British forces in New York, General Knyphausen, who had taken over while General Clinton supervised the assault on Charleston, South Carolina.

The German Knyphausen had written to Clinton, "General Washington having taken up his quarters at a distance from his army, under the protection of a small corps of infantry, it appeared practicable to surprise that body with cavalry and to penetrate to the neighborhood of Morristown."[5] Simcoe had also laid out his plan for Knyphausen, and one has to wonder on the timing of Captain Beckwith's plan. It would be the shot in the arm of a lifetime to be the man responsible for kidnapping George Washington and possibly ending the five-year war in North America. In a sense, Simcoe might have been foolish to think he could keep such a mission restricted to himself and the Queen's Rangers.

General Knyphausen, like many who take an idea and then bring it to fruition, liked Beckwith's plan because it had more assurance of success if only because it was a more ambitious operation involving many more troops. Essentially the difference between Beckwith's and Simcoe's plans was the employment of a diversionary tactic that Knyphausen saw as lessening the risk for disaster. Simcoe's plan, like his romp through New Jersey, was based on secrecy and speed, with the entire raid hinging on hitting the Americans so fast they could not mount a force to intercept the kidnapping party. It was built for a small unit of the Queen's Rangers and it had the tang of a brilliant yet highly risky assault as planned by one man with a possible vendetta to fulfill. Beckwith's plan was more a classic military operation. "Beckwith proposed staging various diversions in New Jersey. By different movements from Staten Island, British forces would attack at Cranes Mills, Elizabethtown, Rahway, and Woodbridge. Then according to Knyphausen, 120 dragoons were to cross the North Hudson River from the city of New York to penetrate by a particular route to the neighborhood of Morristown and in their retreat to fall back upon a body of infantry posted at Newark to receive them."[6]

The mounted men would be composed of sixty men from the Queen's Rangers and sixty from the British 17th Dragoons. Simcoe was not unlike the man who comes up with an invention only to have a powerful company take it over and relegate the inventor to a minor role. Knyphausen wanted to go ahead with Beckwith's plan, and Simcoe was now part of the diversionary force. Others would be used for the actual kidnapping force, and the glory of snaring George Washington was not to be Simcoe's. Beckwith ordered the lieutenant colonel to send him the Queen's Rangers as Knyphausen began to prepare for the raids in late January. The glittering ice of the Hudson River was not to be the spangled banner of John Graves Simcoe's planned revenge.

Lieutenant Colonel Samuel Birch and the British 17th Light Dragoons would go to the Ford Mansion for the capture of Washington. The dragoons had sailed from Ireland and fought at Bunker Hill with their trademark "red jacket with white facings, buckskin breeches, blacktop boots, and a leather helmet with a skull-and-crossbones above the words 'or glory.'"[7] The helmet was topped with a red, flowing crest of dyed horsehair. The dragoons were armed with a single-bladed straight saber and a light carbine.

These mercenaries were known for their savagery at Bunker Hill, and many were thought to have impaled patriots to trees with their sabers. George Washington's life was in the hands of men who would like nothing more than to mount his head on a pike as a warning to all. Planning began in earnest for the mission to kidnap George Washington. The only wild card was the weather. The ice must hold, and surely the snow would cease at some point.

CHAPTER TWELVE

The Seeds of Mutiny

January 1780

ZERO OUTSIDE. MAYBE TWENTY DEGREES INSIDE. ROLLED UP INTO A human cocoon to try and find warmth. Snoring. Coughing. Hacking. The men all around knew what was coming. Outside, the snow of course was still falling. It was piled up by the door. There were no windows, and at five a.m. it was still dark outside. Still, it was better to be wrapped in the blanket in the cold cabin than outside in the bitter cold and snow. Then . . .

The drum roll in the cold darkness. The fire long gone out in the hut; the temperature was just touching zero. The smell of woodsmoke, sweat, urine, and bits of horsemeat that had been overcooked and fallen to the floor. But the drum never stopped, and though the blanket was thin, it was still a warmer situation Private Martin found himself in than what the "retreat roll" signified to every man in the 1,000 huts of Morristown. Dawn was still just a thin line behind the stars, and they were expected out on the parade ground, and Private Martin knew he was no longer destined to lie in his bunk.

And in that cold, smoking air the men of Morristown assembled. It had been this way ever since the July night of 1776 when Connecticut farm boy Joseph Martin joined the Continental Army at the age of fifteen. He initially signed his enlistment papers for only six months, but it would be seven years before he was finished with his tour of duty and now, four years after he had joined up, he found himself in the "hardest winter" of his life, where he was literally starving. There is nothing unique about Joseph Martin's experience in the winter of 1779 to 1780 except that one day he would write it all down and provide one of the few eye-witness accounts of life in the Continental Army. Morristown would test Private Martin in more ways than he could ever have imagined. "I tell a simple truth that I felt more anxiety, undertook more fatigue and hard-ships away from the battlefields than I ever did in fighting the hottest battle I ever engaged in."[1]

Martin's account of life in Morristown begins with building his hut along with the other men. And then the monotony of camp life took over and Martin slowly began to starve. "I do solemnly declare that I did not put a single morsel of victuals into my mouth for four days and as many nights, except a little black birch bark which I gnawed off a stick of wood, if that can be called victuals. I saw several men roast old shoes and eat them, and I was afterwards informed by one of the officers' waiters, that some of the officers killed and ate a favorite little dog that belonged to one of them."[2]

Washington's army was starving, and it was worse than that; the men were keenly aware that outside the snowy, frozen confines of their encampment were farmers with fattened cattle and stored wheat, but in a coda to all the suffering the men of the Continental Army endured, the American populace had grown weary of the war, and as with all great causes, the zealotry had faded to grudging irritation they should give anything to the army. They generally gave nothing, and George Washington for the first time was considering requisitioning food from every county under the threat of the bayonet.

But this did nothing for the average soldier, and Martin and the rest in the frozen months of January 1780 went about the grim business of trying to survive on nothing. The food, when it did come in, would come in sporadically and then not at all. In December, soon after the huts were nearly finished, the last of the food began to give out. "The fourth day, just at dark, we obtained a half pound of lean fresh beef and a gill of wheat for each man. . . . When the wheat was so swelled by boiling as to be beyond the danger of swelling in the stomach it was deposited there without ceremony. After this we sometimes got a little beef, but no bread. . . . We continued here starving and freezing."[3]

In a taunting reminder of what they didn't have and would never get, the soldiers in the beginning of the war had been promised what now was a king's feast. Each man's weekly rations were to be composed of:

1. One pound of bread

2. Half a pound of beef and half a pound of pork

3. One pint of milk or one gill of rice

4. One pint of spruce or malt beer

5. One gill of peas or beans

6. Six ounces of butter

7. One pound of common soap

8. Half a pint of vinegar

This was never to be seen by the soldier of the Continental Army. At best, some salted beef would appear that was mostly spoiled. In the huts was an iron kettle upon which anything soldiers could find would be thrown into the pot with melted snow to create a warm, thin, watery broth that was better than nothing, and nothing was more often the case than not. Meat was often cut up and put on the end of a stick. Bread was coveted, and fire cakes became the norm of Morristown sustenance and were made quickly in the huts' fireplaces. The fire cake had to be eaten immediately before it turned into a round, hardened brick. It was the hardtack of the Civil War, which men could take with them and then soften by putting it back into water, except the fire cakes did not soften and could only be used to hurl at the enemy. Between the freezing and starving and the endless drilling and guard duty that now entailed, the seeds of mutiny began to grow. Guard duty for the men of Morristown was particularly heinous, as it involved going to distant towns that were the lookout posts to watch for the advance of the British. In the snowy zero-degree temperatures of 1779–1780, guard duty could become a matter of life and death. Joseph Martin described it this way.

> *I must march from the parade at eight o'clock in the morning, go a distance of ten miles and relieve the guard already there, which would commonly bring it to about twelve o'clock stay there two days and two nights, then be relieved and take up the afternoon of that day to reach our quarters at Westfield where as soon as I could get into my quarters and generally, before I could lay my arms, headed for Elizabethtown the next day . . . so far from the troops and so near the enemy, we had to be constantly on the alert.*[4]

Men froze to death on guard duty or on the snowy roads of Morristown that led to the outlying towns. The army had to keep order, and this was done with the threat of lashings (100 to 1,000) and hangings for more serious offenses. There was no break. Sundays were like Mondays, with the endless rounds of reveille, drill, guard, and inspections, and all while men were freezing and starving, and the men had not been paid for years. Desertions skyrocketed. Men would slip off at night in the snowy woods, and the roll call in the morning would reveal just how many had deserted the cause and taken their chances with the elements or being caught by their own army and hanged. It is not amazing that mutiny was considered; it is more amazing that mutiny did not break out before it did. For Joseph Martin and his brigade, in fact, it had happened once before.

The winter of 1778–1779 had proven to be a trying episode of little food and hard conditions in Redding, Connecticut. In a prelude to Morristown, the winter camp pushed the men to their breaking point. Martin wrote soon after arriving, "We got settled in our winter quarters at the commencement of the new year and went in our old Continental line of starving and freezing. We now and then a got a little bad bread and salt beef (I believe chiefly horse beef). The month of January was very stormy, a good deal of snow fell, and in such weather, it was a mere chance if we got anything at all to eat. Our condition at length became insupportable. We concluded that we would not or could not bear it any longer."[5]

The men became desperate and decided to rebel, hoping someone in their home state would see their deplorable condition. The men after roll call turned out and began to parade on their own. Basically, it was an army that had gone on autopilot without leaders. The mutinous soldiers had a general plan to march into the state and get people to sit up and notice. As Private Martin wrote, "We had no need of informing the officers, we well knew they would hear of our muster without our troubling ourselves to inform them. We had hardly got paraded, before our officers, with the colonel at the head, came in front of the regiment."[6]

The officers pleaded with the men and told them their mutinous conduct was not to their advantage and changes would be made. "This latter expression of their sorrow only served to exasperate the men, which the officers observing, changed their tone and endeavored to soothe the yankee temper they had excited and with an abundance of fair promises, persuaded us to return to our quarters again."[7]

Private Martin and the rest returned to their huts and the mutiny was headed off, but it was a warning shot, and the men in their log cabins in Morristown were now being pushed up to that line once again. The only time the men had to themselves was in the evening after the day was over, but even here after the final "sounding of tattoo," which was the signal for men to turn in, they were essentially prisoners in their small cabins.

There were few letters from home, and if any came at all, they were read over like sacrament by the men. Only a fifth of the men were married, and so talk turned to sweethearts, home, better days. When letters did come, they often made matters worse, with wives or family members complaining of dire conditions at home. If there was a ration of rum, this was drunk, or a watery tea or coffee. The conversations would then turn to the inevitable thoughts of rebellion. The catalyst could be the flogging of a soldier for stealing food or when food or clothing was promised and not delivered. There was no money, and the currency had been so devalued that if they did have Continental dollars they would be better used in the fireplace for warmth.

There was no upside for these men. Tired, frozen, hungry, sick, alone, they were the remnants of the "glorious cause," and the real question is why they didn't all just up and leave. It is hard to believe that the cherished ideals of liberty and freedom, esoteric as they were, could keep these desperate men in their cabins in the woods. They were essentially illiterate farmers used to hacking out a living in their fields. The relatively sophisticated concepts of Lockean freedoms by the Founding Fathers could hardly be believed to penetrate the smoke-blackened walls of the huts of Morristown. Maybe it was simply what men in battle experience, a devotion not to a cause but to each other, and in that way, they believed in the cause of the new nation. Their lives had been one of struggle before the war, and so the faint light of a better day might have been a glue, along with their belief in George Washington as the embodiment of that cause. James Thacher's view of Washington was that of many of the enlisted men, but he had a rare opportunity to see Washington up close when he was invited to the Ford Mansion for a dinner. "It is natural to view with keen attention the countenance of an illustrious man with a secret hope of discovering in his features some peculiar traces of excellence, which distinguishes him from and elevates him above his fellow mortals."[8]

Half God, half man. George Washington, for a lot of the men, did walk on water, but Thacher's description of the dinner is illuminating in that it was during the worst part of the winter at Morristown. "His tall and noble stature and just proportions—his fine, cheerful, open countenance—simple and modest deportment—are all calculated to interest every beholder in his favor and to command veneration and respect. . . . A placid smile is frequently observed on his lips, but a loud laugh it is said seldom if ever escapes him. He is polite and attentive to each individual at the table and retires after the compliments of a few glasses."[9]

One can see the young surgeon in awe of the spiritual leader of the American Revolution, who would one day inherit the mantle of "Father of His Country." George Washington was holding it all together behind the tight smile, the dinners with his officers, wondering if his army would disintegrate around him while the British plotted their stratagems of his destruction. One can see him rising from the table and retiring to his bedroom with Martha, utterly exhausted, able to put down the mask for a short while. The man who rarely laughed out loud was barely keeping the pins in place that held together the confabulation that was the American Revolution.

And the men in their huts slept as best they could three miles away from their commander. For now, they were unwilling to mutiny, to throw off their self-imposed shackles. As Private Martin would later write, "We were unwilling to desert the cause of our country when in distress, we knew her cause involved our own."[10] Still, the seeds of mutiny planted in Connecticut would sprout again in Morristown.

CHAPTER THIRTEEN

The Trial of Benedict Arnold

Christmas 1779

BENEDICT ARNOLD WAS NERVOUS. THE CARRIAGE WAS HAVING TROUBLE on the snow-packed roads and the horses several times lost their footing. But that was not what was making him nervous. He would reach Morristown eventually, but the outcome of his court-martial would determine not only his fate but that of his family. Everything he and Peggy had been working toward was now on the line. He had to be acquitted of all charges or he might not be able to sell his services to the British.

Arnold looked out the window holding his hat in his lap. He had had many close calls in battle and somehow always managed to escape unharmed, until he was wounded in his leg. Twice. He stretched out the leg that had healed but left him with a permanent limp. This disfigurement was in the war chest of reasons why he should be compensated for his services in the war. Besides, lives would be saved by what he was doing. The Americans were certainly not going to win the war now, with the populace losing interest and Washington's army falling apart in Morristown. In his view, he was merely speeding up the war to its inevitable finish and in that way saving lives. It was vintage Arnold thinking.

The lacquered carriage rampaged into Morristown, spraying snow from the wheels as the four horses galloped smartly along the packed road and came to a fast halt in front of the tavern. People stopped to stare at the elegant carriage and the finely uniformed coachmen; then the door swung open and out stepped a young, dark-haired two-star general of the

Continental Army. There was the air of the swashbuckler about him, with his trim uniform, high-polished boots, and the limp that was the mark of a man of action. Charisma radiated as his gray eyes flickered over the tavern before he went inside with a flurry that was his habitual manner.

Benedict Arnold had arrived in Morristown for his court-martial carrying a ticking time bomb that was set to go off when he assumed command of West Point. No man present had any idea that the general had made a deal with General Clinton that he would procure command of the highly prized fort and then basically turn it over to the British, with a big fat bow of prisoners and supplies as well. That was why it was more important that he be done with this court-martial and it reach a favorable conclusion; nothing could mar his chances now of assuming command of the jewel of the Hudson River.

It was understandable that people should stare at Arnold. He was ruggedly handsome and had the joie de vivre of a man who had cheated death many times and, not unlike some swashbuckling pirate, had managed to come out on top and swing right into another important battle, making sure he was a prominent player. He did have a large nose, but his dark skin and piercing gray eyes only made the appendage the bow spar of a very imposing personage. The Indians called him Black Eagle, and the name fit. Benedict Arnold was getting ready to swoop down on his largest prey yet: George Washington and the American Revolution. How had it come to this most promising general giving away all glory and honor for the gold shackles General Clinton had promised him? It was a series of events leading to the road of the court-martial that even now he was walking into.

After taking Fort Ticonderoga from the British, he had returned home to find his wife had died, leaving him with three small boys. Even in this clear victory there was the rock in his shoe that would constantly dog him, and that was that for every accolade there was an asterisk. Yes, he had taken Ticonderoga, but his superiors accused him of mishandling funds and the bulk of the glory had gone to Ethan Allen and his Green Mountain Boys, whom he had been forced to bring along.

Then in 1777 he led the attack on the British in Quebec after a hellish journey through dense swamps, rapids, and rivers that became a survival journey, only to be severely wounded in the right knee and having to retreat after leading a heroic charge against the entrenched British. Again, the charges were financial impropriety, the claim that he absconded with 55,000 of the 67,000 pounds allocated for the campaign. At the very least, there were questions about how the money was spent. Major John Brown of Massachusetts later said presciently of Arnold, "Money is this man's God and to get enough of it he would sacrifice his country."[1]

No matter; he joined Washington's army in winter encampment in Morristown in 1777, but he had made enemies in Congress and he was passed over for promotion while five brigadier generals were promoted to major generals. Benedict Arnold had had enough and submitted his resignation to George Washington. His Excellency soothed the wounded general's pride and convinced him to stay on, but we see a pattern of bitter indignation at not being recognized for his achievements. This was helped by his taking command of an American force at Danbury, Connecticut, where he attacked a British force that had burned depots, barns, and storehouses. Leaving 154 dead, Arnold had a horse shot out from him, and when a British regular approached him with guns drawn and declared him his prisoner, Arnold, who was pinned under the horse, drew his own pistol and shot the soldier dead. Congress awarded the brigadier general a new horse.

The Second Battle of Saratoga saw Arnold in his strangest role yet, that of renegade general going against orders to save the day. General Horatio Gates, who hated Arnold, ordered him to stay away from the battlefield after he returned from the fighting. Arnold, true to form, did not obey the order and raced back to the battle, leading men in charges on various fronts and turning the tide of battle, singlehandedly capturing a redoubt held by General Heinrich von Breymann and his Hessian troops. Unfortunately, Arnold was wounded again in the same leg that had taken a bullet at the battle of Quebec. This time it was much worse, and it would give him the limp he would have for the rest of his life.

The British regarded him as the hero of the battle, while many saw his rushing into battle as theatrics on the American side, claiming the battle had already been won. Even though Congress officially thanked him, Arnold could not catch a break, and he was tiring of the sniping and the absence of recognition. He was finally promoted upon Washington's recommendation to the rank of major general, and then he was appointed the commander of Philadelphia after the British evacuated. This set him on the road to the court-martial in Morristown.

Arnold immediately made himself a target with an opulent lifestyle. His mansion had a "housekeeper, coachman, groom and various other servants where he entertained the wealthy elite of the city."[2] He galloped through Philadelphia in a coach drawn by a matched team of four horses. It was as if Arnold was exacting his own revenge for the glory denied him after years of service and he was determined to build up his personal fortune. Joseph Reed, who was president of the Pennsylvania Supreme Council and Washington's former adjutant, was an enemy of Arnold and launched an investigation, as few could understand his lavish spending unless he was absconding with funds. This is when he met Peggy Shippen, whose family were prominent Loyalists and who counted as her friend Major John André, who would be heading up the British intelligence. It is when Benedict Arnold married Peggy Shippen that he veered for all time into the seas of treason.

But John Reed saw Arnold's downfall as simply one of being guilty of graft and using monies for his personal benefit or selling influence. Washington had a more prescient understanding of Benedict Arnold's plight than many when he wrote, "Few men are capable of making a continual sacrifice of all views of private interest or advantage to the common good. . . . It is vain to exclaim against the depravity of human nature on this account—the fact is so, the experience of every age and nation has proved it."[3] Washington then went on to describe the disillusionment of many officers who had entered the revolution full of patriotic enthusiasm and lately reached the five-year mark at Morristown.

At the commencement of the dispute—in the first effusions of their zeal and looking upon the service to be only temporary, they entered into it without paying any regard to pecuniary or selfish considerations. But finding its duration to be much longer than they at first suspected and that instead of deriving any advantage from the hard-

ships and dangers to which they were exposed, they on the contrary were losers by their patriotism and fell far short even of a competency to supply their wants.[4]

No matter; the investigation produced a court-martial that was now, after being postponed several times, being held two days before Christmas. Reed and others had no idea that the stakes for the court-martial of Benedict Arnold had become much bigger than his being accused of impropriety as his role of commander of Philadelphia. It was for the fate of the American Revolution and whether Benedict Arnold would become the most famous traitor in history.

John Reed was a complicated character. No one was quite sure why he was attacking Arnold, and the truth was that Reed had been contacted by a woman offering him 10,000 pounds if he would assist the British Peace Commission in securing a truce. Reed said he had refused the offer, but in Britain one of the commissioners had let it be known that there was back-channeling going on to destabilize the government of the United States. An old friend of Reed's, Charles Thomas, had his suspicions in a letter he wrote to Reed.

Would it not be to divide the people by every means in their power; to lessen the reputation and consequently the weight and authority of the great council of the United States to poison the minds of the people and prejudice them against Congress by misrepresentation of facts and publications calculated to deceive to seize every occasion of quarreling with Congress and endeavor to bring the other states and particularly the legislature of their own into the dispute; to labor to damn the reputation of . . . general officers of the army, not sparing those of their own state whom they cannot hope to influence; especially such as are distinguished for their spirit and bravery and if they cannot effect their purpose to disparage their past services, pour upon them a torrent of abuse with a gentle salvo of 'as it is reported and believed.'"[5]

This is eerily applicable to the present day, and it was Charles Thomas's prescient view that eventually foreign countries would try and wreck the United States from within. He was pointing out that attacking the character of Benedict Arnold, a very talented general in the Revolutionary cause, was in fact helping Britain by potentially depriving America of one of her fighting heroes. What Thomas didn't know was that he was dead-on; the damage had been done, and Benedict Arnold had already been weaponized and would soon strike. But to Reed, who loathed Arnold, the investigation was pursued to its logical end, which would be a court-martial in Morristown.

Arnold opened up in the tavern in Morristown with a polemic on why he was going to commit treason, though no one knew what was percolating behind the bandy-legged general's words. He stated that he "had sacrificed a great part of a handsome fortune"[6] for his country.

> *The part which I have acted in the American cause has been acknowledged by our friends and by our enemies to have been far from an indifferent one. My time, my fortune, and my person have been devoted to my country in this war. . . . Is it probable that after having acquired some little reputation, and after having gained the favorable opinion of those whose favorable opinion it is an honor to gain, I should all at once sink into a course of conduct equally unworthy of the patriot and the soldier?[7]*

The answer was yes. More than anyone on the tribunal knew. Arnold was taunting his judges with a scenario that he had actualized, and now he needed to be acquitted to clear the way for the grand final act of his treasonous play. The surrender of West Point on the Hudson River was the jewel of his treasonous act. He had to have a meaningful command, and nothing was more coveted by General Clinton than gaining control of the Hudson. If not a death blow to the Americans, it would at the least be a dagger to the main artery of the young republic.

Chapter Fourteen

Valley Forge

February 22, 1778

Two years before, George Washington had undergone another test of fire at Valley Forge. On his birthday Washington was eating scrambled eggs with stewed carrots and onions. Martha looked on while her husband enjoyed the hot food that was so precious in Valley Forge. There was snow on the ground, but it was not deep. It was cold but not freezing. A typical winter's day. George Washington would have rather been blowing out the candles on his birthday cake, but there were no candles and no cake. Scarce provisions did not provide either, and now the man who had just turned forty-six had behind him 8,200 men in the encampment, with only 2,898 fit for the duty because, as Washington noted, the rest were barefoot and naked.

Shirts that had turned to rags on their backs, pants hanging in strips around their knees, and of course no shoes constituted naked in the eighteenth century. The camp's famous bloody footprints attested to the lack of footwear, and the sight of those blooded indentations in the snow carried the ominous knowledge that men were dying by the thousands. There had been no food in camp for seven days, and Martha Washington had managed to scrape up some eggs and vegetables for the general's birthday and even hired a band to play. It could have been a funeral march and it would have been no less apropos. Once again, the lack of food was appalling. Private Martin, who would later be the same witness in Morristown, wrote, "I lay here two nights and one day and had not a morsel of anything to eat all the time, save half of a pumpkin, which I cooked by placing it upon a rock, the skin side uppermost, and making a fire upon it."[1]

But Martha wanted to make her husband feel better and had arrived at Valley Forge to take charge of the general's well-being. As one historian wrote:

> *Martha had traveled little before the war and whenever she joined Washington, he attempted to make her lodgings as familiar as possible. At Valley Forge he had his private baggage, including the family tableware and cutlery, released from storage and shipped to the Potts House. . . . Even after the addition of a new great room—its floor, walls, and roof hewn from the same trees as the huts—the Potts house afforded little privacy. Though secretly dismayed by the cramped living conditions, Martha never complained and instead slipped naturally into her familiar role of convivial lady of the manor.*[2]

The tabula rasa of suffering in the American Revolution was a long, broad cloth punctuated by peaks and valleys where George Washington and the Continental Army came close to dissolution from the combined pressures of the British, lack of food, weather, disease, enlistments running out, defeats, lack of hope, and the real killer: horrible mismanagement by a government just created to run a war.

The dry run for Morristown began here, and if there is a marker for comparison, then it has to begin at Valley Forge The benchmark of suffering in the American Revolution is Valley Forge, and history has handed this to us as the time of a wintry hell that Washington and his troops barely survived intact. Like Morristown, it would be a time of starvation and endurance, but the story and the denouement would be much different.

Albigence Waldo kept a journal in Valley Forge that gives a firsthand account of the suffering the soldiers endured.

> *There comes a Soldier, his bare feet are seen thru his worn out shoes . . . his legs nearly naked from the tattered remains of an only pair of stock-*

ings, his breeches not sufficient to cover his nakedness, his shirt hanging in Strings, his hair disheveled, his face meagre, his whole appearance pictures a person forsaken and discouraged. He comes and cries with an air of wretchedness and despair, I am sick, my feet lame, my legs are sore, my body covered with tormenting itch—my clothes are worn out, my Constitution is broken, my former activity is exhausted by fatigue, hunger and cold. I fail fast I shall soon be no more![3]

The Continental Army began their winter camp on December 19, 1778, after a humiliating defeat at Germantown. Washington had actually considered attacking the British in Philadelphia in early December with pressure from Congress, and the victory by General Gates gave Gates the reputation as a man who engages the enemy, while some whispered that Washington mostly avoided the enemy. Nothing could have been further from the truth, as the Battle of Trenton had shown, but Washington had an aggressive nature that could be detrimental to him and the army.

It was General Nathanael Greene who advised against the attack.

We must not be governed by our wishes. . . . Let us not flatter ourselves from the heat of our zeal that men can do more than they can. . . . The successes of last winter (at Trenton and Princeton) were brilliant and attended with the most happy consequences in changing the complexion of the times, but if the bills of mortality were to be consulted, I fancy it would be found we were no great gainers by those operations. . . . An attack upon the city of Philadelphia appears to me like forming a crisis for American liberty which if unsuccessful I fear will prover her grave.[4]

The commander in chief cooled his heels in a tent while the army constructed a log city, and then he moved into Isaac Potts's house. The suffering at Valley Forge was preordained when months before the British under Generals Knyphausen and Cornwallis attacked a supply depot and hauled off 3,500 barrels of flour, horseshoes, tomahawks, and supplies for the approaching winter. Washington and his men were coming to camp stripped bare. As Private Martin would record in his diary, the suffering began immediately. "We arrived at Valley Forge in the evening. It was dark. There was no water to be found and I was perishing with thirst. I searched for water until I was weary and came to my tent without finding any. Fatigue and thirst, joined with hunger, almost made me desperate. I felt at that instant as if I would have taken victuals or drink from the best friend I had on earth by force. I am not writing fiction all are sober realities."[5]

The differences between Morristown and Valley Forge would be not the suffering but the rate at which men died. Compared to Morristown, Valley Forge was a mild winter. The weather, while cold, was not the killer it would become two years later; the brutal truth of Valley Forge is that men would die because of disorganization within the army and simple greed. The awful reality was that they died needlessly; "the toll to mismanagement, graft and speculation was great."[6] A very rich harvest in Pennsylvania was sold on the "London Trade" to the British, and this, along with total ineptitude by Thomas Mifflin, who was the quartermaster at the time, contributed to the general disorganization that seems to have been the hallmark of Washington's army in 1778. Desertion became horrendous.

The men running out of Valley Forge had hopes of receiving clothing and food from the British even though they would be prisoners of war. The stories of men eating rats and lice in British prison cells still were not as bad as the suffering they were enduring in Valley Forge. Many Americans were imprisoned on British prison barges, where conditions became so bad, they set fire to the ships in a mass suicide pact. Still, when the deserters reached the British, some were offered uniforms if they would fight for Great Britain. Many then deserted back to the Americans once they had their new pants, stockings, and coats. Officers were not treated well when they turned up in British lines and offered their services. They were regarded as men without honor and ended up in the filth of the deep holds of the prison barges. But life in Valley Forge remained a suffering hell.

For those who preserved, stacked like cordwood in their rustic huts, life remained wretched. Much of the firewood was still so green that when the stove lengths did manage to catch flame the cabins were inundated with black choking smoke that left the camp in permanent twilight. And though slit latrines known as vaults had been dug haphazardly about the living quarters, exhausted and hungry men were unlikely to be meticulous about their sanitary habits. Filth rapidly accumulated in and around the cabins and disease spread unabated.[7]

And this brought about the now famous Baron Friedrich Ludolf Gerhard Augustin von Steuben, who arrived on the dark afternoon of February 23, 1778. "George Washington was not certain what to expect when he rode out of camp that afternoon to greet Steuben and his cortege. . . . The man whom Washington encountered was a plump officer ensconced in a grandiose sled adorned with 24 jingle bells and pulled by a team of well-muscled coal dark Percheron horses stepping in sync as if dancing a ponderous waltz."[8]

This Prussian nobleman became the bright light, the counterweight to the story of death and greed and mismanagement that was Valley Forge. Every story needs a payoff, and at Valley Forge there were two: the arrival of Baron von Steuben and the treaty signed by France on February 6, 1778, recognizing the United States, with a commitment to assist in defeating the British and helping the new country toward independence. These two events would round out the Valley Forge *Heart of Darkness* journey and could be used to show that the death of 2,500 men was not in vain. France could now be brought to bear against the British, while von Steuben brought order to the chaos that was the Continental Army in the winter of 1778.

Establishing discipline would be Steuben's primary hurdle, a task for which he was well suited. For perhaps the first time, there was an experienced officer at hand who could instill a dedicated professionalism in the Continental army. Neither Prussian nor American soldiers simply sprang from the earth fully formed. . . . The would-be drillmaster would take on the task of molding the raw material the colonies had provided to George Washington . . . a distinctly martial enthusiasm.[9]

Von Steuben inspected the camp of the Americans and submitted a report detailing "rusting muskets and ammunition tins, a dearth of bayonets and . . . both officers and enlisted men standing guard duty in a sort of dressing gown made of old blankets or woolen bed covers."[10] Von Steuben had new latrines dug farther from camp and instituted regimens promoting cleanliness, order, and discipline. "Each morning and afternoon, in fair weather and foul, the Prussian assembled his small troop on the vast parade ground in the center of camp. Circulating among the soldiers and barking instructions like a rabid drill instructor he preached the dual discipline of mind and body."[11]

What von Steuben discovered was that the Americans had proved they could fight but they had no "institutional memory." They had no training or military culture to fall back on. They were just as disorganized at the beginning of the war as they were at Valley Forge. The only reason they had any success was that they fought like wild animals with the natural skills of backwoodsmen who could shoot accurately and used the forest for cover. "It was only the Americans' spirited tenacity that had prevented them from being completely swept away by polished British and Hessian soldiers at Brandywine and Germantown."[12] Von Steuben was about to give American soldiers the basic training they never received.

He began with basic concepts of military discipline. Breaking his gaunt combatants into ten- and twelve-man squads, the tallest in the rear, he demonstrated for each trooper how to "stand straight and firm upon his legs with his head turned to the right so far as to bring his left eye over the waistcoat buttons; the heels two inches apart, the toes turned out; the belly drawn in a little but without constraint, the breast a little projected the shoulders square to the front and kept back, and the hands hanging down to the sides, close to the thighs."[13]

It was what George Washington could not do. Von Steuben would literally get down in the mud to explain small-arms maintenance or how to dig in and take shelter when under attack. The bayonets owned by the Continentals were mostly used to cook over fires. Von Steuben immediately threw off his coat and showed the correct method of wielding and thrusting. Then at night the Prussian would work on his book of military regulations, which was basically a how-to book for a new army addressing "the gathering and interpretation of intelligence; the proper arms and accoutrements to be carried by all officers and enlisted men, the marching formation and exercises of brigades, regiments, companies, and platoons, the instruction and inspection of new recruits and even the correct method of executing an about face."[14]

The book would be finished in the spring and would emerge as *Regulations for the Order and Discipline of the Troops of the United States*.[15] Von Steuben understood the American character in a way the British did not, and they should have taken notes from the odd Prussian and probably could have avoided the American Revolution altogether. Von Steuben had commanded an undisciplined light infantry of Magyars who were Frederick the Great's shock troops. Von Steuben realized that like the wild Hungarians, the iconoclastic Americans who had been isolated in the backwoods of the continent did not understand an order as being valid until they understood the *why* behind the order. And von Steuben explained the why for all of his rules and regulations. He explained the reasons for all of his tactics and found the Americans then took them on as their own.

His hard-won respect for the Americans soared as he came to understand what they had endured. "No European army could have been kept together under such dreadful conditions,"[16] he mused. Von Steuben's sense of order was contagious, and "cleanup crews were suddenly scurrying across the cantonment digging new latrines, filling in old vaults and hauling away several months' worth of accumulated filth and nastiness."[17] George Washington took notice of the changes and felt von Steuben was responsible for the new pride he saw in the average soldier. They had succeeded in spite of themselves, and von Steuben believed that if the American soldier could be trained and organized into a cohesive military machine, he would be unbeatable.

Von Steuben was rebuilding the American army from the ground up, and he was equally pleased with the progress made by the soldiers. "My enterprise succeeded better than I had dared to expect," he wrote a friend. "I had the satisfaction, in a month's time, to see not only a regular step introduced into the army, but I also made maneuvers with ten and twelve battalions with as much precision as the evolution of a single company."[18]

Von Steuben had intuitively improvised his training for the unorthodox style of American fighting. The image of the American Revolutionary soldier is one of a traditional battle with the men crouched down and firing their muskets. But in fact, they had no real discipline in firing as an organized unit.

> *What military experts of the era called "fire discipline" required three rough components. First infantry battalions on the march had to be able to change formations while maintaining cohesion. Then, upon meeting the enemy, each soldier required the discipline to stand and hold fire when so ordered even if the man next to him was torn to pieces by cannon fire. Finally, in engaging, the ability to load, fire and reload rapidly and efficiently through the noise and smoke of a battlefield had to become second nature.*[19]

Von Steuben broke through the theoretical nature of other foreign experts and gave the men hands-on advice for tasks from digging a latrine to building breastworks around the camp. "For the first time there was an experienced officer at hand who could instill a dedicated professionalism in the Continental army. Neither Prussian nor American soldiers simply sprang from earth fully formed and von Steuben's years of developing the clockwork efficiency of an unremarkable group of German peasants and serfs had enabled him to provide the leadership the American soldier required."[20]

The road to the winter of Morristown had the lessons of suffering at Valley Forge built into the army. Organization was better, and combating disease, starvation, desertion, and enlistment expirations was now well-trod ground thanks to Valley Forge. And the army was a more cohesive, well-trained unit. It is just that the ante had been upped at Morristown, with each side looking for a knockout blow and the wild card of the worst winter in a century switching the tables on both sides. A final asterisk to Valley Forge was that soon afterward General William Howe was replaced with Henry Clinton as the commander of the British forces. General Clinton would be the man Washington would face at Morristown, a very different general in every way.

CHAPTER FIFTEEN

The Manic-Depressive

New York, 1779

HE WAS THE OVERALL COMMANDER OF THE BRITISH IN AMERICA, AND he was convinced he was a hated man by not only the Americans but those on his own staff. He just wanted to leave. He wanted to go back to Britain and forget all about America and George Washington. In his mind, the Howe brothers had left him a hell of a mess, and it was now up to him to somehow bring this five-year debacle to a close. But he was surrounded by stupid men. Only a fool would want his job. He would rather just be a foot soldier. It was all so depressing that sometimes he didn't even want to get out of bed.

The fact that British general Henry Clinton might have been a manic-depressive did not come to light until his papers were published in 1926. Then the self-doubts and meanderings of the strangely paralyzed general were revealed and people could finally connect the dots as to why General Howe's successor seemed so indecisive. He controlled New York, and Washington was holed up in Morristown, and yet he was filled with self-doubt, if not self-loathing. He revealed himself many times to his junior officers in letters that would cast light on his malady. "Believe me my dear Colonel Smart, I envy even that soldier who is passing the door and would exchange with joy our situations. No. Let me advise you never to take command of an army. I am detested—nay hated—in this army. But I am indifferent about it because I know it is without cause. I am determined to return home; the minister has used me so ill that I can no longer bear with this life."[1]

He quarreled with his own officers, stewed, doubted his own decisions. He despised his appointment as commander of the British forces in America and pined to return to Britain. He thought Washington might come across the frozen Hudson and attack New York from Morristown before promised reinforcements could arrive. He worried about the thousands of Loyalists who had fled to New York and made it essentially a Loyalist stronghold, and that at any minute the French fleet might appear and attack New York. He was the opposite of the decisive commander who chose a course and stuck to it; he called himself an introvert and a "shy bitch," and in his papers, released by the William L. Clements Library at the University of Michigan in 1926, he comes across as neurotic at the least and maybe bipolar.

But this was the man George Washington was facing in the winter of 1779–1780, and his own sporadic behavior made it hard for Washington to gauge his intentions. After the crossing of the Delaware, Clinton, as the second in command under General Howe, prompted him to attack the commander of the Trenton-Princeton campaign. He accused General Howe of having "the most consummate ignorance I ever heard of in any officer above a corporal."[2] A month later, Clinton headed back to Britain, vowing never to come back to America and never to serve under General Howe again. After being knighted, he withdrew his resignation and returned to serve once again under Howe, until the general was relieved and Clinton took command. He then wrote a running critique of how General Howe had botched the war in America.

Had Sir William fortified the hills around Boston he could not have been driven from it; had he pursued his victory on Long Island he had ended the rebellion; had he landed above the lines at New York, not a man could have escaped him; had he operated with the Northern army he had saved it; or had he gone by land to Philadelphia he had ruined Mr. Washington and his forces; but as he did none of these things, had he gone to the D—l before he was sent to America, it had been the saving of infamy to himself and indelible dishonor to his country.[3]

96

So much for General Howe. In a way, things never looked better for Henry Clinton in 1779. He had risen to the top of the British military. He was living in the luxurious Archibald Kennedy House on Broadway and had country homes at his disposal. He was commander of the crown jewel of America, New York City. And George Washington's army was shivering, starving, and coming apart in Morristown while his own army enjoyed every amenity New York could offer. The corpulent general was kept well served by five farms, and he put on elaborate parties that consumed his expense budget while putting on plays and himself playing the violin in an orchestra in his home.

When the weather broke, he slept in the afternoons in the gardens behind the Kennedy House overlooking the Hudson River. This became well-known, and Captain Henry Lee of the Virginia Light Dragoons proposed kidnapping Clinton while he napped. His plan was for soldiers to wade ashore at low tide, snatch the sleeping general, and bring him to Morristown. It would seem everyone had kidnapping on their minds. Alexander Hamilton cancelled the plan, saying, "It would be our misfortune, since the British government could not find another commander so incompetent in his place."[4]

But then food for his troops became a problem for Clinton as well when the brutal winter descended in 1779. The ice-bound harbor kept out British ships, while foraging parties that ventured into New Jersey were intercepted by American soldiers. Wood had also fallen into short supply in New York, and many Loyalists were freezing in their beds. The wood situation became a crisis in January when below-zero temperatures gripped the area. It became so bad that a vessel loaded with cargo was detained and then the ship hacked into firewood. Accommodating the Loyalists and the British troops pushed New York to the breaking point when a fire broke out and destroyed many homes and stores. These were problems that besieged Clinton in the winter and he still had no concrete plan to end the war.

Then the reinforcements arrived, and Clinton was flabbergasted to find the army had sent him only 3,400 soldiers. One hundred men had died on the trip over and many were ill. Clinton received an order from London to head for Charleston and oversee the attack there, and he and his second in command, Cornwallis, left with the fleet in December. Cornwallis was a man whom he did not like as well: "he is insipid good-natured Lord and the worst officer—except in personal courage—under the Crown."[5] Clinton really didn't like anybody, including himself.

The vexing problem of George Washington and his army at Morristown would have to wait for now. While Clinton was gone, Hessian general Wilhelm von Knyphausen would be in command. All General Henry Clinton could do now was stare out from his ship heading south and ponder the innumerable problems of ending the war quickly. He really needed a knockout blow. Something to bring this obnoxious war to a close once and for all. There were the ongoing negotiations with Mr. Moore (Benedict Arnold), as the British knew him. His aide Major John André said he was supposedly in George Washington's inner circle and he might be the answer. But what they really needed was something bold right now, something that would bring the Americans to their knees. Something that would decapitate the patriot cause and have them sue for peace. General Clinton stared toward the Jersey coast from his ship and knew that somewhere in that forest was his nemesis, George Washington.

Chapter Sixteen

Preparing to Kidnap George Washington

January 1780

Captain Beckwith's plan to kidnap George Washington was put on the front burner of the British high command. The freezing of the Hudson had taken what was before a fantastical idea and put it in the realm of having a high degree of success. Spies had pinpointed Washington's location exactly and provided detailed maps of the roads leading to Morristown. Deserters confirmed the number of Life Guard soldiers guarding Washington, and most importantly, the main force of Washington's army was three miles away.

This was no half-baked idea inspired by a man who had been wrongly imprisoned by the Americans, but it was now a full-scale military raid based on the sound principles of diversion, speed, redundancy, secrecy, and finally execution. After accepting Captain Beckwith's plan, General Knyphausen went full speed ahead. He would need many more men than Simcoe had initially proposed, including infantry along with the strike force of cavalry. While the frozen Hudson gave the British their opportunity, they realized the Americans could use it as well and might just pour across the ice at any time.

The situation was fluid, partially because of the weather but also as a result of Washington shifting troops around and forcing the British to reevaluate their plan. At one point Knyphausen also planned to send men across the ice to simultaneously attack the American outpost at Paramus, which was reported to have 200 to 300 men, while another British force would attack the outpost at Newark Mountain Meeting, which was said to have another 300 men. This would prevent these soldiers from interfering with the returning force of men with the captured general, but then word came that Washington had pulled back his troops from the outposts and Knyphausen canceled the attacks.

At its heart, the kidnap raid remained unchanged. Charge across the Hudson River and then up toward Morristown under the cover of darkness; disarm, kill, or silence any soldier of the Life Guard present; snatch Washington from his bed, where he presumably would be sleeping; and then ride like the wind back to the Hudson and cross the ice to Staten Island with the prize of the American general in tow. Simple. But the logistics of the raid were not so simple.

In late January, Knyphausen assigned a new regiment of infantry to the British outpost at Paulus Hook, who would wait for the returning men from Morristown and give them cover as they galloped across the blue ice. If they were being chased, then the men of Paulus Hook would cut down the Americans as they came across. Then came the news from a James Jones, a deserter from the American army at Morristown, that George Washington was still using the Ford Mansion as his headquarters. On February 15, Jones, who was originally from Merionethshire in Wales, conveyed to William Tryon in New York that "the horse cavalry had been sent to distant quarters. Washington had a few about him and a small foot guard."[1] Jones might have deserted in late January and probably ran into Simcoe and Beckwith before going to New York.

The main cavalry strike force remained at 120 men, with 350 infantrymen in a support function. William Smith, a Loyalist, reported in his diary that 400 to 500 men would cross the ice. There are conflicting reports; the strike force may have been expanded; "About seventy German cavalrymen were reported to have ridden from Long Island to Richmond on Staten Island on February 4th."[2] They did this to ride with the Queen's Rangers, which they commonly did. If the force had been expanded to 300 men, then the composition would have been 175 of the British Light Dragoons, 60 hussars from Simcoe's Queen's regiment, and 70 of Diemer's Black Hussars.

The British 17th Light Dragoons commanded by Lieutenant Colonel Samuel Birch would actually ride to Morristown and capture General Washington. As stated before, they were a regiment from Ireland that had arrived in Boston prior to Bunker Hill. They participated in major skirmishes around Boston and had a sister regiment, the 16th Light Dragoons, that had captured General Charles Lee. Many of the men from the 16th joined the 17th, with their headquarters at Hempstead on Long Island and men patrolling the lines around New York City.

Their appearance was designed to instill terror, with a skull and crossbones on their hats with OR GLORY beneath and a straight saber and a light carbine. The men were trained to fire from the saddle at full gallop, an early version of the blitzkrieg concept used by Adolf Hitler where speed and terror were used with deadly force.

The Black Hussars were made up mostly of escaped prisoners of war who had come with General John Burgoyne's army and had a reputation in New York for being unruly. "The men wore a hussar cap and black coat with blue trousers and boots of the Hussar style (short with the trousers tucked in)."[3] The Queen's Rangers dressed much the same, with green wool jacket and trousers tucked into a short boot with a belt over the right shoulder. Birch had gained a reputation for stealing the possessions of Loyalists and allowing his soldiers to pillage as well. He had ordered a Quaker meeting house torn down and sold off the wood on Long Island. One could say it was a renegade force of cavalrymen led by a renegade. These would be the men who would greet George Washington in the dead of night.

Not a man to leave anything to chance, General Knyphausen added more soldiers to Stirling's Elizabeth-bound troops, led by a brigadier, Cortland Skinner, who at one time had been the attorney general in New Jersey. "Stirling commanded two regiments of British regulars and Skinner commanded his first and fourth battalions of New Jersey volunteers, for a total of 1200 men."[4]

Final preparations were put in place. On February 6, the British procured eighty-six sleds from the locals to transport military supplies to British posts on Staten Island and Paulus Hook. It was noted that the ice on Newark Bay was so thick and hard that the twenty-four-pounder cannon pulled across the ice left no grooves. Major General James Pattison later wrote that it was "an event unknown in the memory of man."[5] Then on February 7, Simcoe and his Queen's Rangers rode across the ice from Staten Island to New York along with Diemer's Hussars. The 17th Regiment of Light Dragoons left their post in Queens County and joined them the next day.

The mission to kidnap George Washington depended on moving down thirty miles of roads swiftly and efficiently, and to this end the British enlisted the help of Loyalists in getting accurate maps "detailing the network of roads between Elizabethtown and Washington's headquarters and the more distant Continental camps at Morristown."[6] Everything was in place, and the tentative date of February 8 would begin the operation to decapitate the American Revolution by depriving the army and the emerging nation of its leader. On the evening of February 7 it began to snow.

CHAPTER SEVENTEEN

Mr. Moore's Unspeakable Treason

December 23, 1779

THE TAVERN SMELLED LIKE SAWDUST AND OLD BEER. MAYBE PICKLES. The sawdust was put on the floor to soak up the beer, but the planks of the floor had absorbed many a sloshed beer over the years and now the august generals sat breathing what would later become the smell of any bar in America after closing time. The men chewed on tobacco, smoked cigars, slid their heavy boots across the planks, trying to get comfortable in the cold tavern that even with the roaring fire was probably just above fifty degrees. But it was Morristown, and it was always cold.

Benedict Arnold did not want to leave anything to chance at his trial. Nothing must affect the deal he had struck with the British. Mr. Moore (his spy name) needed money to keep his beautiful young wife Peggy Shippen happy, and that was no easy task. His beautiful young wife had a habit of losing her mind when things didn't go her way and becoming hysterical, almost manic, screaming, crying, beating her fists on the bed, tearing at her hair.

Mr. Moore was alarmed that if things did not work out Mrs. Moore might just go off the deep end, and to that end she had been orchestrating the communication with Major André, who passed the communications to General Clinton. A final salvo by Mr. Moore ensured he would be paid even if he was not able to turn over West Point and had his cover blown. Ten grand. He wanted to be ensured that he and his wife would get $10,000 if the whole thing blew up. The British shrugged. Give Mr. Moore what he wants, and let's see if he can deliver.

But now Mr. Moore was on trial, and he had made quite a show of limping into the courtroom like the war hero he was and taking off the two-inch lift in front of the gathered men of his court-martial in the Morristown tavern. He had worn his spit-shined boots and his best uniform, and his hair was immaculately smoothed back. Mr. Moore must appear to be a man who has been wronged, as nothing but honor would be his due, or put another way, nothing could get in the way of his deal with the British. Mr. Moore, like many who marry up and find themselves with a wife who expects a standard of living that she is accustomed to, had to emerge from this trumped-up court-martial untarnished.

He had already tried an end run around Washington back in May with a hysterical letter: "If your excellency thinks me criminal, for heaven's sake let me be immediately tried, and if found guilty, executed, I want no favor, I ask only justice."[1] Washington yawned. He was used to the histrionics of his high-strung general and assured him it would all be worked out in the court-martial, shrugging away Mr. Moore's falling-on-his-sword ploy. So now the would-be spy was meeting with fourteen generals, among whom were William Maxwell, John Stark, Henry Knox, and William Smallwood. These were his peers, and Mr. Moore promised a tour de force of his career so far, and he delivered on that promise. He showed his erudition and elegance, and mixed in Latin phrases, finally winding up with the statement that he was being "charged with practices his soul abhors."[2]

For shame. For shame. The indignities he had been accused of weighed down Mr. Moore's soul. The first charge addressed was of giving the ship *Charming Nancy* a pass so it could come into the harbor and conduct business. Of course, Mr. Moore kept it to himself that he was part owner of the ship. The second charge was that while commander of Philadelphia, he had closed all shops to prevent anyone from making purchases while he went on a shopping spree and "privately made purchases for his own benefit."[3] Mr. Moore was indignant. He began to weep. "If this is true, I stand disgraced as the vilest of men. I stand stigmatized with indelible disgrace,"[4] he proclaimed, weeping copiously.

What about the third charge of getting a sergeant to do personal tasks for him and his wife? Mr. Moore sighed and brushed it all away, proclaiming that a soldier must follow orders whatever those orders are. Hmmm. Then how about this one: Why did Mr. Moore procure a wagon and have the cargo of *Charming Nancy* removed when a British foraging party was reported to be nearby? Ha. Mr. Moore explained that he didn't want the goods to fall in British hands! The board blinked. Really.

And then Mr. Moore had to wait until January 26 to find out the verdict. Mr. Moore was not acquitted. His shenanigans with his ship *Charming Nancy* had stuck. Of course he was profiteering. The generals were not that stupid. And the sentence was to be a reprimand from General Washington. Mr. Moore was very concerned. What might General Clinton and André think of this reprimand when they returned from Charleston? Well, there was always the ten grand. Mr. Moore, aka Benedict Arnold, would have to wait then to commit his unspeakable treason when the British returned. He still had to get his appointment to command West Point so he could turn it over to the British. Mr. Moore hoped the reprimand from George Washington would not be too bad.

CHAPTER EIGHTEEN

He Was but a Man

January 1780

MARTHA WASHINGTON COULD NOT SLEEP. EVERYONE HAD BEEN ON edge. There were reports of the British getting ready for an attack and amassing men on Staten Island. There had been rumors of a plot to kidnap her husband. Martha knew there had been a plot to kidnap her from Mount Vernon, and nothing could be discounted. Her husband had been very unhappy lately and working late many nights. Martha was used to going to bed by herself. It happened with married couples, and Washington worked with his aides late into the night. She listened for George sometimes, but most of the time she just fell asleep and he was there in the morning when she woke.

The glow from the snow outside poured in the long windows like three blue coffins. It was very bright outside. Martha shut her eyes and fell asleep. Sometime after midnight she opened her eyes and was not sure if there was a knock or not. She opened her eyes in the cold room as the door burst open and three large uniformed men burst in with muskets at the ready and went to her window, throwing up the window to the subzero air. The fire had long gone out in the fireplace, and while the room was cold enough that her nose was always cold when she woke up, now came a blast of frozen air that rushed right through the three blankets she had on top of her. Then came the fear, and this brought the shivering while the men peered into the darkness with their rifles by their cheeks, looking for the approaching enemy.

Then George Washington rushed into his wife's bedroom with his own Life Guard soldiers standing not ten feet away from her, who lay in bed with the covers up to her neck. Some of the Life Guard might have thought she was Washington's mother, as Martha Washington was short, dowdy, frequently wore bonnets, and had a matronly air about her. Now the strapping George Washington was standing next to her bed speaking in soothing tones while soldiers with loaded muskets peered into the frozen darkness. This had happened before.

The reports of the British gearing up for an operation against the Americans had become numerous. "News of British preparations was speedily conveyed to Washington and his commander of American outposts in northern New Jersey, General Arthur St Clair."[1] Washington felt like he had taken adequate actions and that "our main body cannot be surprised."[2] The commander in chief suspected all the preparations were to destroy magazines of powder, and he never suspected that the British activity was for an action that had him squarely in the crosshairs. Besides, he was well protected by his Life Guard, and they had a set protocol that would curtail the possibility of surprise.

The Life Guard were constantly on patrol, with two sentinels in the back and two in the front. His guards were barracked in eleven huts about one hundred yards east of the Ford Mansion. The increased action by the British and the expectation and rumors swirling around put everyone on edge, and this led to jittery men who saw soldiers in the darkness approaching the mansion. As two historians noted in 1846, "Several times in the course of the winter false alarms were given of the approach of the enemy. First a distant report of a gun would be heard from the most remote sentinel, and then one nearer, and so on until the sentinels by the house would fire in turn. From them it would be communicated on towards Morristown, until the last gun would be heard far to the westward at camp."[3]

Jockey Hollow was three miles away and the troops would immediately begin turning out, but the Life Guard was already on automatic pilot. When they heard the shots, "the lifeguard would rush from their huts into the Ford House, barricade the doors, open the windows, and about five men would place themselves at each window, with their muskets brought to a charge, loaded and cocked ready for defense. There they would remain until the troops from camp were seen marching, with music, at quick step down towards the mansion."[4]

Obviously, this was predicated on the Life Guard being alerted. Simcoe's and Captain Beckwith's plans were both predicated on surprise. If all went according to plan, then they would be in and out of the mansion before any shots were fired in alarm. But the false alarms also led to a lessening of tension that this was in fact a real attack. One can imagine Mrs. Washington having to endure the men in her bedroom with guns while her husband tried to soothe her nerves. A historian, Benson Lossing, noted that "these occasions were annoying to the ladies of the household, for both Mrs. Washington and Mrs. Ford were obliged to lie in bed, sometimes for hours, with their rooms full of soldiers and the keen winter air from the open windows piercing through the drawn curtains."[5] It was then Washington who had to stay by her bed until the alarm was over. The Life Guard was surely ready for any assault they could detect, but a stealthy expedition able to penetrate the house without alarm like the one Simcoe envisioned could succeed by the fact that the Life Guard would not be in position and could be cut down as they bolted from their huts.

And so the winter at Morristown progressed, punctuated by these moments of terror, boredom, and then, strangely, parties and entertainment. For Washington and the officers, that is. In a strange incongruity to the suffering going on in Log City, George Washington did enjoy a life of plentitude. This went along with the assumption that officers in the eighteenth century were expected to enjoy a better life than enlisted men. And they did, and Morristown was no exception.

George Washington was a mortal who needed release as well from the pressures of the war, and to that end he would appear in his finest at tables set for a king, and some of these dinners that turned into parties got out of hand and led to an incident so incongruous with the deity that is the George Washington who has come down to us through history. The conjugal relations between Martha and Washington had to be strained for any moments of intimacy. The Ford Mansion was full up, but add to that the fact that at any moment soldiers of the Life Guard might break into the bedroom, and it is not hard to see the frustration of the husband who has been alone for many months.

But first let's paint the picture of the strange bacchanalian events that went on in Morristown while men were literally starving. Lieutenant Erkuries Beatty arrived on Christmas Day and then wrote his brother a letter on his own rum-fuzzed day. "I am just down from dinner about half drunk; all dined together upon a good roast and broiled, but in a cold hut, however grog enough to will keep out the cold for which there is no desiring. Tomorrow we all dine with the Colonel. Which will be another excellent dinner and I think you may call that fair living."[6]

The rum that Beatty drank was fifty pounds a quart, which was eight times the monthly income of a private. We compare Beatty's letters to those of Private Martin, and it is as if there were two different universes. Martin was reduced to considering eating leather or eating nothing at all, while the lieutenant followed up with another letter describing a party binge he had been on. "Afterwards I was at two or three dances in Morristown and I had been at a couple dances at my Brother John's quarters at Bottle Hill where I spent the evenings very agreeable and when I can frolic nowhere else I do it at home with some of my friends. I am determined to drive all care away."[7]

And so, he and the other officers did drive all cares away, along with Washington, with women who were brought in from northern New Jersey. Was Washington a ladies' man? Yes. He enjoyed the company of high-spirited, pretty women. He attended dinners and every type of social gatherings along with the small parties he gave in the Ford Mansion. Washington worked from dawn to dusk along with his aides. Tedium was a factor, and the socializing gave him release, but not the sexual release he must have looked for in some form. After being the father of the revolution and the country, he was still a man in his mid-forties.

George Washington was maybe not a libertine, but he was an epicurean and really always had been, especially at Mount Vernon. This side of Washington was more indulgent than history would like to recount. Indeed, some historians have had a hard time interpreting the extreme suffering of Morristown with this strange interlude of sensual pleasure. Yet they did exist side by side, and Washington, while willing to go into battle with his men, was not willing to share their hardships. He was not above passing on a residence that was not ornate enough, as he did outside Boston in 1776, and when Martha Washington came to town, he ordered a custom coach for her from Philadelphia with ornamental moldings.

Many officers fixed up their huts and had small parties. The huts were different from those of the enlisted men in that they had wood floors and windows with real glass. There were two or three bunks in officers' huts, compared to the twelve that were crowded into the common soldiers'. Then there were the girls who came to Morristown. And George Washington the man of flesh and blood comes through in a party thrown by Colonel and Mrs. Clement Biddle. At many parties Washington was the first to dance. Once he opened with Lucy Knox, the wife of Brigadier General Henry Knox. Washington would later appear at social gatherings in Washington in a black velvet suit. He was a dandy. But at the Biddle party, thrown in rented quarters, Washington was there with Nathanael Greene and his wife attended, as did two civilians, Mr. and Mrs. George Olney.

Mrs. Olney was said to be very beautiful, and George Washington loved beautiful women. But then came the moment that was most inconsistent with the image of George Washington handed down to us through history. Here he was enjoying himself while the world swirled around him, betting on his demise, scheming coming from his very inner circle as well as from the outside, and who can blame him for veering from the high horse of moral granite? To put it bluntly, George Washington became handsy. The rum was flowing, the music was playing, people were dancing, Martha was not to be found, and the story handed down was that Mrs. Olney screamed at George Washington that "if he did not let go of her hand, she would tear out his eyes, or the hair on his head, that tho he was a General, he was but a man."[8]

Obviously, George Washington had stepped across a clearly defined line. He had had a lot to drink, as was his custom, and Martha had retired with her bonnet to the bedroom upstairs at the Ford Mansion, waiting for the soldiers to burst into her room and her ever attentive husband to come to her side. The Washingtons had a great friendship and a good relationship, but one must wonder if the physical part of it had flickered out. And so maybe he took Mrs. Olney's hand and held it too long, pressing it to his chest, whispering closely, who knows, but if it had no merit it would have died away. It did not.

The talk, innuendos, and rumors persisted, and a year later Washington's aide-de-camp Tench Tilghman offered a formal explanation, essentially confirming the incident had occurred. The aide said it all really had to do with Mr. Olney, who had refused to drink with Washington and the other officers, and so they had grabbed him while he was talking with Mrs. Olney and taken him over to drink with the men. It was the scuffling that Mrs. Olney responded to, and it was "just a happy rumpus as any good-natured person must suppose." The aide went further and said Mrs. Olney didn't use "any expressions unbecoming a lady of good breeding."[9]

So, there it was. Mrs. Olney would never dare to accuse Washington of impropriety because she was a lady of "good breeding." But the fact is that Washington had to issue a statement, and this shows he stepped over the line and Mrs. Olney called him on it. He was, after all, holed up in a winter encampment with the world on his shoulders. If this incident shows anything, it is that, as Mrs. Olney said, though Washington "was a General, he was but a man." In other words, George Washington was human.

And then the parties and dinners ended as the weather stopped all possibilities of supplies reaching Morristown. Washington settled back into writing Congress and pleading for money, food, supplies, anything to help his starving army. The Life Guard burst into Martha Washington's room, staring at phantoms in the frosted night, completely unaware that men with skulls and crossbones would soon emerge from the darkness.

CHAPTER NINETEEN

The Diversion

February 11, 1780

THE QUEEN'S RANGERS WAITED ON THE HUDSON RIVER WITH THEIR horses breathing steam while the men kept their hands together and hunched down in their collars to conserve heat, but their mustaches already were icy from their breath. The horses shifted about, anticipating they were about to set off on the white and blue expanse of ice, and like the men, they wanted to get to it. No one was more anxious than Lieutenant Colonel Simcoe, who had been quietly biding his time, waiting until General Knyphausen gave the approval to launch the mission to kidnap George Washington.

Colonel Simcoe kept a tight rein on his horse, breathing the super cold air of the blue night. The Hudson glittered before him as an unbroken expanse of snow and ice, and beyond were the frosted trees of New Jersey and beyond that was Morristown, where George Washington slept on the second floor of the Ford Mansion. Simcoe was impatient. He had watched the 300 cavalrymen of the strike led by Colonel Samuel Birch of the 17th Dragoons along with a regiment of infantry cross the river in a hail of snow dust and marching men. Simcoe looked at his watch; it was one a.m. It was time.

He raised his sword and dug his heels into his horse. The Queen's Rangers all entered the ice road as one and galloped across the white expanse. Simcoe's eyes watered as he hunched over his horse with his sword slapping his thigh. His role was diversionary, and he still chafed at being given a supporting role rather than being part of the actual force that would go to Morristown and kidnap the unsuspecting Washington. But as he rode, he felt a solace that the plan he had thought of so long ago was going forward, even if it had been altered and other men were leading the way. Still, his role was an important one: The diversions would pull away the Americans and give the strike force the needed time to get Washington and then be away before the main body of the Continental Army could be alerted. And after all, Simcoe was a soldier in the British army, and soldiers above all else followed orders. And his orders from General Stirling were to attack the American posts at Woodbridge and give "a general alarm."

After reaching the Jersey shore and following the snowy road some distance, Simcoe set up covering his return by leaving Major Richard Armstrong with some infantry and cavalry and a few cannons on the heights above the Old Blazing Star Ferry. He was in enemy territory, and once he aroused the enemy, then it would be a race to get back across the frozen Hudson before being cut off. Simcoe had been an American prisoner once, and damned if he was going to let himself get captured again. After securing his covering force, Simcoe and the Rangers took off at a dead gallop toward Woodbridge.

The moon was out, and the snow-packed road was clear as day with the lunar light speckling the woods and shining on the slung sabers of the Queen's Rangers. The air was clear and brisk; a good night for fighting, Simcoe thought grimly. He had hoped to approach on a less conspicuous road, but the heavy snowfall from the day before forced him to stay on the main road. He saw the Woodbridge post ahead and held up his hand to his men. They came to a stop, and Simcoe examined the darkened fortifications and saw no movement at all.

The post, which consisted of nothing more than some breastworks and a cabin, seemed to be deserted. Simcoe approached cautiously and saw an open door. Someone might have tipped the Americans off, and they had already pulled back. The spy networks worked both ways, and it was folly to assume someone had not made the Americans aware of their preparations. "Still Simcoe was determined to beat up some of the enemy's quarters or fall in with their patrols."[1] He wanted to be sure that his part of the mission was fulfilled and he provided the diversion Captain Beckwith needed.

The Queen's Rangers galloped on through the snowy woods of New Jersey and soon came to the crossroads leading from Perth Amboy to Elizabethtown. Simcoe could see Continental sentries ahead on the road, and just then the Americans called out to them for the password. Simcoe raised his hand, and his Rangers came to a halt and stood still in the snowy quiet night. They were all apparitions against the blanket of white that silhouetted the men and their horses. At this point there was no telling friend from foe.

Then Simcoe heard the sentinels talking in the absolute silence, doubting they had seen the enemy. Simcoe thought surprise was theirs until he heard a horse off to his right. His blood thumping suddenly in his chest, he turned and saw New Jersey militia riding up on his flanks. The New Jersey militiamen could see clearly now, and they shouted out an alarm to the sentries to fire. "They are British! They are British!" Fire exploded in front of Simcoe as the sentries' muskets flashed, and he wheeled his horse around and with "bugle horns, drums and bagpipes,"[2] the Queen's Rangers retreated. "The horse patrol had done his job,"[3] as historian Benjamin Huggins wrote later.

Simcoe heard bullets whining over his head as he and the Rangers pounded down the road, heading back toward the Hudson River. The Americans got organized and set out after Simcoe and his men on the same snow-packed path. The Queen's Rangers stayed ahead of the patriots up until the crossing of Woodbridge Creek, where the Americans finally caught up with them. One of the Rangers had been killed by a lucky shot by the Americans, but so far the Continental soldiers could not flank Simcoe's men because of the deep snow and had to stay on the road. This helped Simcoe, as he could stay just enough ahead and was taking no fire from the sides.

Old Blazing Star Ferry loomed up in the dim light, and Simcoe set his trap for the Americans. He sent Sergeant Wright over the ice to inform Major Armstrong to prepare his cannons, then ordered Captain David Shank with a detachment to a ridge to provide cover for his retreat. Then Simcoe wheeled around his horse, pulled out his sword, and called out to his men. "Simcoe suddenly ordered the remainder of his men to 'turnabout' and charge 'at a steady run' at the pursuing Americans."[4] Momentum was everything, and the disciplined Queen's Rangers bore down the road in a hail of spangled snow clouds as the Americans turned and fled over a distant hill.

Captain Shank's men then rose up from their cover and unleashed volleys upon the retreating Americans at the same time Major Armstrong fired his cannons upon some buildings sheltering some of the Americans. The thundering explosions and the whine of Shank's men firing in perfect order drove the Americans into a full rout. By trapping the Americans so perfectly, Simcoe had given them the impression of a much larger force. The retreating Continentals would now sound the alarm that the British were coming in force by the Hudson River, and this would be the focus, and not Birch's raiders, who were methodically making their way toward Morristown. Simcoe and his men ceased fire and saw that the Americans had vanished. They then turned and rode back across the Hudson without further harassment. Simcoe stared across the blinding snow glare of the river in early morning. He had fought with the local militia and General St. Clair's horse patrols and only suffered one dead and several wounded.

He thought the Americans had suffered greater casualties, but they reported only one killed and later said, "The party at Woodbridge committed no outrage of any kind upon either persons or houses of the inhabitants, but carried off about thirty head of cattle."[5] Still, confusion and panic had been sown, and the second diversion could now take place. However it played out, Lieutenant Colonel Simcoe had fulfilled his part of the mission to kidnap George Washington. It was up to the others now.

Even with Simcoe's expedition, no one in Morristown was notified, which shows a real lack of actionable intelligence. George Washington was practiced at the art of deception. When he put cannons on Dorchester Heights, he did it all in one night and covered the noise of getting the cannons into place with a diversionary cannonade that kept the British occupied while he readied the real attack. He sent out disinformation and cultivated spies who would make the British believe he had more men and was much better armed than he really was. He had fires built to simulate an army encampment while he slipped away in the darkness to fight again. But why didn't George Washington know on the night of February 11, 1780, that 500 men had crossed the Hudson River and were riding toward his headquarters for the sole purpose of kidnapping him?

Washington had been warned months earlier the British might attempt such an operation with the freezing of the Hudson, and yet he had not really taken any precautions and was asleep in his bed with no understanding that there were men riding directly toward him to tear him out of his bed, silence Martha, kill his Life Guard or anyone else who tried to stop the British dragoons, and possibly kill him should he resist. Yet in the porous atmosphere that was New York, with intelligence leaking out from both sides, he had not received any concrete information that such an operation was underway or had been planned for.

The British, by the same token, knew that Washington was sleeping in the Ford Mansion on the second floor, and they knew where the Life Guards were stationed and how many there were and how many had been called away and what their protocol was for guarding Washington. They knew that about half of his army had melted away, and they were starving, and the Americans were breaking, and morale was low. They also knew the roads to Morristown and the exact layout of the log city, and even the layout of the Life Guards cabins. The reason for this was they had better spies and were better at the spy game than Washington and the Americans.

But George Washington was learning. In fact, he was already adept at disinformation. When General Howe sent a spy to Morristown to determine troop strength, Washington showed his cunning by not arresting the spy but by cultivating him. He had every commander send to him inflated troop numbers and then had the spy dine with one of his officers with the troop numbers on a desk. The officer was then called away and told the spy he would not return for thirty minutes. The would-be spy then pulled out the numbers from a desk and wrote down the troop strength, 12,000 men, when in fact Washington was down to 3,000. General Howe received this information in New York and patted himself on the back that he had not attacked Morristown.

This was George Washington's first foray into counterintelligence. From there he began to cultivate spies of his own. Washington cultivated secret meeting places and stockpiled hard money to pay the spies, who could not be expected to accept the devalued Continental currency. A Major Benjamin Talmadge, twenty-four, was chosen to create a Continental spy network.

Talmadge had been friends with Nathan Hale, a Yale classmate who in 1776 attempted to spy on the British, and was caught and subsequently hanged. On the gallows, he famously said, "My only regret is that I have but one life to give for my country."[6] It was up to Talmadge to get a real spy network in place, and he began with Robert Townsend and Abraham Woodhull, who formed "the Culpepper Ring." Talmadge was a merchant in New York with a thriving trade in flax, sugar, and dry goods. Messages were written in invisible ink, which at the time was as sophisticated as a spy satellite is today.

The method to get messages to George Washington in Morristown was clever. Messages were given to a boatman, Caleb Brewster, who had whaleboats in six different Long Island coves. The signal was given by a clothesline belonging to a female spy. If a black petticoat appeared, this was the signal Brewster was ready to row. Then a handkerchief would appear next to the petticoat. One handkerchief meant cove number one and two meant cove number two and so on. Brewster went to the cove after dark and received the messages; then he rowed through English patrols and headed for Fairfield, Connecticut.

There Brewster gave the messages to a courier, who then gave them to Talmadge, who then would get them to Washington in Morristown. But curiously, the spy networks gave Washington no real intelligence on any attempt to kidnap him or that a raid had even been launched toward Morristown. There were rumors, but Washington didn't act on them and sincerely believed no one would attempt any type of raid in the snow and subzero temperatures. He could not have been more wrong.

CHAPTER TWENTY

Desperate Measures

January 1780

SOME OFFICERS KILLED A DOG FOR FOOD. OTHERS WOULD TAKE THE leather from a shoe and put it in hot water. Still others gnawed on hard corn for the horses, and some ate the lice off their own bodies. Many just disappeared into the forest in the night and took their chances with the elements and hoped they might reach the British. Some went and stole from surrounding farms, and Washington began to look the other way, finding it hard to lash men who were starving.

A month before Simcoe took off across the ice to implement the kidnapping of George Washington, the leaders of the soldiers at Morristown had come to the conclusion that only desperate measures would alleviate the suffering. At the end of 1779, the United States was bankrupt, with a worthless currency and no ability to pay soldiers or to procure food. After printing 201 million in Continental dollars, Congress stopped the presses, with 1 silver dollar worth 99 Continental dollars. A wheelbarrow of Continental dollars was worth only the value of the wheelbarrow . . . the paper currency good for little more than starting fires.

Even though Washington's table was sumptuous, he understood that his army was starving and Congress could do nothing. He had written to Joseph Reed, president of the Congress, on December 16: "We have not three days bread on hand or anywhere within reach. When this is exhausted, we must rely on the precariousness of neighboring country. . . . We have not experienced a like extremity at any period of the war."[1]

He had Colonel Biddle grind all the Indian corn that was being held to feed the horses into flour for the men. Horses would starve, but better the men had some biscuits or fire cakes. The three-day blizzard in January brought the situation to a head when no supplies could reach the stranded army. Soldiers headed off into the blizzard looking for food, begging surrounding farmers for anything they could spare. After mid-January there was no more begging; soldiers began to steal. Washington could do nothing.

"The men have at last been brought to such an extremity that no authority or influence of the officers, no patience or virtue of the men themselves could any longer dictate their obeying the orders."[2] The despicable truth was the farmers around Morristown had fattened cattle and grain bins that were full. They were willing to sell, but only to army buyers with hard money, and the only buyers with real cash were the British, who ended up with the food after it passed through intermediaries and prices were driven even higher.

The London Trade was basically the market upon which the farmers could sell their cattle or grain to the highest bidder, and that was usually the British. Washington had enough, and on January 5 he acted. Desperate times required desperate measures. He ordered all the brigade commanders to dismiss men whose enlistment expired on January 31. Fewer mouths to feed. It was simple math and took thousands off the army rolls.

Then Washington got tough with the farmers. On January 18 he let the magistrates of several counties know that there would be quotas of food that must be supplied to the army. There would be no exceptions. And the wagons and manpower to transport the food to army storehouses must be supplied by the counties as well. If there was noncompliance, then the foodstuffs would be seized by the army with no compensation. If done voluntarily, then a pay voucher would be issued, or they would be paid in the inflated Continental dollars if available.

Washington framed it all under patriotic duty and described the plight of the starving soldiers, who bore "their sufferings with a patience that merits the approbation and ought to excite the sympathy of their Countrymen."[3] Washington explained that the time had come for everyone to contribute to the cause. But the magistrates were not fooled by the appeal to a higher calling. Each county's quotas were carefully spelled out with specific numbers of bushels of grain and cattle. But if there was noncompliance or even hesitation, then the quotas would be taken forcibly. Washington would not let Congress know until January 27 that he had ordered the first impressment of food in the United States for a standing army. It was the rationing of the day, which would surface again in every world war. After the food began to come in, Washington issued standing orders that anyone caught stealing would receive a hundred lashes on the spot. He understood stealing when there was no food, but stealing after food had arrived could not be tolerated.

It was historic, and it was the first time Washington demanded that those other than the army contribute to the "glorious cause." It would cause grumbling around the countryside of New Jersey, but there was compliance, and Congress passed a resolution of gratitude for the patriotism of the citizens of New Jersey. It was a small recompense, but the starving in Morristown had slowed and Washington and his men could look toward spring, when surely warmer weather would come. But so would the British, and sooner than George Washington would ever believe.

Although Washington's winter at Valley Forge has been well documented, such as in this painting, a far harsher winter awaited him and his troops at Morristown a year later.
LIBRARY OF CONGRESS

George Washington's troops spent the winter of 1779 in a log city with eight men in a single cabin. PHIL DEGGINGER/ALAMY

The Ford Mansion (seen here in 1901) became Washington's headquarters and the place the British intended to kidnap him from. LIBRARY OF CONGRESS

The Ford Mansion today is managed by the National Park Service. George Washington was miles from his troops in the Ford Mansion, which made him vulnerable to a kidnapping plot.
NATIONAL PARK SERVICE

The brutal winter forced Washington's troops to remain in dark, smoky cabins where they slept, starved, and died. NATIONAL PARK SERVICE

British General Simcoe (center) planned the expedition to kidnap George Washington after bad treatment at the hands of the Americans. TORONTO PUBLIC LIBRARY

The once-in-a-century winter of 1779 turned Morristown into a frozen wasteland of suffering and allowed the British to cross the Hudson River to attempt to kidnap George Washington.

George Washington ran his army from his room in the Ford Mansion, and this was where the British planned to take him while he slept. LIBRARY OF CONGRESS

CHAPTER TWENTY-ONE

The Coldest Night

February 11, 1780, five a.m.

SOMETIMES HE DREAMED OF MOUNT VERNON. THE SUNNY PLACIDITY of his plantation was now a dream. The life of foxhunts, fine whiskey, cigars, his own farms brimming with tobacco leaves, had no place in the frozen world he now occupied. So many times, when sleep finally came, he found himself drifting back in time to life before the war. Then he would hear the wind howling outside the window, hear the ice pelting the window, feel the cold draft of the house, and he knew the world that he knew before no longer existed.

George Washington tossed and turned in the cold bedroom in the Ford Mansion. The firelight flickered against the windowpanes; logs snapped and crackled with small explosions of steam. The snow swirled outside the window, danced, then blew sideways. Martha's breathing was low and rhythmic, and Washington moved against the heavy covers in his nightshirt. He was a man of habit and had the farmer's habit of going to bed early and rising with the dawn. He would have tea, honey, and biscuits for breakfast and then sit down at his desk and clear away as much paperwork as he could in his nightshirt. He was a man who never wasted a moment and prided himself that he was able to accomplish many tasks before the sun even rose.

At Mount Vernon, he would ride to his farms and many times strip off his coat and work alongside the men. He was known for his prodigious strength and stamina and would sometimes throw a leaded ball in the front yard with much younger men, throwing the weight with his coat still on, yet sending it farther than anyone else. It was his strength and endurance that had seen him through the wilderness campaigns with the French and the British, attacks by Indians, excursions into the wilderness in the dead of winter, surviving ordeals that weaker men would have perished under. George Washington had rude health and ate the same thing every day, fish for dinner with a bottle of madeira to finish off the evening. And then he went to bed and usually slept soundly.

But tonight, his teeth were aching. He had bad teeth; many had been pulled, and he had a habit of keeping his mouth closed. Eventually he had dentures that pinched the inside of his mouth. Washington stared at the window again, where a snowstorm raged. He didn't believe the weather was conducive to any assault against his army, but he had taken precautions. He believed his force at Morristown would be safe with the local militias and Continental soldiers manning posts, who could sound the alarm if they saw the British coming. "Our main body cannot be surprised,"[1] he wrote to Major General Arthur St. Clair on January 30. To that end he had several brigades moved west of Elizabethtown to watch for any raiding parties coming from Staten Island, while St. Clair ordered guards at "Rahway, Carnes Mils, Connecticut Farms, Elizabethtown and Newark. In addition, the New Jersey militia could be called into the field on an alarm. Washington also kept a detachment of about 200 infantries at Paramus."[2]

The fireplace was now just licking orange coals. Bedrooms became very cold at night in eighteenth-century dwellings, and people often took hot bricks to bed and slept under mounds and mounds of blankets. Washington could hear the wind now. The night had been clear with a bright moon, and now another snowstorm had moved in. It was all he could do to keep from going mad. He was a man of action, and yet all he could do was keep watch and make sure the British did not surprise him. He was a man who was very circumspect until he wasn't, and then he moved with the boldness of a daredevil. He liked the unexpected, the bold move that could change the board and allow him to checkmate his opponent. He wanted to make a bold move against the British in New

York, but he could do nothing until this brutal winter ended and he got his troops back up to fighting strength.

Washington turned in the bed and stared out the window again. It would be madness for anyone to launch an attack on a night such as this. The weather was his best barrier against the British, with ten-foot snowdrifts that could drown a man. The roads were mostly impassable, with only a few packed down enough to allow men and horses to march on the snow-hardened pathways. Yes, the Hudson River had frozen, and this offered opportunities for both sides, but then it was thirty miles to Morristown. In the subzero temperatures and incessant snow, no army could traverse the roads to wage an attack. Silas Condict had said he might be the target of such an attack. Washington stared out the window. Yes, kidnapping was a tactic, but it was always a long shot, and in this type of weather the ability to get men and horses and artillery to launch such a mission would be almost impossible. Besides, someone would take his place if he was kidnapped. He was not indispensable.

Chapter Twenty-Two

The Indispensable Man

1776

In the beginning, General Howe didn't recognize George Washington as the leader of anything. When he sent him a letter in 1775, it was addressed to George Washington Esq. Washington refused the letter, and Howe protested that rank was only conveyed by the crown. He sent another letter and Washington refused again. This went on for some time until Howe finally addressed the letter to General Washington. But he didn't regard him at all. To the British, George Washington was a failed officer who at one time wanted to join the British army but had been rejected. That assessment changed quickly.

Now the British regarded George Washington as indispensable. He had proved it at Boston. The colonial rebellion, even after Lexington, Concord, and the drubbing at Bunker Hill, was seen as something that had flamed up but could be quickly tamped down when the right amount of pressure was applied. General Howe, who had holed up with the army in Boston and barricaded himself in, took the attitude that once reinforcements arrived the rebels would come to their senses and realize that their best interests still lay with Great Britain. If the Americans didn't come to their senses, the ragtag army would be crushed with British might and Hessian savagery.

The Hessians were brutal. At Bunker Hill, when the patriots ran out of powder and the Hessians attacked with bayonets, they spiked many colonists to trees with their swords, watching them squirm like bugs tacked to a wall. They gave no quarter, and when the Americans tried to surrender, they ran them through with their broadswords. It was a blood-bath, and these mercenaries saw the ragtag soldiers as nothing more than unruly peasants. Now the British had taken over Boston and were going to ride out the winter and wait for reinforcements.

They knew George Washington had taken command, but no mat-ter. He had been a planter for the last fifteen years and his military service was less than illustrious, so much so he was turned down when he tried to enlist in the British army as a young man. The Americans could do nothing. They had no artillery, and without artillery an army could not lay siege. General Howe entertained himself with the theater, fine dining, and his concubine while the Americans froze, starved, and were ravaged by disease.

In a letter to Joseph Reed, Washington questioned even taking com-mand of the army. "I have often thought how much happier I should have been if instead of accepting command under such circumstances, I had taken my musket upon my shoulders and entered the ranks or . . . had retired to the back country and lived in a wigwam."[1] His real problem was gunpowder and lack of artillery and the fact that half of his 10,000 troops were barely fit for service. His men had little to eat, and every time he proposed an attack to his council of generals, they declined to approve his plans. "Could I have foreseen the difficulties which have come upon us . . . all the generals upon earth should not have convinced me of the propriety of delaying an attack upon Boston at this time."[2]

General Howe regarded the American army as a rabble that would be crushed in the spring when the fighting resumed. Washington was at an impasse, but he had been eyeing the Heights of Dorchester for some time. The Heights were a windswept, desolate hill that overlooked Boston. Washington knew instinctively that this was an Achilles' heel for the British and that if he could place cannons upon the Heights he could quickly drive the lobsterbacks out of Boston. But the only artillery was at Fort Ticonderoga up on Lake George, and it had been poorly manned when Ethan Allen and Benedict Arnold took it at dawn. There were sixty tons of artillery in the fort, including 5,000-pound cannons that would put the British fleet in range. But the fort was 350 miles away, and frozen lakes, rivers, and mountains separated the cannons from the man who could use them.

Enter Henry Knox, a twenty-five-year-old Boston bookseller who had recently left Boston with his wife to join the cause. Knox had trained with an artillery unit in Boston and had read everything to do with the use of cannons and military engineering, filling his store with books on military strategy and military history. He was heavy and boisterous, and saw the inevitable break with Britain. "The future happiness or misery of a great proportion of the human race is at stake—and if we make a wrong choice, ourselves and our posterity must be wretched. . . . And that is to separate—an event which I devoutly pray may soon take place and let it be as soon as it may be."[3]

Knox turned up in the Continental Army, soon coming under the favor of George Washington. Washington was taken with his intelligence and his can-do attitude. He was the man to go retrieve the cannons from Fort Ticonderoga. Washington's generals were skeptical, but Washington overrode them, and on November 16, Henry Knox and his brother William set off for Fort Ticonderoga. The plan was to transport the cannons using oxen and sleds and for hired teamsters to assist Knox and his men. When they reached Fort Ticonderoga, Knox was disappointed to find many of the guns in disrepair. He selected fifty-nine cannons, including three 5,000-pound cannons. They loaded the cannons on flat-bottomed boats and set out across Lake George.

This began a journey of incredible suffering for Knox and his men, in boats that were now weighed down with 120,000 pounds of iron. Knox began to keep a diary of the expedition. He recorded days of heavy rowing against unrelenting headwinds—four hours of "rowing exceedingly hard" one day, six hours of "excessive hard rowing on another."[4] In places the boats had to cut through the ice. Knox's brother William wrote, "Beating all the way against the wind . . . God send us a fair wind."[5]

Finally, Knox's fleet of cannons reached Fort George. After some difficulties, the sleds and oxen were finally in place. "We shall cut no small figure in going through the Country with our cannon mortars drawn by eighty yokes of oxen."[6] Henry's train was a hybrid composition of teamsters, oxen, and horses. As historian Alexander C. Flick described the train, "Horses as well as oxen were employed. Instead of moving in a single cavalcade, the drivers were divided into companies which were often many miles apart."[7]

Before setting off south, Knox sat down and wrote Washington, informing him he was on his way with the cannons.

> *May it please your Excellency, I returned to this place and brought with me the cannon. . . . It is not easy to conceive the difficulties we have had getting them over the lake owing to the advanced season of the year and contrary winds, but the danger is now past and three days ago it was uncertain whether we could have gotten them until next spring—I hope in 16 or 17 days' time to be able to present your Excellency a noble train of artillery the inventory of which I have enclosed.*[8]

Knox finally got underway and had to deal with varying weather conditions, from too much snow to no snow at all. There would be four crossings of the Hudson River, which Knox anticipated by cutting holes into the river to flood the ice and thicken the surface. Warming temperatures made each crossing an adventure, with thousands of pounds of cannons, oxen, and men liable to break through any moment. He wrote his wife, "The thaw has been so grave that I've trembled for the consequences, for without snow my very important charge cannot get along."[9]

Knox wrote Washington while waiting for the Hudson to freeze enough to cross.

> *I did myself the honor to address your Excellency from Fort George on the 17th. I was in hopes that we should have been able to have had the cannon at Cambridge by this time. The want of snow detained us some days and now a cruel thaw hinders from crossing Hudson River which we are obliged to do four times from Lake George to this town—the inevitable delays pain me exceedingly as my mind is fully sensible to the importance of the greatest expedition in the case.*[10]

It was at Albany the catastrophe occurred. The method for crossing the river was for a teamster to walk along next to the sled with an axe, ready to cut the oxen free if the sled should go through the ice. John Becker Jr., who accompanied his father, wrote of how they crossed. "My father took in charge a heavy nine pounder [2,800 pounds], which required the united efforts of four horses to drag it along.... The method adopted was this; a rope forty feet long was fastened to the tongue of the sleigh and the other end was attached to the horses. The first gun was started across in this way and my father walked alongside the horses with a sharp hatchet in his hand, to cut the rope, if the cannon and sled should break through."[11]

They were almost across when a 5,000-pound sled went through the ice and created a fourteen-foot hole. Knox had to ask the townspeople for help in pulling the cannon from the river, but over two days the task was accomplished. The next formidable undertaking for Henry Knox and his noble train of artillery was the Berkshire Mountains.

The teamsters who accompanied Knox did most of the heavy lifting, literally. John Becker Jr. wrote a journal entry about transporting the cannons and the eeriness of the countryside. In passing through a forest, he had a scare that stayed with him as he led his wagon along the road.

> While I was thus in spite of myself giving way to the most unpleasant feelings, my leading horses, which had been jogging along on a pace quite inconsistent with my views of propriety, made a sudden halt and fell back upon the pair next to the sled.... My father came swiftly up, when I informed him of what had occurred. A diligent search was then made along the road by persons in our company. What should the cause of my anxiety prove to be but a drunken soldier, who had, in some unaccountable way, fallen asleep on the road, overcome by fatigue and exhaustion.[12]

Without the teamsters, Henry Knox's task would have been impossible. The Berkshires were frozen, jagged peaks that looked to be the end of Knox's journey. "It appeared to me almost a miracle that people with heavy loads should be able to get up and down such hills,"[13] he wrote in his diary. Drag chains and pulleys had to be used to pull the cannons up the mountains and then again to keep the sleds from breaking free and running down the sides of the steep inclines. They cleared the mountains, and news of the noble train had gotten out and the townspeople came out to see the men and the cannons. The young teamster wrote, "We were the great gainers by this curiosity, for while they were employed in remarking upon our guns, we were equal pleasure, discussing the qualities of their cider and whiskey. These were generously brought out in great profusion."[14]

It took three months for the twenty-five-year-old bookseller to get back to Cambridge with the cannons, and Washington lost no time in putting the artillery up on Dorchester Heights. The plan was to get the cannons up on the Heights in one night and surprise the British in the morning with a bombardment. The problem was the Heights of Dorchester had an elevation of 112 feet and the ground was frozen rock-solid. To cover the noise of the work parties dragging the cannons up on the Heights, Washington had Knox begin to shell Boston with some low-level cannonades. Washington let his troops know what he expected of them on the eve of the attack. "As the season is now fast approaching when every man must expect to be drawn into the field of action, it is highly necessary that he should prepare his mind, as well as everything that is necessary for it. It is a noble cause we are engaged in, it is the cause of virtue and mankind, every temporal advantage and comfort to us, and our posterity depends upon the vigor of our exertions."[15]

Dr. James Thacher recorded his impressions of the men on the Heights just before the cannons were unleashed. "Each man knows his place and is resolute to execute his duty. Our breastworks are strengthened and among the means of defense are a great number of barrels filled with stone and sand."[16] At dawn Henry Knox unleashed his cannons and the 5,000-pounders hurled shells into the sleeping town of Boston.

The shelling of Boston by the Americans shocked the British, but more than that, the entire British fleet was in range of the 5,000-pound guns and the admiral told General Howe they would have to leave as the exploding cannonballs fell around Boston. General Howe, who had spent the night with his concubine, could not believe his eyes. "My God, these fellows have done more work in one night than I could make my army do in three months."[17]

A London paper would later publish a letter from a British officer.

This I believe, likely to prove an important day to the British empire as any in our annals. We underwent last night a very severe cannonade, which damaged several houses, and killed some men. This morning at daybreak we discovered two redoubts on the hills of Dorchester Point and two smaller works on their flanks. They were all raised during the night, with an expedition equal to that of the genie belonging to Aladdin's wonderful lamp. From these hills they command the whole, so that we must drive them from their post, or desert the place.[18]

General Howe immediately made plans to attack the Heights and drive the Americans off, but in a strange confluence of weather and circumstance, the landing boats were nearly swamped when a northeaster swept in, and Howe cancelled the attack. A meeting was called, and Howe realized the inevitable. As a Captain Roberts later wrote, "After waiting some time Captain Montresor came down from the general and told me had been in the council and had advised the going off [embarkation] altogether, that Lord Percy and some others ascended to him, and that the general said it was his own sentiments from the first, but thought the honor of the troops concerned. So, it is agreed immediately to embark everything."[19]

Howe let Washington know he would evacuate if they were not assaulted further. If the Americans did not cease shelling the town, Howe would burn Boston to the ground. James Thacher, the young army surgeon, recorded the British evacuation. "Nothing of consequence occurred to observation till Sunday morning, March 17th when at an early hour it was perceived that the royal army commenced their embarkation on board of transports. . . . We enjoyed the unspeakable satisfaction of beholding their whole fleet under sail, wafting from our shores the dreadful scourge of war."[20]

The British evacuated Boston and gave the Americans their first victory. General Howe had new respect for the Virginia planter who had come to take charge of a motley crew of state militias. Underestimating George Washington would be a hallmark of the early years of the war.

Washington wrote to his brother soon after the victory over the British in Boston. "We have maintained our ground against the enemy under a want of powder and we have disbanded one army and recruited another within musket shot of two and twenty regiments . . . and at last have beat them in a shameful and precipitate manner."[21]

It was only after the success of the siege of Boston that Washington could let down his guard about what he had faced. Unburdening himself to his brother again, he wrote, "I believe I may, with great truth, affirm that no man perhaps since the first institution of armies ever commanded one under more difficult circumstances than I have done."[22]

George Washington became a master at prevailing against unbelievable odds. In 1776 it happened again. When the British had chased Washington from New York and nearly bottled up his entire army, the war had come close to ending. Once again in the winter General Howe assumed the spring campaign would finish the bleeding and weak Continental Army after the defeats in Brooklyn. Howe left a holding force of 1,500 Hessians in Trenton, New Jersey, while he took up winter quarters in New York. Washington had been chased to the other side of the Delaware River with barely 6,000 men fit for duty. The assumption was the war would be over by spring.

Joseph Reed, his adjutant, wrote Washington a prescient letter on December 22. "Will it not be possible, my dear General for our troops or such part of them as can act with advantage to make a diversion or something at or about Trenton? . . . I will not disguise my own sentiments that our cause is desperate and hopeless if we do not take the opportunity of the collection of troops at present to strike some stroke. Our affairs are hastening fast to ruin if we do not retrieve them by some happy event. Delay with us is now equal to total defeat."[23]

George Washington kept the bold plan always in his back pocket. And like sending Henry Knox on his impossible mission, he came up with another plan that was just as risky and fraught with the very real possibility of being a complete disaster. In the dark days after the Battle of Brooklyn, Washington had told Congress, "We should on all occasions avoid a general action or put anything to risk unless compelled by necessity."[24] But he always held the possibility of the "brilliant stroke."

Washington decided they would attack the Hessians at Trenton on Christmas night. They would cross the Delaware in flat-bottomed boats at three places and surprise the Hessian forces. The actual crossing was slated for Christmas night. Spies had told Washington there were 2,000 to 3,000 men at Trenton. "By marching through the night, the two columns were to arrive at Trenton no later than five in the morning. . ." Officers were to have a piece of white paper in their hats to distinguish them. Absolute secrecy was demanded. A "profound silence" was to be observed, the orders read, "and no man to quit his ranks on pain of death."[25]

Then the weather turned as a northeaster crashed into the east coast, bringing ice and snow and wind, whipping the river, which was littered with large sheets of ice. Washington scribbled three words on a piece of paper. It was a password. "Victory or Death." James Thacher wrote in his journal of the Christmas night crossing. "The passage of the boats was rendered extremely difficult and hazardous by the ice and part of the troops and cannon actually failed in the attempt."[26]

The flatboats, called Durham boats, were used to transport pig iron and were low-sided and in constant danger of being swamped. Painted black and forty to sixty feet long, they could carry up to forty men standing up, but they had a shallow draft and could be brought to shore. Henry Knox supervised the crossing with his booming voice, along with Washington, who made sure every man made it across by three a.m. John Greenwood, a sixteen-year-old fifer, later wrote on the conditions of the crossing. "Over the river we then went in a flat-bottomed scow . . . and we had to wait for the rest and so began to pull down fences and make fires to warm ourselves, for the storm was increasing rapidly. After a while it rained, hailed, snowed, and froze, and at the same time blew a perfect hurricane."[27]

The storm was so bad that artillery could accompany the men. Wind, rain, and hail ruined many of the muskets for firing. Washington should have considered turning back, but as he later wrote John Hancock, "I well knew we could not reach Trenton before day was fairly broke, but as I was certain there was no making a retreat without being discovered, and harassed on repassing the river, I determined to push on at all events."[28]

Washington's situation quickly grew worse when General James Ewing, leading one of the attacking columns of the army, decided the weather was too bad. Washington had no way of knowing he had lost one of his pincers. Then General John Cadwalader called off the attack as well. An officer wrote of the conditions that faced the men that night:

It was as severe a night as I ever saw and after two battalions were landed, the storm increased so much that it was impossible to get the artillery over, for we had to walk one hundred yards on the ice to get on shore. General Cadwalader therefore ordered the whole to retreat again, and we had to stand at least six hours under arms—first to cover the landing, and till all the rest had retreated again—and by this time the storm of wind, rain, hail and snow with the ice so bad that some of the infantry could not get back till next day.[29]

George Washington was on his own now. It would be a bayonet charge now, as the soldiers' muskets were soaked, and many thought they would turn back. A nine-mile march to Trenton on a slippery, icy, skidding road made it hard for men to walk, much less see in the stormy darkness. John Greenwood remembered barely moving and freezing in the darkness. "I recollect very well that at one time, when we halted on the road, I sat down on a stump of a tree and was so be-numbed with cold that I wanted to go to sleep. Had I been passed unnoticed I should have frozen to death without knowing it."[30]

Two men did freeze to death. The 2,400 men stayed together for five miles up to a crossroads, Birmingham, where the army split onto two roads, both slick with ice and snow. They would come into Trenton from two different directions and catch the Hessians between the two claws of the army. Washington admonished the men: "For God's sake keep with your officers."[31] General John Sullivan reported to Washington that his men's muskets were also too wet to fire. Washington shot back a message: "Tell the general to use the bayonet."[32]

They reached Trenton in the morning and attacked the Hessians at eight a.m., firing the few muskets that were still dry. They "reached the village about seven o'clock in the morning with such promptitude and secrecy as to attack the enemy almost as soon as his approach was discovered."[33] The 1,500 Hessians retreated as the 2,400 Americans attacked like crazed men in the snowy morning darkness. Henry Knox had set up his artillery, and when the Hessians poured out of their barracks, he opened fire and cleared the streets. "When the Hessians retreated into the side streets, they found General Sullivan's men coming at them with fixed bayonets. For a brief time, a thousand or more Americans and Hessians were locked in savage house to house fighting. It was all happening extremely fast in wild confusion and swirling snow made more blinding by clouds of gunpowder smoke."[34]

A Hessian cannon was seized and turned on the Hessian soldiers, and they retreated to an orchard on the edge of town and surrendered, with their commander, Colonel Johann Rall, mortally wounded. It was all over in forty-five minutes, and the Americans took 900 prisoners, with 21 Hessians killed and 90 wounded. At the finish of the fighting, General St. Clair rode up to George Washington where the commander of the Hessian troops, Rall, was surrendering. "I . . . rode up to him at the moment Colonel Rall supported by a file of sergeants was presenting his sword. On my approach Washington took me by the hand and said 'Major Wilkinson this is a glorious day for our country,' his countenance beaming with complacency; whilst Rall who the day before would not have changed fortunes with him, now pale, bleeding and covered with blood, in broken accents seemed to implore those attentions. . . . How awful the contrast."[35]

The British were astonished at the American victory. They could not believe the audacity of the plan, crossing the Delaware in such a storm on Christmas and then attacking with complete surprise the crack Hessian mercenaries, who had no choice but to give up. The Americans fought like wild animals and showed the world they could win against even the mighty British Empire. Then Washington followed up with a bold attack on Princeton. James Thacher wrote of Washington's brilliant use of deception in the attack.

General Washington ordered a great number of fires to be lighted up and leaving a sufficient number of men to keep them burning during the night, to deceive the enemy, stole a march with his main army, taking a circuitous route, and at nine o'clock the next morning, attacked three regiments of the British who were posted at Princeton, routed them, and drove them from their redoubts. By this masterly maneuver the enemy lost about five hundred in killed and wounded and prisoners.[36]

For the British, the lesson was that George Washington was a force to be reckoned with. Many thought he *was* the American Revolution, and that without Washington the war would quickly end. And they were right. George Washington was the spiritual leader of the Revolution and the man with the golden touch. He was indispensable, and to that end, the indispensable man was now asleep in a mansion far from his troops. And the British were closing in.

Chapter Twenty-Three

The Black Hussars

February 12, 1780, six a.m.

THE SNOW HAD BEGUN IN THE NIGHT. IT HAD BEEN LIGHT AT FIRST, AND then fat wet gobs began to fall. The temperature was just below freezing and not unpleasant, but then the wet snow began to soak the men and the temperature began to fall. The horses slipped on the snow-packed road, but the men stayed bent over their manes, staring straight ahead toward their destination. So far, the weather was a bother but nothing that would stop them in their mission to kidnap George Washington.

While George Washington slept, Lieutenant Colonel Samuel Birch led the 17th Light Dragoons in a fierce gallop down the snow-packed road, which soon gave way to a road of frozen snow. The snow in fact had begun to fall hours before and the temperature plummeted to less than zero. Birch loved a good fight and delighted in the more daring raids that gave his Dragoons exposure and him acclaim. The Dragoons were trained to ride hard and fast, and Birch hoped the diversion under Simcoe had done the trick. Surprise was everything in a raid like this, and he had allowed himself to think about the accolades that would follow when he returned with a manacled George Washington.

Birch detested the rebellious Americans, and after his regiment arrived from Ireland shortly after Bunker Hill, he had taken great pleasure in riding in the Old South Meeting House, where the rebels had fomented their new tactics and outlined their government. Birch thought it fitting that the British should ride their horses there and have them defecate all over the sacred meeting house the Americans called the cradle of liberty. The war had dragged on way too long, and this bold raid would put the Americans in their place and make them sue for peace or accept the terms the British imposed.

The Black Hussars were riding with the 17th Light Dragoons, and Birch glanced over at the swarthy Germans with greased mustaches under their hussar caps. The 17th had adopted the copper-rimmed caps bearing the skull and crossbones and OR GLORY. Birch felt this summed up his attitude, but he didn't want things to get out of hand. Many of the Black Hussars had been German prisoners at one time, and he had already told the men to be on guard against atrocities. Birch did not want the Black Hussars ruining his mission by pillaging or molesting women. They did have that reputation. The 17th Light Dragoons had fought in many battles, "including those of Long Island, White Plains, and Monmouth as well as dozens of skirmishes in New Jersey and around Philadelphia."[1] It was always the Hessians who were the most brutal and shocked even a battle-hardened commander like Birch.

Nor did he want things to get out of hand when they captured Washington. He did not want a dead general on his hands. He had led the force that captured General Lee in the tavern outside Philadelphia, and that had gone very smoothly. They had surrounded the tavern when they found out General Lee was inside and then taken the old general away on a horse, still in his nightshirt. It didn't pay to be away from your troops even to cavort with a prostitute. It was a feather in his cap that the 17th Dragoons had captured the general many regarded as Washington's right-hand man.

But General Lee wasn't George Washington. This was the most audacious plan yet to end the war. Washington was wily and had slipped away many times when the British had him cornered. Captain Beckwith and General Knyphausen had a lot riding on this, and General Clinton had been informed of the operation though he was still in Charleston. No, this war should have ended many times over, but Washington refused to take on the British head-on, melting away overnight into the forests of this benighted country that gave him succor while the British stumbled around, not sure who was friend or foe. But now he was in one place, and better, he was miles away from the main force with only the Life Guard unit to protect him.

Colonel Birch looked again at the Black Hussars riding ramrod straight with that peculiar German expression best described as one of benign neglect. They barely spoke the King's English, but they could take care of the Life Guard soldiers while he and the 17th raced into the Ford Mansion and grabbed Washington from his bed. If all went to plan, he would have him on a horse in a nightshirt riding back toward the Hudson while the Americans tried to make sense of what was happening. If things went well, there would be no alarms and Washington would be headed for New York by the time anyone discovered that the leader of the American Revolution was missing.

Colonel Birch looked up toward the false dawn. The snow had thickened, and the horses were already fighting the crusty frozen surface of the road. This weather could kill a man quickly; the mercury was down to zero and the snow stung his cheeks like tiny pins. Yes, it would be a great moment to be back in his quarters by the fire with George Washington sitting opposite him. Really, almost unbelievable. But first they had to get there, and they had miles to go. Stirling wondered suddenly if Washington was an early riser; if he was, would it be hard to find him? All the latest intelligence said that Washington slept on the upper floors toward the back of the manse. Birch huddled down against the increasing snowfall and thought the only thing that could stop them now was the weather.

CHAPTER TWENTY-FOUR

The Insomniac General

February 12, 1780, three a.m.

THE HEAVY BREATHING OF HIS WIFE. THE CREAKS AND GROANS OF THE house. It was but three a.m., and the leader of the American Revolution lay in his bed with the cold air above. Eighteenth-century homes were terribly inefficient. Most of the heat went up the fireplace chimney. Many people warmed a brick and took it to bed with them. They slept like mummies under piles of blankets with several layers of clothes. By morning a glass of water by the bed would have a skim of ice.

But this was not what kept George Washington awake. The fire was now out, and the snow pelted the thin windowpanes of his bedroom. Martha's rhythmic breathing was a tonic to his strained nerves, but his mind raced, and short of drinking some grog or wine he could do nothing to slow it. Washington used the night to go over his game. Like a master chess player, he preferred an overview of the board and liked to strategize ten moves ahead. With his natural tendency to obsess about numbers and plans, he now saw only problems innumerable.

"Many a mickle makes a muckle." The Scottish idiom was his philosophy of life; small things add up. And conversely, so did big things. Washington turned in the bed, going over the last few months and like a sportsman evaluating his game and the games of his opponents. The soldiers had chopped down 2,000 acres of timber for their log city of 1,000 huts. Washington liked that equation. It made sense to him. What didn't make sense was Mrs. Ford not giving up the two rooms on the first floor and forcing the Washingtons to share the floor with her family. George Washington was not an intimate man, and the crowding into the kitchen of Mrs. Ford's family along with his own eighteen servants and aides made getting work accomplished, much less cooking dinner, almost intolerable. He had an addition built for his aides, but he still lived in cramped quarters, and the twenty-one snowstorms he had counted so far had given everyone in the Ford Mansion a severe case of cabin fever.

Washington glanced at the window. He was a farmer and mindful of the weather, and a bit of an amateur scientist when it came to weather patterns. He had never seen so many violent snowstorms in a row, and this had pushed his army to the breaking point, blocking the roads, sealing them in with little food. Add to this that there was not a single pair of shoes in the army depots, nor were there overalls, shirts, or blankets. The men were literally freezing, and he was powerless to do anything.

Washington stared into the shadow light falling on a basin and a pitcher of water. Yes. There were no blankets, and there was no money for the troops either. Three cents to a dollar. That was another figure, but that one made no sense. Congress had stopped printing money, and the rumors were that the British were swamping their currency with counterfeit dollars to further debase the currency. His own personal fortune was slipping away even as he lay in the bed. Like all Virginia planters, he had large loans that were now to be paid with the Continental dollars. He had recently written to his brother, "I am now receiving a shilling in the pound in discharge of bonds which ought to have been paid me and would have been realized before I left Virginia but to my indulgence to the debtors."[1] He estimated his personal losses had swollen to 10,000 pounds. By the war's end, he could well be broke.

Washington turned again, trying to get comfortable and closing his eyes. It was folly to ruminate like this all night, but this is what he did, and many nights he slept not at all. He had heard of reports that in New York there were mutinous sentiments in the militias for lack of food, and of course this could easily spread to Morristown. But his real concern was General Clinton. He knew his situation, he was sure of it, and had written to New Jersey governor Livingston that Clinton "is not ignorant of the smallness of our numbers. . . . He cannot be insensible of the evils he would bring upon us by dislodging us from our winter quarters."[2] The only thing saving him right now was the impassible roads, but in the spring Clinton would return from Charleston and he would attack. He had written Congress many times, finishing up by saying, "Unless some expedient can be instantly adopted, a dissolution of the army for want of subsistence is unavoidable."[3]

Even the requisitioning of food had not proven to stop the hunger in camp. It burned up Washington that his countrymen would let their army starve and provide little sustenance from their fat and swollen stores. This above all else put him in foul moods he could not shake for days. Nathanael Greene had summed it up: "A country overflowing with plenty are now suffering an army, employed for the defense of everything that is dear and valuable, to perish for want of food."[4] His personal aide-de-camp Alexander Hamilton also later wrote, "We begin to hate the country for the neglect of us."[5] Washington smiled in the darkness. It had not been all darkness for Hamilton; he had met and fallen in love with General Schuyler's daughter, Elizabeth, over the winter. At least there was a bright spot in the darkness.

Washington turned to his back, clasping his hand over his chest. He couldn't escape the conviction that what America really needed were professional soldiers, not short-term enlistments that expired with rapidity. The country needed a national army with allegiance not to the states but to the national cause of America. The Congress must have more power as the government in general. Men must shake their home state allegiances. "Certain I am," he had told Joseph Jones, a delegate from Virginia, "that unless Congress speaks in a more decisive tone, unless they are vested with powers by the several states competent to the great purposes of war . . . our cause is lost. . . . I see one head gradually changing into thirteen."[6]

Washington shook his head in the darkness. They really needed more money. The country needed money to wage this war, and without it the cause was not sustainable. He had thought on this a lot and realized that it was not Britain's navy or her soldiers that made her invincible, but the credit that she could draw on to wage war indefinitely. Money was the coal for the engine of war. It was that simple. He had written his aide

Joseph Reed, "In modern wars the longest purse must chiefly determine the event."[7] Washington knew Britain, with its well-funded debt, could crush America, with its inchoate financial system that every day seemed to be on the verge of collapse. "Though the British government is deeply in debt and of course poor, the nation is rich, and their riches afford a fund which will not be easily exhausted."[8] Washington was dead on, of course, and Hamilton would construct a financial system with a strong central bank that could provide this credit. The lessons of the war for Washington and others were that a strong central government was key to waging war, raising money, and running a large country of diverse interests such as the thirteen colonies.

Finally, Washington felt sleepy. No problems would be solved tonight. He turned on his side and stared toward the windows. He had been cross with his aides lately, and he made a note to change that. Washington was not a man to let his emotions show, but even he could not keep the titanic pressure of his situation at bay. "The great man is confounded at his situation, but appears to be reserved and silent,"[9] Nathanael Greene wrote to Joseph Reed. Martha told her brother-in-law, "The poor General was so unhappy that it distressed me exceedingly."[10] Quiet and reserved was how George Washington usually handled stress, but it was taking a toll. He needed sleep and closed his eyes. Things could not get any worse, at least not tonight.

CHAPTER TWENTY-FIVE

The Second Diversion

Elizabethtown, two a.m.

THE WHOLE CONCEPT OF THE DIVERSIONS WAS TO CAMOUFLAGE THE men who were galloping toward George Washington in the ever-increasing snow. Continental soldiers and local militia would react to the incursions by Simcoe, and this would divert any soldiers who might interfere with the kidnapping expedition. One diversion was good. Two diversions were better. If the patriots thought the British were attacking on two fronts, it would create utter confusion, and even if someone discovered George Washington had been abducted, chances were the information would be lost in the fog of war.

Brigadier General Cortland Skinner was fighting the snow that George Washington watched outside his window, except now it was a blowing ferocity of ice and snow that forced the men to keep their heads down, looking up every now and then to see where they were going. The First and Fourth Battalions of the New Jersey volunteers had been marching through the ever-deepening snow with their horses frosted white from the combination of snow and ice. The wind whipped through the valley and further punished the men as they approached Elizabethtown. Skinner's mission was much the same as Simcoe's, to set up a diversion so the Americans would be pulled into the feint while Birch and his men approached Morristown and the Ford Mansion.

Skinner was part of a large detachment under General Stirling's two regiments of British regulars who were headed for Elizabethtown. The combined force, numbering 2,000, headed for the second diversion point not knowing that St. Clair's 50 men guarding the post had already been tipped off on the approach of the overwhelming British force and might have heard of Simcoe's attack. At any rate, the men retreated right before Stirling's regulars reached the post, with Skinner's New Jersey regiments close behind.

Skinner's soldiers fired at the retreating Americans and managed to wound a few, but quickly turned to looting the town, breaking into homes, dragging out suspect rebels in the cold snowy night. "A number of houses in the town have been stripped of everything," American general St. Clair would later write. "And ten or twelve of the inhabitants carried off."[1] A newspaper, *The Pennsylvania Packet*, would later write of the Elizabethtown raid, "After terrifying the women and children, they heroically marched off with their plunder and five or six prisoners."[2]

The diversion was to create havoc, panic, and let the general populace and by proxy the American soldiers know that an attack had taken place. In this way, looting worked in their favor, creating outrage that funneled the news into a vortex, making many think the attacks were part of a larger operation. This was combined with a third attack at Rahway by British soldiers. The three prongs of the diversion pulled any suspicion away from the kidnapping force galloping straight toward Morristown and George Washington.

General Stirling and Skinner let the men plunder for a bit; then they began to pull back away from the town. As soon as the British left, St. Clair's soldiers and local horse patrols reoccupied the town and they began to pursue the British force. The Americans claimed to have wounded several of the raiders, but there was no confirmation in British reports that this was the case. It would seem Stirling and Skinner had pulled off the perfect diversion, including sucking the patriots into pursuing them. It was a classic feint, where few could see the bigger picture at play, and who would question why the raids had taken place on such a snowy night unless there was something else at play? It made no sense for the British to attack these outposts as ends to themselves. There was no real plunder to be had, and to attack and retreat made no sense. But no one was prescient enough to see that the real show was already behind them as the Black Hussars and 17th Light Dragoons raced toward the sleeping George Washington.

CHAPTER TWENTY-SIX

Simcoe's Payback

Six a.m.

THE TEMPERATURE HAD PLUMMETED. THE SNOW THAT HAD BEEN FALL-ing in great tufts before had thinned, and now what had been freezing rain had become thin balls of ice. The men felt the wintry mix as needles on their cheeks. The horses were coated in a shiny layer of ice. The men could no longer feel their fingers or their toes. The horses began to struggle, punching holes in the crusting snow.

The snow had given way to ice that came down like icicles, pounding into the frozen Hudson and onto the shoulders and heads of the men and their horses. Soldiers were used to harsh weather, but this . . . this was something different. How the snow had given way to this torrential onslaught Simcoe had no idea, but he was standing with the Queen's Rangers now on the far side of the Hudson River. He was tired and to some degree frozen, and now this miserable rain was falling on top of the snow and immediately freezing, making it difficult for the horses to proceed.

Simcoe stared toward New Jersey and then looked farther up, where he imagined General Birch and the 17th Light Dragoons and the Black Hussars were making their way. It should have been him, but no matter, if the outcome was the same. He imagined the horsemen approaching the Ford Mansion. He recommended leaving the horses behind and approaching on foot to obtain complete surprise. Undoubtedly the Life Guard soldiers would put up some sort of fight and several would be dispatched quickly while the flying force of men who would take Washington entered the house. Simcoe would have all operations move simultaneously, killing off the sentinels while others moved in and then toward Washington's room, which was reported to be on the main floor along with Mrs. Ford and her family.

If all went well, then Mrs. Ford and Mrs. Washington would be unharmed and maybe even undisturbed, but that would require more stealth than was realistic. And the Black Hussars were sure to raise an alarm if Birch did not keep a tight rein. Simcoe saw Washington's face as the men burst in the bedroom. Oh, that would be a sight! His Excellency staring up as the Dragoons took him from his bed in his nightshirt, with Mrs. Washington in shock, told to not make a sound for the sake of her husband.

And then the hustling through the house, running down along the planked flooring with one man on each of Washington's arms, taking him out into the snow and cold while he stared in shock at his captors, who by this time were patrolling, making sure any Life Guard soldiers were cut down as they came out from the huts. And then the lifting of Washington onto a horse with his hands now bound. A blanket thrown over his shoulders, he would then be whisked off with the dawn into the snowy forest, the men galloping as fast as their horses could go, heading down the way they had come with the breath of wind, snow, and ungodly cold rushing across their faces. And the staring eyes of one George Washington, who would know that a prison cell and possibly a noose awaited him.

And then Simcoe considered a different outcome. Washington might resist. Yes. He was a proud man, and if a kidnapping victim went easily, many times it was felt to be in bad form if not collusion with the kidnappers. So, Washington might resist and fight the men in his bedroom, which would bring force, which might result in gunfire or the unintentional killing of Washington with a body blow or the butt of a musket. Simcoe had worried about this when he first conceived of the kidnapping plan. It might just go badly, and Washington might be killed in the process. This was not the desired outcome, but in a sense, the result would be the same. The snake would have no head, and Simcoe thought it fitting that the rebel flag was a serpent with the motto DON'T TREAD ON ME.

Simcoe felt his eyes water from the wind and felt the freezing rain breaking apart on his tunic. Yes, after tonight the serpent would have no head and the cause would have no leader and the country would have no rallying force. Simcoe had come to believe, along with the other British generals, that after Boston, the amazing vanishing retreat after the Battle of Brooklyn, the victory at Princeton and Trenton, the melting away after each seeming defeat only to reconstitute somewhere else, that George Washington embodied the whole of the American Revolution spiritually, physically, and for all purposes terrestrially. He was America, whatever that was, and if you dispensed with George Washington, you dispensed with America.

Simcoe stared at the increasing icy rain. One could only hope the weather would not hamper General Birch and his men. It would be difficult, but he could not escape the feeling that he would be watching the leader of the American army coming across the Hudson River, a shivering old man on a horse with a blanket upon his back. It was his dream, one he had postulated in a dark American cell a year ago.

CHAPTER TWENTY-SEVEN

George Washington's Fate

Five a.m.

THERE WAS NO CONTINGENCY PLAN FOR THE WEATHER. KNYPHAUSEN had delayed the mission a day because of the snow, but then the decision was to go. There was no plan for a second shot. This was the mission to kidnap George Washington, and it had to go forth as planned. There might not be another opportunity. Washington could move from the Ford Mansion. The Hudson River could start to break up. More troops could be moved to protect the leader of the American Revolution. No, this was it. Now was the moment to strike, weather be damned.

While Simcoe waited for the return of the raiding party on the other side of the Hudson River, the man who had replaced him as the architect of the plan to kidnap George Washington was waiting for a very different sort of deliverance. Captain George Beckwith was waiting, hoping that the incessant snow that had just turned strangely into freezing rain would stop. He had replaced Simcoe as the originator of the plan to kidnap the leader of the American Revolution, and so it was important that his plan should succeed. The diversions should have occurred by now, and so far, the 17th Light Dragoons under General Birch, along with the Black Hussars, had all been riding steadily on the narrowing, snow-packed road.

But this was Beckwith's plan that Knyphausen had embraced. The diversions, using the Black Hussars, the 17th, and the Rangers, were all his and General Knyphausen's innovations. The plan had some redundancy, and the Americans should have been disorientated as a result of Simcoe's and Stirling's attacks. Simcoe was an able general, and it had been his plan in the first place, but a plan of this magnitude with the possibility of ending the war demanded a bigger canvas than the one Simcoe envisioned. No, it required more troops, more cavalry, more firepower, timing, and stealth, and it had to go all the way up the chain to General Clinton.

Captain Beckwith hugged the mane of his horse, feeling the icy rain like small arrows on his cheeks. The temperature was zero, certainly, and the ice made a strange musical *tink* when it hit the top of the snow. All the men hunched down; they were being soaked by this freezing onslaught and they were getting very cold. Already Beckwith felt the tip of his nose had frozen and the tips of his fingers were numb. No matter, they would proceed on, and he allowed himself to see the Ford Mansion with the sleeping George Washington being rousted out of his bed and hurried to a horse. It must be done quickly and with as little commotion as possible.

Captain Beckwith believed in his plan. He believed they could get Washington even before his Life Guard was alerted. There were two sentinels in the front and two in the back. They could be dispatched quickly without gunplay. A knife to the throat or quick bayonet, and they were in, and then if they moved quickly, they would be out and on their way within ten minutes, and then it would be a race to the Hudson. All they had to do now was reach Morristown.

Captain Beckwith felt something like a crack and felt his horse stumble. He reined back and saw the snow had suddenly deepened and they had entered a section of the road that had formed a top crust of ice much like a pond, but now the horses' hooves were breaking through the top layers of frozen snow and plummeting down three feet. Beckwith felt his horse jump again and again, trying to break clear from the imprisoning ice, and then he saw blood in the snow. The horse jumped again, and he saw General Birch's horse doing the same, and he saw the same blood in the snow, but where was it coming from?

His own horse jumped again, leaving a ridge of bright red blood against the jagged, frozen snow, and then Beckwith saw the fetlocks of his horse. The final joint of the leg above the hoof was pulsing bright red blood like a leaky fire hose. Beckwith held up his hand and came to a stop. Birch's horse and many of the Dragoons' horses were bleeding from the fetlocks. The silence of the snowed-in forest moved in, except for the musical rain hitting the hardened ice glaze on top of the snow. The horses stood in place with the men breathing hard, their hands frozen, their coats soaked through.

Beckwith urged his horse forward, but the ice slashed the fetlocks deeper and the horse jumped in pain and confusion. He did not remember what he said exactly, but later Simcoe would write, "Beckwith had found it impossible to carry his attempt into execution, from an uncommon fall of rain, which encrusting the top of the snow, cut the fetlocks of his horses and rendered it absolutely impossible for him to proceed."[1] But this was after Beckwith and his men had continued for a half a mile, leaving a trail of blood behind them, and they feared the horses could soon be lame and they would not be able to return. The rain was entombing the men in ice, and it was here that Captain Beckwith stopped and stared into the false dawn.

This winter. This once-in-a-century winter that had opened up opportunities with the freezing of the Hudson River had now struck again, but this time with a pernicious hammer blow. Men had frozen on post. Inlets and bays that had never frozen were rock-hard. Snow fell with such rapidity that men were dwarfed by ten-foot drifts. The temperature plunged below zero and stayed there for weeks. This was all known. This brutal winter, like none that the denizens of the region could ever remember, had given him and the British a brilliant opportunity to end this war.

George Washington was less than twenty miles away. He was in a mansion with only a small Life Guard unit between him and Beckwith's men. His army was three miles away from him. The diversions had taken place. The spies had given them detailed maps leading directly to the mansion with the best roads to take there and back. Deserters had confirmed that Washington slept on the second floor of the mansion along with Mrs. Ford and her children and Martha Washington. All they had to do was get there and swiftly dispatch the Life Guard sentinels and take George Washington and essentially end the war of colonial rebellion that had dragged on for five years.

Beckwith stared down the road, which was now a plane of ice, with the rain, hail, and snow hitting the surface like pebbles on a frozen pond. The horses could go no farther, and they were too far away and the weather was too harsh for the men to go on foot. Beckwith felt the freezing rain running down his collar and freezing the tip of his nose. The ice had formed a jeweled bridge between the ears of his horse. They would all soon be severely frostbitten and might not be able to make it back if they proceeded any further.

The British captain shook his head slowly. The wily general had done it again. Somehow this American cause seemed destined to survive the day. It had happened time and again. Fate, providence, call it what you will, always seemed to come to the rescue of this . . . this ragtag army in this benighted country of farmers and frontiersmen, these towns of displaced Englishmen who acted with such impudence, and this general who seemed to have the favor of God on his side. They could have plowed on through snow, cold, and wind, but this strange confluence of freezing rain and dropping temperatures had turned the roads into jagged icicles that slashed the horses' legs. What were the odds?

Not a Life Guard unit, not a call in the night, not an alarm, not a fleeing at the last minute had foiled their mission. No, it was simply the uncontrollable variables of the elements that Beckwith had considered but then chosen to view as on their side. It had given them the ice bridge over the Hudson, and it had made Washington complacent, thinking he was in a snowed-in fortress. That was the reason he had taken up residence so far from his troops. Morristown had been chosen for its seeming invulnerability to attack, but Washington had miscalculated. Simcoe and Beckwith had taken in the situation, calculated the odds, and determined that the possibility of success was high . . . and now George Washington had been saved not by his Life Guard or his troops, but by providence, by the weather that would prove to be a rare confluence of snow, ice, zero-degree temperatures, and twenty-eight consecutive snowstorms, a once-in-a-century convergence of horrible meteorological events that showered favor upon the leader of a rebellion who was fighting the most powerful nation on earth for the birth of a new nation.

Captain Beckwith looked at his men and their bleeding horses, man and beast now exhausted and frozen, and realized they would have to turn back and get back across the frozen Hudson before they perished from the cold. All the planning that had gone into his operation had been for naught. The one wild card he had not considered was not the Continental Army or local militia patrols or spies, but something only God could control, and He had decided in his divine wisdom to stop his mission with only miles to go.

Captain Beckwith reached down and pulled out five rockets from his rucksack and swung down from his horse. He crunched through the snow, and one by one he shot the rockets in the early-morning sky and watched their brilliant red arcs against the darkness. The rockets said only one thing, and that was that the mission was over and that if the diversions had not yet occurred, then the British forces should turn back. It let all the moving parts know that it was time to get back across the ice, for George Washington would remain sleeping in his bed on this night, and maybe forever. The freezing of the Hudson River was a once-in-a-century event and a once-in-a-century opportunity. Beckwith knew as he remounted and turned his horse around that there would not be another.

A William Smith would later write in his diary, "There went over the river last evening a party of 4 or 500 and 200 more from Staten Island but they all returned on account of the depth of the snow. I suspect Washington was the chief object and the sallies from Staten Island feints."[2] It would turn out that the snowstorm of February 7 and 8 was Beckwith's undoing, but he had recorded in his diary on February 8, "A fall of nine or ten inches of snow in the night from the northeast."[3] If Washington's men had been able to clear the road between Hackensack and Morristown, the raiders would have made it all the way to the Ford Mansion. It was the strange confluence of snow, rain, and freezing temperatures that created the perfect storm for stopping a group of men on horseback, a group of men who had but a singular mission: to end the American Revolution on a frozen February night.

INTERLUDE

If a bird flew over Morristown, it would see rows upon rows of tidy cabins with smoke whipping from mud-and-stone chimneys. The bird would see mummified men walking not far from the cabins to urinate or defecate and then scurrying back into the smoky warmth of coughs and crackling fires, with the wind whipping snow across the doorways of the 1,000 cabins.

Inside, the men huddled around smoky fires that blackened their skin while they slept away the worst winter any could remember. The hunger persisted through the winter. Men too weak to go on guard duty. The morning roll call showing an army that had slipped to 4,000 men. Every night the blooded footprints going into the forest. Better to take your chances with the snow than to starve in the dark hell of Log City. And the deserters told the British of an army on the brink. Disease, starvation, dwindling enlistments. They said George Washington was at a low point and an attack by General Clinton would surely finish off the Continental Army. Still the snow came. Twenty-eight storms that kept the men huddled under thin blankets, dying, starving, wondering if the winter would ever end.

PART 2

SPRING AND SUMMER

CHAPTER TWENTY-EIGHT

The Circumspect General

March 1780

WINTER FINALLY LESSENED HER GRIP. THE SUN CAME BACK, AND MEN emerged from their cabins, the men who had survived, blinking in disbelief that the bright star had returned, and they felt the warmth as something foreign. There had been many strange rumors flying around, and the strangest one was that there had been a kidnapping attempt by the British to take George Washington from the Ford Mansion.

But the kidnapping of George Washington had failed, and the revelation that a spy was among the British Dragoons would have given Captain Beckwith more of a reason for the unsuccessful mission than the weather. Though the weather was enough. The frozen snow crusted into a hardened sheet of ice broke and became knives that sliced the horses' fetlocks and made it hard for man or beast to proceed more than a few feet at a time. The mission had come to a virtual standstill. The spy's account of the mission was reported back to General St. Clair.

The party from Paulus Hook consisted of about three hundred horse and landed at Hackensack. . . . They proceeded some distance into the country and from the route they pursued, he thinks, intended to have passed the Cedar Swamp, and were very particular in their inquiries about the situation of your quarters, and where I was quartered, and the guards that were posted between Hackensack and Morristown. He says particularly that, after marching some ways into the country, he heard an officer ask the commandant where they were going. He replied that he could not tell him, but they had more than thirty miles to march that night. In a short time after this, finding the snow very deep and the roads not broken, they returned, and the spy was dismissed.[1]

General St. Clair later wrote to Washington, "If their design was an attempt on your quarters . . . I hope you will pardon me for hinting that there is not a sufficient body of troops near enough to render you secure. Had they designed to have fallen on our rear, which they might have done, they had troops enough to have given us a full occupation, and them the opportunity."[2]

St. Clair knew how close the British had come to reaching Washington and that were it not for the frozen snow they might have succeeded. Washington in his understated way communicated that he had been vulnerable. He wrote back that "he had just taken precautions to guard against an attempt by a party of dragoons as might be able to reach his Morristown headquarters."[3] This was the kidnapping mission he described, and he immediately increased his Life Guards, with soldiers posted in each bedroom and six men guarding the top of the stairs. The Hudson River, which had given both sides opportunities, now was viewed as a liability by Washington by giving the British a straight road to his headquarters. "I hope that a short continuance of this weather will make the ice impassable by horse; from the foot there is no danger at this distance,"[4] he wrote back to St. Clair.

The temperatures warmed in late February and the ice on the Hudson broke up. The British essentially put on hold any further plans to kidnap Washington. The thaw made the roads that led to Morristown passable, but that would have involved an amphibious assault across the Hudson, and this was something Washington did not see as a realistic operation for the British. But Captain Beckwith did not give up so easily. He had made the decision to turn back and canceled the mission, but he kept up with his spies to see what changes Washington had made to his personal guards. The intelligence did not bode well for another operation. "General Washington's bodyguard is now augmented to 350 men . . . one third of them lodge every night in the lower part of the house."[5] Then Beckwith received further intelligence that "General Washington's guard is augmented to 400 men. The caution against being surprised is sentinels being posted on every road leading to headquarters. The discharge of a musket is an alarm."

Washington had come a long way from dismissing Silas Condict's letter back in December when he warned him of the possibility of such an attempt to kidnap him. Then on March 16, a late snowstorm brought nine inches of snow to Morristown and the temperatures plummeted again. Washington was now very cognizant that another raid could be launched against him and "ordered two soldiers from each regiment and one sergeant from each brigade to join his Life Guard at the Ford mansion."[6] Even as late as May 16, 1780, a Jeremiah Greenman wrote in his diary that he "went on his Excellency's guard where there were four log houses built to post the guard in case of an alarm."[7] This meant that Washington was having even more Life Guard huts built nearby to augment his personal force.

Still Beckwith monitored Washington's movement, and this more than anything shows that he was not willing to give up the idea of kidnapping Washington. He had come within twenty miles on the February attempt, and he was convinced the mission would have succeeded had it not been for the inclement weather, Even as late as July 28, 1780, Beckwith received a report from a Hessian intelligence officer that Washington had moved his headquarters to Joseph Appleby's house and a female spy who worked in the house doing laundry passed on information as to his whereabouts. "The woman is returned from Washington's headquarters,"[8] wrote Lieutenant Carl Levin Marquard. "She saw him herself and says that Washington sleeps in the back bedroom; that there were two French sentries yesterday at his door; that his guard consists of French and rebels, which she judged to about 30 or 40 men; that she saw no men there; that there was no camp in the rear of his quarters . . . that Appleby's was about a half mile back of the Rebel camps."[9]

It is easy to imagine Beckwith not willing to give up the idea of snatching George Washington when he was so close before. On August 11, he received a report from a rebel deserter that Washington's house was now about a quarter of a mile in the rear of the army and that he had a guard of eight men who never left his side. Beckwith did nothing with this information. The British had moved onto another secret weapon to defeat the American army. This one had a very good chance of succeeding and went all the way to General Henry Clinton. It was a war of secret weapons, submersibles, kidnapping plots, and Benedict Arnold.

CHAPTER TWENTY-NINE

The Stressed-Out Family Man

April 1780

FINANCIAL PRESSURE DESTROYS MANY MARRIAGES. THE FAMILY EXPANDS and the house grows, and suddenly there is simply not enough money. The great dissatisfaction that was Benedict Arnold now turned to a bitter conviction that he had given much but received little. His deal with the devil, his Faustian pact with the British, was in his mind, and what George Washington, the government, nay the country owed him for his service that had cost him his fortune (perceived) and his health (his leg), and besides, it was all for the good of humanity to stop this bloody war that dragged on and on.

His wife had just given him a son in March, and now the Arnold household consisted of his sister Hannah and his youngest son from his prior marriage, and he had the two older boys in school in Maryland with bills innumerable and without any real way of paying them. Like many people, he tried to obtain a loan and inquired with the French ambassador, Chevalier de La Luzerne, but was turned down.

And so, the Arnolds had to tighten their belt by downsizing. This was a humiliating admission that he had lied about his finances to Peggy and her father. The family gave up their residence at the Penn Mansion, which he had procured with a loan on which he could barely keep up with the payments, and moved into a home owned by Peggy's father. Insult to injury, the proud general had to go hat in hand to the in-laws.

Benedict needed to get the court-martial at Morristown behind him so he could strike his deal with the British, and then all his financial woes would be solved. He had been waiting for Washington's reprimand for some time, and while he was waiting, he proposed to His Excellency that he take several hundred soldiers on a naval expedition. Arnold probably wanted to plunder any ships he captured or, worse, surrender his ship to the British for a price. Who knows? Washington did not give him his appointment, but on April 6, Arnold was given his reprimand. "The commander in chief would have been much happier in an occasion of bestowing honors on an officer who has rendered such distinguished service to his country as Major General Arnold, but in the present case a sense of duty and a regard to candor oblige him to deliver that he considers his conduct in the issuance of the permit as peculiarly reprehensible both in a civil and military view, and in the affair of the wagons as impudent and improper."[1]

It was but a slap on the hand for his chicanery involving the ship *Charming Nancy*, but André and General Clinton were still in Charleston and he had no way of knowing if this would diminish his value as a traitor to his country. Washington genuinely liked Benedict Arnold and saw his value as a fighting general who was brilliant, brave, and foolish all at the same time. He was a bit like a younger Washington in the frontier wars, and to that end he followed up the reprimand with a personal letter.

Our profession is the purest of all. Even the shadow of a fault tarnishes the luster of our finest achievements. The least indiscretion may rob us of public favor, so hard to be acquired. I reprimand you for having forgotten that, in proportion as you have rendered yourself formidable to our enemies; you should have been guarded and temperate in your deportment to your fellow citizens. Exhibit anew these noble qualities, which have placed you on the list of our most valued commanders. I will myself furnish you, as far as it may be in my power, with the opportunities for regaining the esteem of your country.[2]

In other words, Washington would still attempt to give Arnold what he desired, and what the stressed-out family man desired most was West Point. This strategic fort eleven miles up the Hudson would give the British the ability to cut the country in half and disrupt the supply chain for the American army and possibly end the war. This would be the fort he would hand over to the British, and they would hand him the princely sum they had agreed on—20,000 pounds was kicking around in Peggy's and Arnold's heads by now. A bonus was that there was housing at West Point for his wife and children and they could all leave America together with their chest of gold.

He quickly enlisted the help of Philip Schuyler in procuring the command of West Point. Schuyler headed up a congressional committee that was evaluating the state of the army, and he consented to speak to Washington on Arnold's behalf. The family man was impatient and wrote Schuyler a letter in May. "I have not yet had the pleasure of receiving a line from you since you arrived at camp . . . and know not who is to have the command at the North River."[3] Everything was riding on his appointment, and Arnold had many sleepless nights staring financial ruin in the face should his commission not come through. Finally a letter arrived from Schuyler telling Arnold that Washington "expressed a desire to do whatever was agreeable to you . . . and intimated that as soon as his arrangements for the campaign should take place that he would properly consider you. . . . If the command at West Point is offered, it will be honorable."[4]

Done. As far as Arnold was concerned, West Point was his. Now all he had to do was set up the deal. Major André and General Clinton were still 750 miles away at Charleston, but he could get the ball rolling and to that end reached out to General Knyphausen, who had been instrumental in the plot to kidnap Washington. He must have seen this as another opportunity to knock America out of the war and pursued it with the same zeal as he had pursued the operation back in February. It wasn't a kidnapping, but the control of West Point and the Hudson was a body blow with almost the same import as taking the general.

He told Arnold he would have to wait for Clinton's return to finalize the details, but it was as good as done. Benedict began to tie up loose ends and left for Connecticut in early June to oversee the selling of his home in New Haven. He would go by Morristown first and lock down his appointment. Benedict now felt time was on his side, and on June 12 he wrote Knyphausen, using his new spy alias, "Mr. Moore expects to have the command of West Point offered to him on his return."[5]

The family man breathed a little easier.

CHAPTER THIRTY

Some Violent Convulsion

April 28, 1780

CONGRESS WAS SICK OF THE LETTERS. DOOM AND GLOOM. THE LETTERS coming from Morristown painted a horrible picture of starvation, naked men, no money, no equipment, and worse, hints that at any minute the army might simply dissolve into its parts and slip away. There were even hints of mutiny in Washington's letters. This was all not to be believed, and if it was to be believed, then Washington and his officers were to blame. Not Congress. But saying all that, prudence dictated a fact-finding mission to find the true source of the demise of the Continental Army.

George Washington watched the three men on horseback ride up to the front of the Ford Mansion. The three members of Congress had seen better days, with mud-spattered clothes, drooping hats, their boots the same color as the sandy brown mud that now coated man and beast since the spring thaw. The last snowstorm in late March had brought fat heavy flakes of snow that piled up to nine inches and then melted in a great rush when unseasonably warm temperatures came with the beginning of April. It seemed every day now Washington woke to the sound of water dripping from the roof, the branches, and sometimes the heavens. It had been a wet, wonderful spring; it was wonderful in that it brought to an end the juggernaut of snowstorms that had pummeled Morristown.

They had all emerged like bears after a long hibernation, blinking against the bright sun, not quite sure whether to believe the snow and miserable subzero temperatures had finally left. But the awful winter that had left Washington with half of his original soldiers—10,000 had shrunk to 5,000—had been a long time of starvation and disease and desertion, and this he had documented to Congress all winter long. He had been writing to Congress about the state of the army since 1775. "The military chest is totally exhausted. The Paymaster has not a single dollar in hand. The Commissary General assures me he has strained his credit to the upmost for the subsistence of the army. The quartermaster general is precisely in the same situation, and the greater part of the army is not in a state far from mutiny."[1]

This same letter could have been written five years later in 1780. "I know not to whom to impute this failure, but I am of the opinion, if the evil is not immediately remedied and more punctually observed in the turn, this army must absolutely break up."[2]

And this was the case in 1779–1780. The American army, as the British knew better than Congress, was in the process of slowly withering away. As James Thacher, the army surgeon, wrote, "Our sacrifices are incalculably great and far exceed the bounds of duty, which the public can or right claim from any one class of men. Our wages are not punctually paid we are frequently five or six months in arrears and the continental money which we receive is depreciated to the lowest ebb. . . . This is the trash which is tendered to requite us for our sacrifices for our sufferings and privations while in the service of our county."[3]

Washington kept up the steady stream of letters, and Congress finally voted to send a three-man investigative committee to Morristown and see if there was any truth to Washington's claims. The three men left Philadelphia in early April: Philip Schuyler of New York state, John Matthews of South Carolina, and Nathaniel Peabody of New Hampshire. Schuyler was the only military man, as a former general in the army. "A committee have arrived in camp from Congress, for the purpose of investigating the circumstances and the condition of the army,"[4] James Thacher wrote in his journal. He then foreshadowed the mutinous mood that would grip the men in the spring. "Four battalions of our troops were paraded for review by the committee of congress, in the presence of George Washington, they were duly honored with the military salute. We are again visited with the calamity of which we have so often complained, a great scarcity of provisions of every kind. Our poor soldiers are reduced to the very verge of famine; their patience is exhausted by the complicated sufferings and their spirits are almost broken."[5]

When the congressmen reached Washington, he learned of their instructions. Basically, they had been charged with talking with the commander to see where they might reduce troops and costs. The initial charge of the committee was hopelessly blind to the real problems of Morristown and showed the skepticism of a Congress that had no real idea of the suffering that had occurred over the winter.

First, they were to ascertain the need to cut the troops. Second, they were to make sure officers did not have too many horses. Third, the committee was to suggest to Washington "such plans for the convenience of the officers with respect to clothing and commissary supplies as will tend to remove all just ground for complaint."[6] It was as if Congress wanted to apply a Band-Aid when a tourniquet was needed to stanch the bleeding. The committee was there to find out if Washington and Quartermaster Greene had let the army slip into the disastrous state Washington described.

It got even worse. The committee was to have broad-reaching powers to restructure the army where they saw fit. "You are to abolish unnecessary posts, to erect others, to discharge useless officers, to stop rations improperly issued, and are hereby further authorized to exercise every power which may be necessary to effect a reformation of abuses and the general arrangement of those departments which are in any wise connected with the matters committed to your charge."[7]

A different man might have been offended by the tone of the committee, but Washington welcomed the three congressmen, who listened to his view of the situation of the army and then set out to investigate themselves. Two weeks later, Congressman Matthews galloped back to Philadelphia with the committee's report under his arm. It was a bombshell. Instead of implicating George Washington for the deplorable state of the army, the report stated that the army was in worse shape than could be imagined. The report said there was no money, few supplies, and that the foraging system was not adequate for the needs of the army. "Before we had an opportunity closely to view and examine into the real state of things, we had no conception of the almost inextricable difficulties in which we found them involved."[8] The committee report then veered and said the soldiers were at the end of their patience after the long winter of scant food, and "it has had a very pernicious influence on the soldiers."[9] The summary drove the point home.

Their starving condition, their want of pay, and the variety of hardships that they have been driven to sustain, has soured their tempers, and produced a spirit of discontent which begins to display itself under a complexion of the most alarming hue. If this spirit should fully establish itself, it must be productive of some violent convulsion infinitely to our prejudice, at home and abroad, as it would evince a lack of means, or want of wisdom to employ them, either of which must bring our cause into discredit and draw into its train consequences of a nature too serious to be complicated without the deepest anxiety.[10]

The violent convulsion was mutiny. This jumped out at the committee members as they made their way through Log City, talking to the soldiers. There were three things Congress must do to head off a possible mutiny: pay and clothe the troops and arm them. Matthews left the report with Congress and then went back to Morristown to continue the investigation. The committee then concentrated on Quartermaster General Nathanael Greene. His department spent $407,393 a month on the war, a staggering amount of money for the time, but the war machine was monstrous. He had hired 3,000 men and employed 28 deputy quartermasters. The committee could find no corruption in the department.

On May 13, Congressman Schuyler recommended that Washington be imbued with dictatorial powers to implement sweeping reforms to the army. If not, then a full-time committee should be appointed to stay with the army and augment change. It was all too little too late. General Clinton had a great victory in Charleston and was headed back to deal with George Washington and his army in Morristown. There was still no money, no food, no ammo, no uniforms. And once Clinton returned, Benedict Arnold would finalize his agreement with the British and Washington would unwittingly hand him the keys to the kingdom with the appointment as commander of West Point. The violent convulsion was on the way.

CHAPTER THIRTY-ONE

The Volcano Explodes

May 1780

WE THINK OF MUTINY AS OCCURRING ON A SHIP. MAYBE THIS IS BECAUSE of books and movies, most famously *Mutiny on the Bounty*. In this fantasy we see the men with swords and eyepatches taking over the ship and then having the captain walk the plank. It is never quite clear what happens after the mutiny, as the mutineers then must become the rulers. But we don't have much familiarity with an army turning against its commanders. How does it start and where does it end? In the American army it was almost unthinkable.

Spring had come to Morristown, and one would think the winter of suffering had ended, but it was not true. The splendor of the blooming dogwoods with their white flowers, not unlike the snow that had just passed, and the meadows brilliant with blue wildflowers were in harsh contrast to the men who were starving in the grimy rows of Log City. On May 21 the rations that had been trickling into Morristown stopped entirely. The thin gruel that had passed for food through the winter was not to be had, and this last egregious deprivation seemed to be the straw that broke the camel's back.

"The men were exasperated beyond endurance," Joseph Martin wrote. "They could not stand it any longer. They saw no alternative but to starve to death or break up the army, give it all up and go home. This was a matter for the soldiers to think upon. They were truly patriotic; they loved their country, and they had already suffered everything short of death in its cause; and now, after such extreme hardships to give up all was too much, but to starve to death was too much also. What was to be done?"[1]

The insult to injury was that the country was enjoying a war-fueled economic boom, and prosperous farms around Morristown gave only what was required by Washington's requisitions. The army was simply starving to death, and George Washington reached out to Joseph Reed, president of the Pennsylvania Supreme Executive Council. "All our departments, all our operations, are at a stand, and unless a system, very different from that which has a long time prevailed, but immediately adopted throughout the states, our affairs must be desperate beyond the possibility of recovery."[2]

The spark was in the powder keg of neglect. The mutiny by the men from Connecticut was symptomatic of a larger ill. The country had not graduated from a collection of states that thought of only their own needs. The national cause, for the most part, had devolved into a collection of competing interests who were unwilling to pay for a national army. America had grown tired of the war, and while they were not willing to pay taxes imposed by the British, they were also unwilling to pay taxes imposed by their own government. The result of this lack of resolve was the starving army in Morristown. Like all causes begun in a flash of enthusiasm and energy, the Revolution had dragged on so long that people had simply lost the ability to see any reason why they should contribute money to what might be a lost cause.

"The rascally stupidity which now prevails in the country at large is beyond all description,"[3] twenty-five-year-old Lieutenant Colonel Ebenezer Huntington from Connecticut wrote, expressing the sentiments of soldiers who had started the war full of patriotic pride. In a letter to his brother, he implored him to join the fight and bring others.

Send your men to the field. Believe you are Americans . . . you don't deserve to be freemen unless you can believe it yourselves. . . . I despise my countrymen. I wish I could say I was not born in America. . . . The insults and neglects which the army has met with from the country beggars all description. . . . I am in rags . . . and only a hunk of fresh beef and that without salt to dine on this day; received no pay since last December. Constituents back home complaining and all this for my cowardly countrymen who flinch at the very time when their exertions are wanted and hold their purse strings as though they would damn the world rather than part with a dollar to their army.[4]

In this way, Benedict Arnold was a weathervane for the way popular opinion seemed to have turned against the cause. Most people would still not sell out their country, but Arnold was not far wrong when he compared the struggle of America to "the pangs of a dying man, violent but of short duration."[5] Why shouldn't it be every man for himself? Certainly, the soldiers were beginning to glean that this was now the case. Benedict would later justify his treason by framing it as a man necessitating the end of the war on humanitarian grounds. "Our cause was hopeless: I thought we would never succeed, and I did it to save the shedding of blood."[6] And to make a lot of money, but that is getting ahead of ourselves.

In the microcosm of camp life in Morristown, the men from Connecticut had had enough. They had staged a small rebellion in January where they paraded in front of their huts after evening roll call. Officers immediately appeared and talked the men into returning to their quarters. Several days passed, and the men formed up again, ready to march through Connecticut, fully armed. Once again, they were convinced to return to their cabins. The crisis had passed, but the seeds of rebellion would sprout again on May 25.

As before, the men from Joseph Martin's Connecticut brigade lingered on the parade ground. Things went from bad to worse quickly. A man sang out, "Who will parade with me?"[7] The whole regiment joined in, and the drummer beat out the signals. "On the first drum roll, the men shouldered their arms. On the second, they faced to the front, and on the third, the regiment moved out, with music playing toward the other Connecticut regiments."[8]

They then marched to another Connecticut brigade and brought them into their cause and began parading around the camp with drums and fifes playing merrily in the warm evening air. The young surgeon James Thacher recorded the mutiny: "Other causes of discontent has produced a considerable degree of relaxation in discipline and an unusual number of desertions from our ranks. An event still more alarming occurred on the 25th instant. Two regiments of the Connecticut line took the liberty to parade without their officers, and in the spirit of mutiny resolved to march into the country to relieve themselves from present difficulties and to furnish themselves with provisions at all hazards."[9]

Once again, the officers approached the men and demanded they return to their quarters. This time it didn't work, and the officers realized the men had mutinied. "Colonel Meigs in attempting to restore order, received a blow from one of the mutineers."[10] An officer tried to drag one soldier from the group to make an example of him, and the soldiers surrounded the officer with bayonets. Then the officers tried to lure the men with the promise of food and claimed that cattle had been driven into the camp.

Lieutenant Colonel John Sumner then tried to order the men back into submission. The soldiers stared at him as he demanded they shoulder arms. This more than anything let the officers know the chain of command had been severed and the order of military discipline was no longer to be seen. The Connecticut men were a body unto themselves, an armed group of men parading around the camp looking for revenge, food, pay . . . no one was quite sure, but they were a bit like a dog that has suddenly become rabid with the final solution one of violence.

The Connecticut regiment continued to march while the officers ordered a Pennsylvania regiment into the surrounding trees to cut off the men if they should try and leave the camp. But the Pennsylvanians became sympathetic to the cause of the mutinous men, and one man yelled out, "Let us join the Yankees!"[11] The Pennsylvanians were sent back to their huts and the Connecticut men continued to march around the camp. If the Pennsylvania regiment had joined the men from Connecticut, the army might have experienced a full-scale mutiny, effectively ending the Continental Army.

It was logic and a willingness to listen that stopped the mutiny. Colonel Walter Stewart walked through the men and asked why they had not gone to their officers. The men scoffed, but Stewart persisted. "Your officers suffer as much as you do,"[12] he pointed out, explaining that the officers were just as broke as the men. "I had not sixpence to buy a partridge that was offered to me the other day."[13] But it would seem the gentle, engaging tone of Stewart had allowed him to relate to the men. He asked the men "how much you injure your own character by such conduct?"[14] Stewart then appealed to the men's pride. "You Connecticut troops have won immortal honor to yourselves the winter past, by your perseverance, patience and bravery, and now you are shucking it off at your heels."[15]

The rage that had propelled the mutineers forward seemed to dissipate, and the men gradually returned to quarters. There was food soon after the mutiny, and Joseph Martin wrote, "Our stir did us some good in the end, for we had provisions directly after, so we had no great cause for complaint for some time."[16] But the mutiny showed that the American army had reached the breaking point, and George Washington knew how close they had come to losing the war right there in Jockey Hollow. He would later write that mutiny "has given me infinitely more concern than anything that has ever happened, and strikes me as the most important, because we have no means at this time, that I know of, for paying the troops, but in Continental money, and as it is evidently impracticable from the immense quantity it would require, to pay them."[17] There would still be no money for the soldiers, and Washington knew he was on borrowed time. Then he received news from Charleston that changed the entire war once again.

CHAPTER THIRTY-TWO

Bonnie and Clyde

June 1780

BONNIE AND CLYDE WERE LOVERS AND PARTNERS IN CRIME. THEY FED off each other. Bonnie thought Clyde had more potential than he did. They dared each other. Their crime spree across the country made them legendary. Without Bonnie, Clyde would have been just another two-bit bank robber. But once they came together, they became mythic, something bigger than life. They knew their time was limited and knew they would die together one day. And we still know their names. Notoriety has no morals.

Benedict Arnold stared at the jewel of the Hudson. He had been on his way to Connecticut when he stopped off to see his prize. It was a jewel. A great big diamond in the middle of the "River of Mountains," as the Hudson had been designated. One million years before, a glacier had carved out the river and left the Hudson Highlands: a collection of hills extending from Stony Point and continuing eleven miles up the river. In sheer size the Hudson River is larger than any other river on the Eastern seaboard. The 400,000 gallons a second pouring out from the Hudson creates its own tidal currents in the ocean.

The West Point fort that Arnold wanted to give to the British was the key to the continent. The natural S bend in the river along with the craggy heights had given Washington and his engineers an opportunity to make navigation of the river almost impossible for an enemy ship. "The two forts on either side of the river—a series of redoubts on Constitution

Island to the east and Fort Arnold to the west—commanded the river but they in turn were commanded by the heights behind them, requiring that an interlocking series of fortifications be constructed that fit like puzzle pieces into the complexities of the surrounding hills."[1] To back this up, the Americans had strung a sixty-five-ton chain across the river at the S curve, with each of the 1,200 links two and a quarter inches thick. The chain rested on log rafts and would in theory stop any ship trying to navigate up the Hudson.

Benedict toured the fort with General Robert Howe and then quickly communicated his opinion of the fort to the British. He claimed the fort was in serious disrepair and said he was "greatly disappointed in both the works and garrison. There is only fifteen hundred soldiers, which will not half man the works."[2] He then pointed out some weaknesses the British could exploit in Redoubt Number 4. "I am told the English may land three miles below and have a good road to bring up heavy cannon at Rocky Hill. This redoubt is wretchedly executed, only seven or ten feet high and might be taken by assault by a handful of men."[3]

What was Arnold doing here? He was proving his worth to the British and whetting their appetite for the grand prize, West Point. He was building the value of the prize that would set him and Peggy up for some time in Britain. He then cast doubt on the iron chain across the river. "I am convinced the boom or chain thrown across the river to stop the shipping cannot be depended on. A single ship large and heavy load with a strong wind and tide would break the chain."[4]

After sending off his assessment, Arnold made his way to New Haven to tie up some loose ends in anticipation of leaving the country. His high-strung wife, Peggy, meanwhile, was doing her part by seducing one Robert Livingston with her feminine wiles. Livingston was a congressman from New York whom Peggy convinced to send a letter to George Washington demanding Arnold be given command of West Point to ensure the security of the fort. Peggy was not above using her stunning good looks to get what she wanted, so much so that her sister wrote to Arnold saying the two of them had "frequent private assignations and . . . numberless billets-doux."[5] But no matter, Bonnie and Clyde each had a role to play, and Peggy did get Livingston to request that Arnold get command of West Point. Washington responded, clearly puzzled by the letter. "I am under no apprehension now of danger to the post at West Point."[6]

The truth was that Washington had no real reason to replace Robert Howe as commander, but Benedict and Peggy had just begun their campaign to wrangle the appointment. George Washington had a much bigger problem now than who would be the commander of West Point.

CHAPTER THIRTY-THREE

The Darkest Hour

May 1780

THE LIGHT FILTERED DOWN THROUGH THE TREES AS THE RIDER
passed under the dappling trees and kept his head toward the horse's
mane with the close leathery scent of the saddle in his nose and the
horse's labored breath in time with the hooves pounding the packed
road. Under one arm he kept the wrapped package that he had not let
go of the entire way. He saw the mansion peeking through the trees,
the headquarters of George Washington. The white Georgian mansion
with the black shutters spread out like a monolith, the beating heart of
the American Revolution.

The rider rode up to the Ford Mansion and dismounted, barely
breaking stride, and waited for George Washington before giving up the
package he held tightly under his arm. Colonel Elias Dayton had given
him strict instructions to ride like the wind and show the package to
only Washington. The commander thanked the express rider, tearing off
the sheaf of paper and reading the headline in the *Royal Gazette*, a Tory
newspaper edited by British writer James Rivington. There was a scribbled note as well that Washington held up to the light. The note said the
headline was probably a lie. Washington looked back at the paper with a
sinking feeling. If only that were so. CLINTON CAPTURED CHARLESTON!
Washington quickly read the article, which cited regiments and generals
in Charleston that he knew to be accurate.

He asked the messenger to wait and wrote a quick squib to Dayton. "I most sincerely wish that your suspicions of the truth of Rivington's publication may prove well grounded, but I confess it bears too many marks of authenticity."[1] He then ordered Dayton to ready the defenses of Elizabethtown. Three days later, Washington had his confirmation when the British frigate *Iris* sailed into New York. It was worse than he believed. General Clinton would be returning soon to turn his sights on Washington and his army at Morristown. First the mutiny at Morristown, and then five days later the collapse and loss of Charleston. On May 31, Washington wrote to Joseph Jones, an attorney from Richmond, "I fear our cause is lost."[2]

The British could now finally focus on George Washington. He had escaped being kidnapped, but the simple math of a large invading force of British regulars was undeniable. His fighting force had slipped below 5,000 men and the British had had all winter to beef up their army and now could turn from Charleston. Washington would now face an army and a general riding the crest of victory. The only question was when General Clinton would arrive. This was also the question on commanding general Knyphausen's mind as well.

One might look at the British campaign in the winter of 1779–1780 as a three-pronged attack. The first prong was the attempted kidnapping, the second prong was Benedict Arnold, and the third prong was an all-out attack on Washington in Morristown. Logic would say that at least one of these prongs would be successful. The British knew of Washington's weakened army, and the pressure to attack had become unbearable for Knyphausen in New York, whom Clinton had left in charge with no return date.

Loyalists in New York led by former New Jersey governor William Franklin clamored for an attack by General Knyphausen. They believed New Jersey was practically defenseless and had become frustrated with Knyphausen's refusal to do anything until Clinton retuned. Franklin's spies told him of massive desertions, lack of food and munitions, and mutinous activities in Morristown. This spoke of an army in its death throes, and in May he urged Knyphausen to attack. But the Hessian general's default position was to do nothing until Clinton returned. Even when the message came on May 28 that Charleston had surrendered, there was still no information about when the commander might return.

General Knyphausen's larger fear, more than the American army at Morristown, was the New Jersey militia, rumored to be about 16,000 soldiers. Franklin thought this a fiction and believed local militias were no match for the British army. But Knyphausen knew the power of the homegrown American soldiers, who had been picking the eyes out of squirrels for years with their long rifles. The guerilla style of fighting was no match for the lined-up British, who took heavy casualties from these hit-and-run insurgents.

But more than all that, Knyphausen was a German officer and German officers above all else followed orders. To take matters into his own hands and launch an attack on Morristown before Clinton returned was unthinkable. He had already had one failure on his hands with the kidnapping debacle. He did not want to have to tell General Clinton of another failure when he returned. So the Hessian bided his time, but by June the pressure had become even more intense. The risk of acting without the approval of his superior, General Clinton, started to fade with the enormous pressure to act.

By all reports the American army was at its lowest point. If the deserters and spies were to be trusted, then there might be a once-in-a-lifetime opportunity for a knockout blow. It was the same psychology that was used for the kidnapping attempt across the Hudson. For Knyphausen it was a decision fraught with risk, but some glory as well should he be able to smash the remains of George Washington's army.

He made the decision to launch the attack. At midnight on June 7, Hessian and British troops landed at DeHart's Landing near Elizabethtown. Their flat-bottomed boats came in silently, and they disembarked for an hour. The element of surprise seemed to be with them while boat after boat unloaded men. And then a musket flash. And another. The long wait that began in November when Washington went into winter camp at Morristown was over.

Spies. Kidnapping plots. Benedict Arnold's grand scheme. It all came down to this moment. The muskets flared on both sides, with the leaded balls finding their targets. No surprise then. The hope for a quick route and possible charge toward Springfield and Morristown was no longer a reality. They would have to fight their way inland. The first muskets fired belonged to Washington's Life Guard. The commander had become nervous about the security around Elizabethtown and sent his own personal bodyguard unit of 150 men with Major Caleb Gibbs in command.

The British boats had stood out in the moonlit water. Caleb waited for the men to come ashore and then opened up. Brigadier General Thomas Stirling was commander of the invasion force, and he was one of the first to go down with balls slamming into his hip. The men had to pull back with Stirling, and this slowed the British by an hour and a half. It was in that time that a messenger galloped toward the Ford Mansion and another raced to alert the soldiers stationed in the gap at the Short Hills. Then beacons atop the mountainous peaks were set ablaze, and beacons along the Watchung Mountains were lit as well. These were triangular structures packed with wood and dry tinder that could be seen for miles. Cannons boomed into the night and awakened sleeping militiamen. The battle of Morristown or for the control of New Jersey had finally begun.

CHAPTER THIRTY-FOUR

The French Component

May 1778

THE FRENCH SAW IT AS A WAY TO STICK IT TO THE BRITISH ONCE AGAIN. They were their mortal enemy, and depriving Britain of her colonies would level the playing field and be a dagger to the heart of her economy. Besides, the Americans had shown they could fight, and George Washington was a charismatic leader who could be depended on to bleed the British dry in their efforts to snare the wily leader and his ragtag army. They would come in on the side of America and gain a new ally in the emerging New World.

But for George Washington and the Americans, the entry into the war by the French was a bit like a winning lottery ticket that simply wouldn't pay. It was infuriating for George Washington that this major European power could tip the scales of the war but never seemed to engage. The French treaty with the Americans had been signed in 1778, and there was an assumption that this would end the war once France entered on the side of the Americans. Washington was still in Valley Forge when the treaty was ratified by Congress. On May 6 a celebration was held, and John Laurens wrote to his father about the news.

> *Yesterday we celebrated the new alliance with as much splendor as the short notice would allow. Divine service preceded the rejoicing. After a proper pause, the several brigades marched by their right to their posts in order of battle, and the line was formed with admirable*

rapidity and precision. Three salutes of artillery, thirteen each, and three general discharges of a running fire by the musketry, were given in honor of the king of France, the friendly European powers, and the United American States. Loud huzzahs! The order with which the whole was conducted, the beautiful effect of the running fire, which was executed to perfection, the martial appearance of the troops, gave sensible pleasure to everyone present.[1]

It was a tantalizing trump card that never seemed to get played. Washington received a letter on July 14, 1778, from French vice admiral Charles Hector that the Count d'Estaing had just arrived at the base of the Delaware River with "a fleet of twelve ships of the line and five frigates."[2] This was what Washington had been waiting for, a sizeable French force to strike at the British and give America and France naval superiority. But there were problems at the start. It had taken the French twice as long to cross the Atlantic (eighty-seven days), and they missed their opportunity to trap the British in Philadelphia and force General Howe and his brother to surrender.

Instead, d'Estaing reached Sandy Hook on July 11; this was essentially a shoal where ships waited for favorable tides before sailing into New York Harbor. General Howe lined up his ships in a line and, while outgunned 850 to 534, his ships were like stationary outposts that guarded the channel leading from the Hook to the harbor.

In what would become an unfortunate repeating scenario of French procrastination, d'Estaing sat for ten days and pondered what to do. He was nervous about confronting the British, who were behind a sand bar outside of Sandy Hook, where a draft of only twenty-two feet was the maximum for any ship attempting to pass. D'Estaing's flagship, the *Languedoc*, drafted twenty-five feet, and he waited for a high tide. On July 22 the French made their move, but then d'Estaing had second thoughts as he approached the sand bar, and he headed out to sea.

Still, Washington continued to hope the French would confront the British fleet and thought Newport, Rhode Island, might be where the confrontation would take place. But again, the French demurred when Admiral Howe and thirty-one British ships appeared on the horizon.

D'Estaing did not want to get trapped in Narragansett Bay, and he headed out to sea to engage the British. For two days the two fleets circled each other, trying to get the "weather gauge" which meant the advantage of having the wind behind while coming up on the enemy ship. Suddenly a gale-force wind rippled across the ocean and a squall came on that had both commanders thinking now only of their own survival.

D'Estaing's flagship *Languedoc* was tossed around violently, lost all her masts, and then her rudder snapped. She now was at the mercy of the storm and was thrown about like a wooden duck helpless to paddle against the violent contortions of gale-force winds. Men went overboard, cannons broke loose, and then the British ship *Renown* approached the helpless ship and began firing cannonballs into the ship's transom. Several cannonballs went through the commander's stateroom as sailors brought in cannons to his suite and fought it out with the British from there. The British and the French exchanged fire, and then the British broke off until morning, when two French ships came to d'Estaing's rescue and the battle was over.

When the French commander finally sailed into Newport, his ship was in tatters and any hope of an assault against the British was gone. He eventually went into Boston for repairs, and as Washington headed into winter camp at Morristown, he watched the French fleet turn away from America and head for warmer waters to wait out the winter without firing a shot. And then in the spring on May 10 came word from General Lafayette that the French fleet under Count de Rochambeau was headed for America with 4,000 soldiers and a fleet of warships. "Here I am my dear General," Lafayette had written him after returning to America, "and in the midst of the joy I feel in finding myself again one of your loving soldiers."[3]

The French had played with Washington, and one could argue that in the beginning they did more harm than good. There was a feeling that the French would now do the fighting, so why suffer for the cause when in fact it would be a foregone conclusion? When the French assistance failed to materialize, this quickly turned to a darker view that the French might not be reliable and could pull out at any moment. Certainly, in the long winter of Morristown, it was hard for soldiers to believe anyone was coming to their aid, much less a foreign power.

But with the spring came the promises again, and Washington envisioned a French-American attack on New York. It was even worse. Benedict Arnold had fed the news of the French movements to the British, and when the formerly depressed neurotic Henry Clinton returned with André (Arnold's chief contact), he came back a new man. He was not bent on resigning, as he had been when he left, but was focused now on defeating George Washington and ending the war once and for all. He quickly made plans to defeat Washington's weakened army at Morristown in June, but then he found out that Knyphausen had already launched an attack on Morristown that was literally ongoing as he arrived.

Simultaneously Benedict Arnold had come up with intelligence that the French fleet was headed for Newport and Clinton might be able to trap the fleet in Narragansett Bay. Arnold was also offering to turn over the fort of West Point on the Hudson. Clinton verified Arnold's information on the movements of the French fleet and then began to raise a force of 6,000 for an attack on Newport.

Washington's hopes would once again be dashed when French commander Rochambeau said he needed time for his men to recover from the long voyage across the ocean and could not risk an attack on New York. He also did not have the promised uniforms and equipment for Washington's army. The French would be a card waiting to be played. The French component would not really come to fruition until the final defeat at Yorktown. For now, George Washington was on his own.

CHAPTER THIRTY-FIVE

Americans Fight Like Bulldogs

June 7, 1780

THE SAILS LIFTED WHITE AND BRILLIANT IN THE MORNING SUN. THE breeze from the ocean blew in cool and felt good after the stifling humidity of the past few days. The British flagship rode the waves and the general, looking out, knew he had done something bold. It was really the final battle. George Washington had been hiding out in Morristown like a thief in the night, and now, finally, he and his motley army would be dispatched once and for all. It was a good day to be a British officer in the King's service.

The ocean sparkled below. General Knyphausen breathed the ocean air and felt good about the offensive. The first wave had already gone, and victory might be theirs. George Washington's army was weak and by all reports in no fighting shape at all. What a moment it would be when he could tell General Clinton he had just defeated the rebel army and possibly turned the tide of war. The German officer stared out from the bridge and saw a forest of masts on the horizon. He squinted; an ant had crossed his line of vision. A small boat had left the forest and was heading directly for him.

Knyphausen spread out his hands on the railing and watched the boat becoming larger and larger. The early-morning sea breeze was a tonic to his overwrought nerves, but he felt better now that he was out of the pressure cooker that was New York. He had made his decision and he would have to live with it. He held his hand up against the sun and felt the gentle sway of the ocean. What was this boat doing? It was coming straight for him, and now a man was signaling with a flag. Good God! He felt the pleasant day disappear. It looked to be the flag of General Clinton's fleet.

The invasion of New Jersey had just begun, and it could not get any worse for General Knyphausen. He had agonized over the decision to invade New Jersey, with the pressure from the Loyalists forcing his hand, telling him that now was the time to strike while Washington's army was on its knees. The Prussian general did not like to disobey orders. He did not like to assume anything, and he would much rather wait for General Clinton's return, but he had given in and against his better judgment sent his troops to invade New Jersey and hopefully to finish off Washington's army in Morristown.

The first boats had already gone and Knyphausen was on his way to Staten Island when the boat signaled to come about. Knyphausen's flagship met the small boat, and Major William Crosbie, General Clinton's adjutant, bounded aboard with amazing news that the general had just reached Chesapeake Bay with his fleet and his army and was headed for New York. Knyphausen blinked in dismay. He could not pull back now. His men were ashore, and if Crosbie had reached him five hours earlier the attack would have been called off, but he couldn't pull his troops back, and worse, now the operation was not going well.

His reinforcements had landed at Staten Island many hours behind schedule, and then they had to be transported to Elizabethtown. It was well after dawn and all elements of surprise might be lost. The Hessians and British then headed inland. The Americans faced the British with the 150 men under General Gibbs from Washington's Life Guard, 741 from General Maxwell's New Jersey brigade, and 360 militiamen. The British were attacking with a force of 5,000 highly trained soldiers, with 2,500 more on the way. It would seem to have been highly stacked on the British side, but the invasion quickly became mired down with the guerilla tactics the backwoodsmen of New Jersey had perfected through lives spent hunting in the forests. Screams were heard among the soldiers marching on New Point Road and proved the colonials were highly skilled shots. The soldiers fired back at the musket flares.

Maxwell's men fought a rearguard action, trying to slow down the British as much as possible until reinforcements arrived. Brigadier General Thomas Stirling took a bullet in his hip, and this slowed the invasion down by an hour and a half as the wound was cared for. The Hessians and the British headed for an area known as Connecticut Farms (in present-day Union Township). But the alarm had been given to the militia and townspeople of New Jersey, and they appeared out from the trees as if providence had placed them there. The farmers, blacksmiths, hired hands, butchers, and bakers fired relentlessly. These were men who knew how to shoot with deadly accuracy, and Knyphausen's men were introduced to the guerrilla tactics the Americans had perfected when facing a force of overwhelming superiority. Each man found a boulder, a tree, a hill, a thicket, a log, anything to take cover behind. Then they would rise up, aim, pick off one of the British soldiers, then hide behind their cover and reload. To the British and the Hessians it was terror, watching the men next to them fall from unseen assassins. The Hessians had never seen this type of fighting before. They observed that the Americans would take a shot and then run away and vanish into the forest.

It does conjure up the Viet Cong, who faced heavily armed American soldiers and learned the fine art of striking and disappearing into the jungle. Hessian captain Johann Ewald expressed his admiration of the fighting tactics of the American militia.

> *What can you achieve with such small bands who have learned to fight dispersed, who know how to use every molehill for their defense, and who retreat as quickly when attacked as they advance again and who always find a space to hide? Never have I seen those maneuvers performed better than by the American Militia and especially that of the province of New Jersey. If you were forced to retreat against these people you could certainly count on constantly having them around you.*[1]

General Philip Schuyler, who was still in Morristown with the committee at headquarters, reflected on the assumptions the British had when they invaded. "I find the enemy were made to believe that if they came out in force, our army would not fight, the Country would submit, and they would possess themselves of all our stores. They were surprised to find the militia so firm—some were heard to say the Americans fight like bulldogs."[2] The Hessians had in theory trained for American-style fighting, but they had no defense for an enemy that fired and then melted back into the forest.

General Maxwell reached Connecticut Farms before nine a.m. and set up his men on two hills overlooking the Elizabeth River. The Hessians came on, and Maxwell's men cut them down as they tried to ford the stream. The Hessians charged several times, some with short-barreled Jaeger rifles, and had to be stopped with bayonets. Fortunately for the Americans, the short-barreled rifles did not have bayonets and the Hessians retreated back across the river.

But Maxwell's force could not hold out for long, and it retreated to the west side of the village as the British and Hessians poured into the town. The scene of carnage was surreal. The British bullets and cannonballs had ripped down trees in the nearby orchard, and the white blossoms from the fruit trees dappled the bloody bodies of the British soldiers. The British then burned the town of Connecticut Farms and made the major mistake of the campaign. They burned the meetinghouse, barns, and chicken coops, but worse, the death of the local parson's wife, Hannah Caldwell, by a stray bullet set the fury of a hornet's nest upon the British.

Militiamen from all over the county headed for the town, and Knyphausen heard that four Continental regiments were also on the way and retreated to Elizabethtown. His army began their retreat in the evening and continued it through the night. One British officer recalled that it was the darkest night he could remember, with severe storms. The British fortified their position in Elizabethtown and waited for General Clinton to arrive in New York. General Knyphausen was only too glad to be a subordinate once again. The invasion of New Jersey had so far not gone well at all, and all eyes were on the hero of Charlestown, who had just reached the Chesapeake Bay. He knew nothing of Knyphausen's disastrous invasion.

Chapter Thirty-Six

The Neurotic Returns

June 1780

THE RHYTHMIC GROAN OF THE SAILS, THE SALTY SCENT OF THE OCEAN, the light dancing outside his stateroom window, his books lined up on the shelves, his quill scratching on the parchment; all was in order. The general felt that things were finally going his way and he was putting the finishing touches on his masterpiece, the defeat of George Washington in Morristown. It was such a glorious thing to be at sea and contemplating the vanquishing of one's foe.

General Clinton dipped his quill again in the inkwell on his desk and continued writing. He was a new man. Gone was the self-loathing and the sniping and the obsessing over perceived slights. Victory had washed clean the neurosis that had plagued him all his life and especially as he climbed the ranks in the British service. He was now the man who had taken Charleston and defeated the Americans, and he was sailing back to defeat once and for all George Washington in Morristown. This would be the crowning achievement of the war; the Americans would sue for peace, and General Clinton would sail back to Britain with laurels bestowed.

But for now, he was looking for a hero's welcome. Why not? He had just taken Charleston and dealt the Americans a mortal blow. Now it was time to finish the job by destroying Washington's weakened force in Morristown. He had used the voyage back to draw up his plan to attack Morristown. The plan was bold and innovative, everything the old Clinton was not, but this new man had the sweet redolence of victory on him as he and his young adjutant general, Major John André, worked out the details. He sent André ahead in a packet boat to let General Knyphausen know his plans.

Four days after the New Jersey attack at Connecticut Farms, Knyphausen had Clinton's plans. The Hessian felt his stomach fall as he read that he should not do anything and wait for "further orders as I Clinton judge requisite for conducting my designs with the proper secrecy and expedition."[1] The general then laid out the main thrust of his plan: "a sudden unexpected move to seize upon their grand depot of military stores at Morristown and capture or disperse the forces that captured them."[2] There would be a two-pronged pincer movement that would trap Washington's army. His soldiers from the Charleston siege would land at Perth Amboy, then go hastily "westward to Middlebrook, head north through Mortdecai's Gap on the southern end of the Watchung Mountains and sweep toward Morristown over lightly guarded roads."[3]

Clinton instructed Knyphausen to be ready to sail from Staten Island to Elizabethtown "the instant the fleet from Charleston arrives at Sandy Hook."[4] He was then to head for Morristown, creating the pincer action of two different armies hitting Washington simultaneously. The only problem was that Knyphausen had ruined Clinton's plan with his blundering attack.

The letter that came was predictable. "I had the mortification to hear by a frigate that joined up that General Knyphausen . . . had already entered the Jerseys with a considerable part of the New York force."[5]

General Clinton knew that surprising Washington now was out of the question and that his original plan would not work. "The whole country was now in arms and every preparation made for opposing me with vigor,"[6] he groused. André took it a step further and declared that Knyphausen had "exposed the troops in the march of a day to loss of more than Carolina cost us."[7]

Three letters waiting for Clinton in New York would change the course of the war. The three strategies to defeat George Washington with a knockout blow were all converging. The first letter was from poor Knyphausen trying to justify his botched landing in New Jersey. The next two letters were from Mr. Moore, aka Benedict Arnold, and were both in code and addressed to André. These two letters sent Clinton in an entirely new direction, one that would capitalize on the secret weapon that was Benedict Arnold's treason.

Arnold first let André know that a French fleet along with 6,000 troops would be landing in Rhode Island in a couple of weeks. This had come to Arnold at the Ford Mansion and was told to him by George Washington during a dinner. Arnold then rammed home his case for treason and for paying him off, pointing out it would be prudent to get between George Washington and West Point before the French ships arrived. In other words, they should do the deal then before the French caused real trouble.

General Clinton changed his entire strategy on the strength of Mr. Moore's letters. He canceled the pincer plan and immediately recalled his troops from Perth Amboy and had them ready to sail up the Hudson toward West Point. Knyphausen's force was essentially abandoned, with only Simcoe's Queen's Rangers sent to help him. One can imagine Simcoe wanting to get back into the fight after the botched kidnapping, and this would give him a second chance to go at Washington and his army.

Washington meanwhile reinforced his men at Elizabethtown for the attack he knew would soon be launched by Knyphausen and put General Friedrich von Steuben in charge of a division of 1,168 local militiamen. Expiring enlistments knocked the force down to roughly 1,000 men. To back this up, Washington had Nathanael Greene and Continental regiments join in. Washington inspected the defensive positions around Springfield on June 19 and was told by spies that Clinton was headed for West Point. Washington wanted to siphon off two regiments to intercept the move toward West Point on the Hudson. Major General Arthur Sinclair was in command of 2,556 men and headed off on June 22 from Springfield.

Five thousand British soldiers marched out of Elizabethtown on June 23, headed for Morristown. They were traveling fast and expected to move through Springfield quickly and then run the gap through the Short Hills and reach Morristown before dusk. A repeat of the June 7 action was in play, except this time Continental regulars had fortified positions near the gap in the Short Hills along with the local militias. Shots were fired by Essex County pickets at the advancing soldiers. They were only an hour out from Elizabethtown, and the patriots quickly fell back toward Connecticut Farms. Once again it was sniping and hit-and-run actions slowing down the British and the Hessians, but also the methodical musketry of the American infantry. The same ravine faced the British, with the Elizabeth River flowing through the center. This time Colonel Simcoe took the initiative with his Queen's Rangers and charged across the water in a hail of spraying water and with lightning speed galloped up the opposite side, where Maxwell and his men fell back under the breathless charge.

The British forded the river quickly and pushed on to the main bridge crossing Rahway River, which was the gateway to Springfield. Colonel Israel Angell along with his Rhode Island troops were dug in on a ridge west of the bridge. Other men were behind stone walls and trees. Six militia regiments had taken refuge in some outbuildings. One hour before noon Knyphausen attacked, with 2,000 soldiers rushing the bridge along with a half dozen cannons blasting the Americans.

The Hessians and British came on in a straight line down the road. The Americans under Angell were only 160 men with muskets and one cannon, but they waited until the soldiers had crowded the road and then opened fire, with the single cannon knocking down the advancing British like bowling pins. The Hessians and British regulars then began wading across, some walking on what was left of the bridge, while Angell's men fired into a shooting gallery of bodies. Their faces blackened from gunpowder, with exhaustion and adrenaline running side by side, the Americans fired and fired and fired. This was the road to Morristown, and it was critical that the enemy was stopped here.

They succeeded in stopping the 2,000 British soldiers, and only when their ammunition began to run out did they fall back. Knyphausen then took control of Springfield and incredibly called for lunch while his men burned the town. Dr. James Thacher wrote of the carnage he witnessed that day, citing amputations he made on the spot and cannonballs landing feet away while he tended the wounded. As Knyphausen had tea,

Thacher reported that "the church and twenty or thirty other buildings"[8] were burnt to the ground. Then came the strangest moment in the military history of the Revolution.

Knyphausen received orders from General Clinton to return to Elizabethtown and to cease all engagement with the enemy. General Clinton had altered all his plans after receiving Arnold's letters, and he had no idea where Knyphausen was or if he was successful. The orders were such a surprise that some of the British were unaware of the withdrawal back to the coast. Colonel Cosmo Gordon and his Cold Stream Guards proceeded far into the gap before realizing they would be slaughtered going against the soldiers ensconced on the steep cliffs.

The retreat by Knyphausen back toward Elizabethtown began at three p.m. and was a painful affair, with the Americans sniping all the way, forcing the British into a full trot. Under a full moon they crossed the floating bridge to Staten Island, never to return to New Jersey. At one a.m. a German regiment destroyed the bridge. The battle for Morristown ended in a soggy whimper as a deluge broke over the glum troops on Staten Island. The reason for having Knyphausen retreat was to pursue Arnold's strategy of getting troops onto the Hudson at Tarrytown, twenty miles north of New York. Then they would be ferried across the river to a position bisecting the Americans from their own fort. It didn't work. The Americans had already taken positions on the high ground, forcing Clinton's soldiers back onto their boats. The truth was that General Clinton's pincer movement plan would have worked, as the diminished Continental Army would not have been able to take a one-two punch that would have been delivered by Knyphausen in the frontal assault and Clinton swinging in from the south. But Benedict Arnold's faulty reasoning and his intelligence on the French, which also turned out to not be true, as George Washington had found that many French promises were not followed up on, had duped Clinton into shelving his own very sensible plan in favor of Arnold's treason, which promised West Point and intelligence, all potential knockout punches, but highly risky.

When all was said and done, the battle of Morristown was fought over seventeen days, with 500 British killed, captured, or wounded and American casualties running under 200. Dr. Thacher speculated on

British motives in the battles: "The particular object of the expedition [the battle of June 23] is not ascertained. . . . If it was to force their way to Morristown, to destroy our magazines and stores, they were disappointed; if to burn the village of Springfield, they are welcome to the honor of the exploit."[9]

General Clinton's objective was the destruction of Washington's army at Morristown. He only swerved when it seemed there might be bigger fish to fry, and yet the price was heavy for both sides when the battle was engaged. As Ashbel Green, who was all of sixteen, wrote after looking at the battlefield outside of Springfield the morning after: "The whole scene was one of gloomy horror—a dead form, a broken carriage of a field piece, a town laid in ashes, the former inhabitants standing over the ruins of their dwellings, and the unburied dead, covered with blood and with the flies that were devouring them, filled me with melancholy feelings, till I was ready to say—is the contest worth all that?"[10]

Benedict Arnold still had his hand to play, and yet for all his treason, he might have unwittingly saved Washington at Morristown. By getting Clinton to move off his original plan, he had diverted the British at a crucial moment and allowed the Continental Army to live to fight another day. In a sense, Benedict Arnold was decisive in the final battle of Morristown and ensured the American army's survival. One could say he was the best spy the Americans ever had.

Chapter Thirty-Seven

Benedict Arnold's Final Play

July 31, 1780

One thing George Washington and General Henry Clinton agreed on was that control of the Hudson River was the key to victory. If the English took control, it would split the southern and northern states and the river would become a conduit to the British troops in Canada and those in New York, where the English headquartered throughout the war except for the brief stint in Philadelphia in 1777–1778. If the Americans remained in control, it would keep the river open as a highway for goods flowing between the mid-Atlantic states and New England.

General Clinton, even as second in command under General Howe, had pressed for an attack to the north on the Hudson. Howe instead moved his headquarters to Philadelphia, but when Clinton took over a year later, he brought the army back to New York and concentrated once again on the Hudson River. So it was no surprise that Benedict Arnold found George Washington on a bluff overlooking the Hudson. It was a bright sunny day, and the Hudson sparkled with diamonds; at least they looked like diamonds to Arnold now that he had set his price with the British. Two weeks before he had told Clinton: $20,000. For the fort, the garrison, ammunition, and all intelligence pertaining to the fort, the whole show would cost the British twenty grand, and Clinton had not declined his offer. To Arnold that was acceptance, and now he would get his appointment and those diamonds dancing on the Hudson below would be his.

But George Washington's mind was elsewhere. It was on the French, as it often was now, because he wanted one thing and that was to invade New York with the French and defeat the British once and for all. His army at Morristown had survived and was getting stronger every day. Washington had just written the French commander Rochambeau, "The only way I can be useful to you is to menace New York, and even to attack it, if the force remaining there does not exceed what I have reason to believe, I am pressing my movements for that purpose with all the rapidity in our power."[1]

Washington was a bit like a new employee who keeps trying to please his employer (the French), looking for favor and assistance. His own inclination toward the bold step and the candy store view of French military power, which literally seemed to sail away just when he thought it might strike, put him in the perpetual role of the eager suitor looking to consummate the marriage as soon as possible. That consummation now for Washington was an assault on New York, and the man in front of him was part of the plan.

Benedict had Peggy's latest harangue ringing in his ears as he faced the commander. He had to get the appointment now! She could be force-ful, that one. His leg had finally healed up, and he was feeling good. All was in order, and now was the final anointment.

He asked Washington "if he had thought of anything for him."[2] Washington nodded and bestowed his gift. Indeed, he had a "post of honor"[3] for him. Benedict would lead the left wing of the army in the assault on New York. Arnold's smile froze on his face. A cloud went past the sun and the diamonds disappeared. Washington would later write about Arnold: "Upon this information, his countenance changed, and he appeared to be quite fallen and instead of thanking me or expressing any pleasure at the appointment, never opened his mouth."[4]

Arnold muttered, stammered, then said he had to think it over. He was reeling. He did not want anything but the West Point command, and without it he had no value to the British. Washington told him to "get something to refresh himself and I would meet him there soon."[5] The truth was the invasion of New York was consuming Washington and Arnold's strange reaction was not a real concern. He had no idea of the tripwire Arnold had strung for him. Benedict told his aide Tench Tilghman that while he would like the command, "his leg . . . would not permit him to be long on horseback and intimated a great desire to have the command at West Point."[6] By the time Washington arrived, Arnold had already left and Tilghman told him of the conversation. Washington ignored it and decided Benedict Arnold should still command the left wing and said so in the General Orders of August 1.

But Benedict Arnold was nothing if not lucky. Peggy was having dinner with banker Robert Morris when she got the news that Arnold was not going to be the commander of West Point. She screamed, cried, and went into one of her famous fits. One account said, "The information affected her so much as to produce hysterical fits." Arnold's aide David Franks described it as "occasional paroxysms of physical indisposition, attended by nervous debility, during which she would give utterance to anything and everything on her mind." Peggy herself would sum up her fits to her father as "a confusion in my head resembling what I suppose would be the sensations of anybody extremely drunk."[7] Today she might be manic, schizophrenic, or maybe on the spectrum, but there was an overarching intelligence behind the fits and she wasn't above using them to get what she wanted, and she wanted her husband to have the command of West Point.

This fit was worse than most, and Franks could not placate her. She might have been having a nervous breakdown after being married to the mercurial Benedict Arnold for over a year, giving birth, and constantly being on the high wire of their brilliant scheme to set them up financially for life. Maybe she had finally gone over the edge. But she did calm down, and the luck of Benedict Arnold ultimately saved them both. Washington's vaunted attack on New York would not happen. General Clinton had returned to New York with 6,000 troops. After Washington called off the attack that was predicted on a weakened British force, he issued another General Order on August 3. "Major General Arnold will take command of the garrison at West Point."[8]

Peggy and Benedict had to dance a jig. The twenty grand was almost theirs. Arnold lost no time in setting up his headquarters. This final secret weapon of the British was coming to fruition. The knockout punch that had not worked with Simcoe and Beckwith's plan to kidnap Washington and had failed with Knyphausen's abortive assault on Morristown would now be redeemed with this checkmate on the Hudson. George Washington had no clue at all what he had done by giving command to Benedict Arnold.

So now Peggy and her child had joined Benedict at West Point, and he increased his communication with Major André, who had become very close to Peggy, some thought too close, but no matter, as all that would soon be behind them. Arnold then disassembled the soldiers at West Point, posting the men to far locations and leaving the fort defenseless.

General Clinton's forces were readied to sail up the Hudson to take possession of the fort. André was to precede Clinton and sail up the Hudson on the British sloop *Vulture*, to receive from Arnold details of West Point along with maps. His covert name would be Mr. Anderson, a name he had used in his communications with Arnold before. General Clinton insisted that André wear a British uniform to keep from being considered a spy. Death by hanging was the quick remedy for both sides for any spies who were caught. A Colonel Robinson would go with Arnold to give him cover by saying he was going up the Hudson to check on his property. The *Vulture* would wait and after the meeting take the two men back to New York.

The fourteen-gun sloop HMS *Vulture* set sail down the green Hudson River with Major André aboard and anchored near the home of Joshua Hett Smith, a Tory. Smith must have thought it odd that a ship named after a bird that feeds off the dead was in view from his back porch that overlooked Haverstraw Bay. Smith was well acquainted with the Arnolds, who had just arrived from Philadelphia with their infant son and had hosted their reunion. Smith was part of Benedict's plan, as he had consented to have his house used for "a secret meeting between Arnold and an informant from New York."[9] Smith knew something serious was happening as he hustled his own wife and child to a friend's home twenty miles upriver.

Smith had no real idea of Arnold's treasonous motives for the meeting as he rowed out to the *Vulture* on September 21. He used two brothers, Samuel and Joseph Cahoon, to do the actual rowing. The brothers had second thoughts, being not sure about the British ship, but ultimately decided to go after being plied with some rum and fifty pounds of flour. The lawyer Smith sat in the stern while the brothers rowed out to the boat a half hour after midnight. Sheepskin had been wrapped around the oars to muffle the oarlocks. They reached the ship, and Smith went below and found himself in front of three men: Captain Andrew Sutherland, Colonel Beverly Robinson, and Major John André. In a bit of confusion, it seems Benedict Arnold had wanted to meet with Robinson, but it was ultimately decided he should meet with André.

At one in the morning, Smith and his passenger, "Mr. John Anderson" as André called himself, and the brothers all boarded the dinghy and headed to shore to meet Benedict Arnold. André went ashore and finally met the American general who might be the man to hand the British the victory they had been looking for. "Arnold and André talked amid a grove of fir trees near where the Long Clove gap . . . on the west bank of the Hudson. Not only was it night, they were in the combined shadows of two mountains and the surrounding trees."[10] One can imagine that neither man could see the other clearly. The countryside was pitch-black and only "their white breeches and André's expensive, white topped boots visible in the gloom."[11] André spoke with a British accent, his speech formal if not flowery. Benedict spoke like the blunt, hard-bitten American general he was and demanded that Clinton agree to the $10,000 as a kill fee if things didn't work out. André could give him no assurance on this matter but said he would persuade the general to give him the higher sum. Even to the last moment Arnold was still negotiating.

It was the classic clandestine meeting of two spies. In the loud, purring buzz of insects near the river, the two men talked and Arnold gave the British officer information on the fort along with detailed maps describing the layout of West Point and the supporting installations. But the meeting ended late, and André decided to rest and return to the *Vulture* the following night, when he could row out undetected. Then things began to go bad.

The sky was beginning to turn pink, and the lawyer Smith had returned from the boat where he was waiting with the brothers. He pointed out that they could now be detected returning to the *Vulture*, and to make matters worse, the brothers didn't want to row against the flooding tide and couldn't make it there and back before the sun was up. No matter, André and Arnold were just beginning to get into the mechanics of turning over the fort, with maps and diagrams showing where the British should approach. They would return to Smith's house and André could go back the following night.

When the party reached Smith's home, the morning air was shattered with the explosion of cannon fire. With dawn's light the two men saw to their horror that the onshore battery at Tellers Point had opened fire on the *Vulture*, which had drifted further north. Colonel James Livingston had become irritated with the proximity of the British ship to his post and started to fire at the ship with a small cannon. There was no wind or current, and it was a turkey shoot for the Americans with the *Vulture* not moving at all. A sailor later wrote, "Six shot hulled us . . . one between wind and water, many others struck the sails and rigging and boats on the deck. Two shells hit us, one full on the quarterdeck and near the main shrouds."[12] The tide finally picked up and the *Vulture* floated downriver, leaving André stranded. There was nothing to do but return to New York by horseback with the documents. Arnold told André to put the documents in his sock under the sole of his foot and provided for Smith to lead Andre back north.

Then came the moment that would change the fate of one Major John André. Smith offered André a coat and shirt to disguise him. "Smith had an old claret colored coat with gold tinseled buttons that fit André perfectly. The brim of an equally old, round-topped bowler style beaver hat would keep his face in shadow."[13] André was reluctant. The second he put on the coat and hat, he could be considered a spy. Arnold pointed out that there were roving gangs along the riverfront that would like nothing more than to catch a British officer. André, in a fateful move, put on the shirt and coat.

Arnold then signed passes for both men, and they waited for dark before setting off. They headed for Kings Ferry and came across some American officers in a tent. Smith had some rum with the officers while André walked onto the ferry. They crossed the river and headed toward the "neutral ground," which was held by neither the Americans nor the

British. It was technically held by the Americans, but there were roving bands of outlaw gangs: Skinners if they were patriots or Cowboys if they leaned toward the Loyalists.

After eight miles an American patrol stopped them. Captain Ebenezer Boyd wanted to know why they were traveling after dark and where were they headed. "I told him who I was and that we had passports from General Arnold . . . that we were on the public service of business of the highest import,"[14] Smith wrote later. They went to a nearby house to use the light to read Arnold's passes. "Mr. Anderson seemed very uneasy, but I cheered him by saying our papers would carry us to any part of the country to which they were directed."[15]

André had good reason to be nervous. He knew that if he was discovered he could be tried as a spy. Boyd seemed satisfied and said there were Cowboys in the area and advised them to go back to a house to spend the night. André wanted to continue, but Smith was caught up in the mysterious mission he was on and they continued back to the house, where they slept in the same bed. "I was often disturbed with the restless motions and uneasiness of mind exhibited by my bed fellow,"[16] Smith mused later.

They continued and later bumped into an American officer riding from the south. André was shocked when he realized it was a man he knew, Colonel Samuel Blachley Webb, who had been a prisoner for a time. André was beside himself thinking it was all up, but Webb seemed to have not made the connection. André later said that meeting Webb "made his hair rise."[17]

They reached the bridge across the Croton River, and on September 23, Smith turned around for home and André traveled on, coming within a few miles of British outposts in White Plains. He stayed on the main road that was patrolled by volunteer militiamen who were looking for any strangers, anyone who might be in sympathy with the British. He was almost home when between nine and ten a.m. three men rode up and stopped him near a bridge north of Tarrytown. In the patchwork quilt of uniforms that was the American side, many patriots donned British coats from the dead. One of the men had on such a coat, and André breathed easy, seeing the lobster red of his countrymen. He then committed the fatal error of blurting out that he was Loyalist too, a British officer, and did not show Arnold's passes, which probably would have let him pass on. The three men were not official militia, more like low-level criminals looking for booty anywhere they could find it. They demanded cash from André and then had him take off his boots.

The West Point documents meant little to the three men, but they thought there might be some sort of reward and took André and the documents to an American post at North Castle. The three men were given "André's watch, horse, saddle, and bridle"[18] as a reward. Lieutenant Colonel John Jameson stared at the pass signed by Benedict Arnold, then slowly looked up at the man in front of him. He did not look like a soldier, more like an officer, and the pass was all wrong as well. He had been alerted to allow a Mr. John Anderson to pass into the lines *from* New York City, but this man was heading toward New York.

Then Major John André admitted he was a really a British officer who had gone to "meet a person who was to give intelligence."[19] Jameson then seemed to play into the conspirators' hands by sending him under guard to West Point to General Benedict Arnold. This would have been fine; Arnold could have accepted the prisoner and then schemed another way to get André back to New York.

But then Jameson did something else. He wrapped up the documents and had them sent by messenger to George Washington. But André left the post under guard, and even if the documents got to Washington, he would be in Arnold's custody and set free once again. But Major Benjamin Talmade spoiled everything when he returned to the post and heard about Mr. Anderson. As the secret chief of Washington's intelligence, he knew something was very wrong and sent soldiers galloping off to bring André back to the post.

On Monday, the world of Benedict Arnold came crashing down. Things seemed to be going his way. Arnold was headed for breakfast at his headquarters at West Point. André had headed back to New York, and by now Clinton had in his possession all that was needed to know about West Point. Clinton would then sail up the Hudson and Benedict would surrender the fort and then Peggy and his son, who were asleep upstairs, would accompany him on a British warship to their new life in

Britain with $20,000 in his pocket. And now George Washington was on his way for breakfast. A final bit of breaking bread with the commander before Benedict Arnold sold them all down the river . . . literally.

But Arnold had no idea of the race that was going on as he walked toward his dining room. The original messenger for Washington had returned to the outpost unable to find the commander. The commander of the outpost, Jameson, sent on a messenger to Arnold at West Point with André's statement and another message advising him of his arrest. Neither message reached West Point until Monday morning.

Benedict was almost to the dining room. Alexander Hamilton and his aide had arrived at nine a.m. and said Washington was running late but to eat without him. Benedict paused and took a message from his aide Richard Varick. The message was old and said all accommodations would be extended to Mr. Anderson. So far, so good. Arnold entered the dining room and had begun eating with Alexander Hamilton and his aide when the other two messages from Jameson arrived. He continued eating and read them very slowly.

Arnold then pulled the messenger aside and told him to tell no one of the messages. He finished his breakfast, excused himself very calmly, then rushed upstairs and told Peggy he had been exposed. Arnold then heard a knock on the door. David Franks, another aide, said "his excellency was nigh at hand."[20] General Arnold opened the door and went downstairs and told Franks to inform Washington that "he was gone over to West Point and would return in about an hour."[21] Benedict left out the front door and then headed down a path to the Hudson River to his barge and told the bargeman to take him downstream to the British ship *Vulture*. Washington, Hamilton, Henry Knox, and Marquis de Lafayette finished their breakfast and then headed over to the fort. The inspection showed Arnold's deception: few men were on guard and the fort was in a state of disrepair. It was now time for Peggy Shippen's greatest performance.

Her husband was gone, never to return, and if she did not play her hand well, she could be hanged for treason. When Washington and his men returned to the Robinson home, she went into one of her fits and began screaming that one of Arnold's aides was trying to kill her baby. She was giving Arnold enough time to make his escape, and Washington offered her safe passage to Philadelphia. Then came a letter from Arnold from the *Vulture*, confessing to the plot but claiming Peggy knew nothing. He then threw André under the bus and sealed his fate.

George Washington was in shock and had no idea whether other conspirators were still at large. He sealed off the house and had a four p.m. dinner, not allowing anyone in or out. Alexander Hamilton realized quickly that West Point was horribly vulnerable to the British and immediately took action and ordered a Connecticut regiment to the fort. Finally, Washington took action to bolster the fort in case Clinton attacked and "served notice that the Continental Army might be deployed on a moment's notice." He also informed Arnold's two aides, Franks and Varick, that he had no reason to suspect their complicity with Arnold but felt duty-bound to place them under arrest, a decision the two understood. The next day Washington announced the terrible revelation to his men: "Treason of the blackest dye was yesterday discovered."[22]

Washington would later point to God for the discovery of Benedict Arnold's treasonous act and say that only through divine intervention was West Point saved. "In no instance since the commencement of the war has the interposition of providence appeared more conspicuous than in the rescue of the garrison of West Point from Arnold's villainous perfidy."[23]

The announcement of Benedict Arnold's treachery was given to the American troops at three a.m. at the American camp near Tappan. Two regiments would be headed for West Point immediately, and the situation was revealed to the soldiers in the General Order.

Treason of the blackest dye was yesterday discovered, General Arnold who commanded at West Point, lost to every sentiment of honor, or private and public obligation, was about to deliver up that important post into the hands of the enemy. Such an event must have given the American cause a dangerous, if not fatal wound. Happily, the treason has been timely discovered, to prevent the fatal misfortune. . . . At the same time that the treason is to be regretted, the general cannot help congratulating the army on the happy discovery. Our enemy, despairing of carrying their point by force, are practicing every base art to effect by bribery and corruption what they cannot accomplish in a manly way.[24]

André was now a prisoner and was being charged as a spy. The intelligent British officer had made a confession in a letter to Washington stating that in fact he was not a spy.

What I have as yet said concerning myself was in the justifiable attempt to be extricated; I am too little accustomed to duplicity to have succeeded. I beg your Excellency will be persuaded that no altercation in the temper of my mind, or apprehension for my safety, induce me to take the step of addressing you; but that it is to rescue myself from an imputation of having assumed a mean character for treacherous purposes or self-interest; a conduct incompatible with the principles that actuate me, as well as my condition in life. It is to vindicate my fame that I speak and not to solicit security. The person in your possession is Major John André, Adjutant General to the British Army.[25]

André then pointed out that the clothes he had worn that branded him a spy had been but forced upon him. "Having avowed myself a British officer, I have nothing to reveal but what relates to myself, which is true on the honor and a gentleman. The request I have to make to your Excellency and I am conscious I address myself well, is that in any rigor policy may dictate, a decency of conduct towards me may mark that, though unfortunate, I am branded with nothing dishonorable, as no motive could be mine but the service of my King and as I was involuntarily an imposter."[26]

Washington wasn't buying, but there was scurrying on all sides for the release of André with letters from General Clinton and talks of a swap. The strangest of these letters of course was from Benedict Arnold, who jumped into the game seeing himself as the savior of young André. His letter was as bizarre as Arnold was himself. Arnold had sent Washington an earlier letter soon after he was discovered that pleaded for mercy for his wife. "The heart which is conscious of its own rectitude cannot attempt to palliate a step which the world may censure as wrong. I have ever acted from a principle of love to my country, since the commencement of the present unhappy contest between Great Britain and the colonies. The same principle of love to my country actuates my present conduct, however it may appear inconsistent to the world who very seldom judge right of any man's actions."[27]

Unrepentant and unwilling to see that he had turned on his own country, Arnold believed above all else he was right and fully delusional that in reality his true motives were money. The only slice of honor in his letter was a plea for his wife. "From the known humanity of your Excellency I am induced to ask your protection for Mrs. Arnold from every insult and injury that a mistaken vengeance of my country may expose her to. It ought to fall only on me; she is as good and as innocent as an angel and is incapable of doing wrong."[28]

Of course, this was a lie too. The real insanity of Benedict Arnold was in his final letter pleading for the life of André that was basically a threat of bloodletting upon Washington's army if André was executed. "I shall think myself bound by every tie of duty and honor to retaliate on such unhappy persons of your army as may fall within my power. . . . I call Heaven and Earth to witness that your Excellency will justly answerable for the torrent of blood that may be spilt in consequence."[29]

Alexander Hamilton made a last-minute appeal to trade André for Arnold, but Clinton turned him down. The feeling was that André was being scapegoated for Benedict Arnold. "To an excellent understanding well improved by education and travel, he united a peculiar elegance of mind and manners, and the advantage of a pleasing person,"[30] Hamilton wrote of André to his friend John Laurens. "His sentiments were elevated and inspired esteem they had a softness that conciliated affection."[31] André wrote again to Washington pleading not to be executed as a spy. He did not want to be hanged as a spy but preferred death by firing squad. "Buoyed above the terror of death by the consciousness of a life devoid devoted to honorable pursuits and stained with no action that can give me remorse. I trust that he requests I make to your excellency at this serious period and which is to soften my last moments will not be rejected. Sympathy towards a soldier will surely induce your Excellency and a military tribunal to adapt the mode of my death to the feelings of a man of honor."[32]

The execution was set for October 1. The army surgeon James Thacher attended the hanging. "I went this afternoon to witness the execution of Major André a large concourse of people had assembled, the gallows was erected and the grave and coffin prepared to receive the remains of this celebrated but unfortunate officer; but a flag of truce arrived with a communication from Sir Henry Clinton making another and further proposals for the release of Major André."[33]

The final negotiations didn't produce a release of the prisoner, and on October 2 he was taken to the gallows. Thacher again was on hand. "Major André walked from the stone house in which he had been confined between two of our subaltern officers arm in arm, the eyes of the immense multitude was fixed upon him who rising superior to the fears of death appeared as if conscious of the dignified deportment which he displayed. He betrayed no want of fortitude but retained a complacent smile on his countenance and politely bowed to several gentlemen whom he knew which was respectfully returned."[34]

André, who had wanted to be shot as a soldier, then balked at the sight of the gallows. James Thacher recorded the moment.

At that moment when he came in view of the gallows, he involuntarily started backward and made a pause. "Why this emotion sir?" said an officer by his side. Instantly recovering his composure he said, "I am reconciled to my death but I detest the mode." While waiting and standing near the gallows I observed some degree of trepidation; placing his foot on a stone, and rolling it over and choking in his throat as if attempting to swallow. So soon however as he perceived that things were in readiness he stepped quickly into the wagon and at this moment he appeared to shrink, but instantly elevating his head with firmness, he said, "It will be but a momentary pang."[35]

André put on his own blindfold and adjusted the rope around his neck. His final words were "I pray you to bear witness that I meet my fate like a man."[36] The wagon rolled out and the rope stretched. Dr. Thacher said death was instantaneous, but another doctor said this was not the case. "André was a small man and seemed hardly to stretch the rope, and his legs dangled so much that the hangman was ordered to take hold of them and keep them straight."[37]

The only man who would ever be punished for the treason of Benedict Arnold was dead. The final secret weapon of Morristown had failed just as miserably as the kidnapping and Knyphausen's aborted attack to defeat George Washington. Benedict made it to New York, where he demanded the $10,000 he had negotiated as a payment if he should be revealed. The British paid him $6,315 and then ignored him.

James Thacher and many others could scarcely believe Arnold's treasonous attempt to give the British West Point. "At three o'clock this morning an alarm was spread throughout the camp. Two regiments from the Pennsylvania line were ordered to march immediately to West Point and the whole army was to be held in readiness to march at a moment's warning. It was soon ascertained that this sudden movement was in consequence of the discovery of one of the most extraordinary events in modern history. . . . It is the treacherous conspiracy of Major General Arnold."[38]

Peggy and her son soon joined Arnold in New York, where he was soon made a brigadier general in the British army. He led an assault on Richmond, Virginia, and then burned the city; then repeated the same outrages in New London, Connecticut, killing eighty-one Americans who had surrendered to him. The traitor to his own country was despised by the British as well as the Americans. General Clinton rebuked Arnold for his barbarity in Richmond and New London. The couple now feared for their lives, thinking either side might turn on them. They were right to be apprehensive about their safety. George Washington had one last card to play. It was payback time.

CHAPTER THIRTY-EIGHT

The Kidnapping of Benedict Arnold

October 21, 1780

WHAT COMES AROUND GOES AROUND. THE BRITISH HAD ATTEMPTED to kidnap George Washington in Morristown and then seduced one of his closest generals into committing treason, though one could make the case that Arnold seduced the British. No matter. The outrage of the Benedict Arnold events stuck in Washington's mind as something that had to be remedied in some way, and his subordinate General Charles Lee had the answer.

Lee himself had been kidnapped by the British and had his own personal score to settle, and so he summoned at midnight on October 21, 1780, a twenty-eight-year-old sergeant major in Henry "Light Horse Harry" Lee's regiment. John Champe was barely awake when he made it to headquarters and faced the grizzled old general. Lee was cryptic and asked the sergeant major if he would volunteer for an extremely danger-ous mission that had been personally sanctioned by George Washington. Champe listened intently as Lee laid out the essence of what Washington wanted, nothing short of the kidnapping of Benedict Arnold in New York and bringing him back to American justice, where he could be hung from the highest tree for his unspeakable treachery against the country. Champe was wide awake now. They had all heard of Arnold's duplicity, and Lee laid out the basics of the operation.

Champe was to steal a horse, take off for the Hudson, and then cross the river undetected and slip into New York. Once there, he would find

Benedict Arnold and then abduct him, tie him up, and slip back across the Hudson at night and bring him to American justice for a swift trial and execution. Simple. Amazingly, Champe consented to the impossible mission, even though there was a real chance he could be shot by American sentinels as a deserter or the British could hang him as a spy. Still, it was an amazing opportunity to fulfill a deep desire by Washington to secure retribution against Benedict Arnold for selling out his country.

Champe was more afraid of being shot as a deserter than anything else. But he had to appear to be a deserter, and to that end he stole his orderly's book to make it seem he was a rogue deserter and then he jumped on a horse without consent and took off at a dead gallop for the Hudson River under the light of a full moon. It was a classic deserter escape from the army, and Champe headed down to the shores of the Hudson and plunged into the cold water. Here his plan might have come to naught if Americans fished him out of the water, but a British patrol pulled him from the water and rowed him into Hudson Bay.

Champe then lost no time in finding Arnold and enlisting as a Loyalist in a new regiment he was creating. His luck held when he was assigned to quarters near Arnold's home. Champe could see Peggy and her son coming and going and considered grabbing Benedict Arnold at night and whisking him to the Hudson River. He found out that Arnold liked to stroll in his garden at night and made plans to abduct him then. His plan was simple. He would sedate Arnold, then bind his hands and gag him and get him down to the river, where he would put him in a rowboat and row all night back to the New Jersey side. By morning Benedict Arnold would be in American hands and Champe would be famous as the man who brought Arnold to justice. George Washington would be immensely pleased.

But of course, the best-laid plans go astray. Champe set the date for December 11 and let General Lee know of his plans. Lee crossed the river that night in a rowboat with several trusted soldiers and waited by the shore. The moon played on the still water. Lee was nervous; he wanted to get back across the Hudson before dawn. If they were detected, they would all be hanged as spies. Lee waited well past midnight and several times went up into the city to watch for the approach of Champe and Arnold. The bells of a church tolled the morning hour and Lee had to leave and recross the Hudson.

Benedict Arnold's luck had held. The night before, the Loyalist legion that Champe had joined had boarded a ship bound for Virginia to attack Richmond. Champe found himself headed for Virginia and stayed with the regiment until he could finally slip away near Richmond. It was a dangerous flight, as he was in a Loyalist uniform and the Americans would shoot him on sight. He eventually escaped to West Virginia with his wife and four children. When the war ended, Champe was a guest at Mount Vernon, and General Lee recounted the failed kidnapping in his memoirs published in 1811. Benedict Arnold had come close to American justice, but like the night he fled after his treachery was discovered, he dodged fate by a whisper one more time.

Chapter Thirty-Nine

Morristown

MORRISTOWN WAS THE BOXING RING WHERE TWO FIGHTERS TRIED TO knock each other out in the ninth round. I used the boxing motif in the beginning of this narrative, and it is applicable at the end. It is fitting that the worst winter in a century occurred in 1779–1780 when George Washington and the Continental Army went into Morristown for winter quarters. It was a brutal winter of subzero temperatures and twenty-eight snowstorms, including four in succession in January that sealed off the camp from the outside world. Inlets and bays from the ocean froze, and for the first time the Hudson River became a bridge to New Jersey able to support men, horses, and artillery. It was a winter of terrible suffering, and the weather mirrored the brutal conditions Washington and his men would have to endure.

Trees split open from the cold; animals died in droves, some suffocating from the snow; while sentinels froze after only thirty minutes on guard duty, some perishing, some surviving with disfiguring frostbite. The thousand cabins the men of the army took refuge in became smoky hells of disease, flu, death, starvation, boredom, and every kind of deprivation that could afflict a large army that is supplied with neither food, clothes, money, nor hope for the future. And still the snow fell and fell and fell, and even George Washington, up in the comparative elegance of the Ford Mansion, was forced to huddle in the kitchen with Mrs. Ford, her children, and his aides and servants, as this was the only place people could find warmth.

And yet during all of this there was the war that had dragged on for five years, and it was during this time of the incredible arctic Armageddon that the British tried to knock Washington and his army out of the war. The story of Morristown is not complete without understanding that the British had become frustrated with war in North America, with Washington and his army hanging on beyond all expectations. And now that the French had entered, it became more important than ever to finish off the Americans before the weight of the French could be brought to bear.

And this brought about the unorthodox methods that would be used against Washington while his army was on its knees from desertion, starvation, expiring enlistments, and a general fatigue with the war and the prospects of victory. It is not surprising, then, that the British would take advantage of the deep freeze and launch a kidnapping mission to snatch Washington from Morristown, thereby depriving the movement of its leader. The fighters were tired and Morristown was an interlude in which they could catch their collective breath; for the Americans it was a time to survive a brutal winter while facing the reality that they were still a country too weak to support a national army, and in that way testing the will of the American people to see the war to its finish. For the British it was time for a neurotic general and his officers to see if they could do what the full might of the British empire could not. Knock out the Americans with one quick blow.

And so the kidnapping was launched and in the great irony of that brutal cold and snow was given life by the weather, with the freezing of the Hudson, and then extinguished when the snow froze and cut the forelocks of the horses and froze the men, forcing them to turn back. And then of course the second knockout blow would be the high treason of Benedict Arnold and his surrendering of the strategic fort of West Point, which would have dealt a mortal blow to Washington and his army. But the very desperation that made men like Clinton embrace Arnold was their undoing. When General Clinton came up with a plan to finally crush Washington's starving, mutinous army, a plan that in all likelihood would have succeeded, Arnold's tantalizing intelligence that the French were landing and the offer of West Point had the commander swing off his own operation for another knockout blow.

It gets worse. He abandoned General Knyphausen, who was fighting his way toward Washington and his army in Morristown, albeit badly, but was given the order to retreat by Clinton, who had bigger plans that would bring more glory on a much quicker timetable and possibly knock Washington out of the war. Clinton, who wanted to leave America, had just come back from a victory in Charleston, but he squandered his new-found momentum on Benedict Arnold, who ultimately would not be able to deliver West Point.

And yet. With his army withering away, George Washington should have been crushed in Morristown. He was unbelievably lucky. While all around him plots of kidnapping and treason and plans to destroy his army in a pincer movement swirled about, he managed somehow to steer a steady course between mountains that at any moment could crush him. This was his winter of discontent, as he realized that the country he and his soldiers were sacrificing so much for had grown weary of the war and was unwilling to give even food, forcing him to requisition from surrounding counties whatever food he could.

The Morristown winter of 1779 was a midpoint in the Revolution, and like any author will tell you, it is the middle of the book where the danger occurs that the plot might be too thin, the characters without substance, and that arc, that hill between the buildup and the ultimate denouement and resolution might just be the undoing of the whole story. This was the midpoint of Washington and the Continental Army's tale. By 1783 it would be all over, so the midpoint from 1775 was the winter of 1779–1780, and it was here that all the enthusiasm for liberty and freedom had evaporated and only two mud wrestlers remained trying to get a grip any way they could.

And so, it could have all ended at Morristown. Even in the spring, when the hellish winter ended, the army was still in the process of becoming unglued. No food to speak of. No money. No uniforms or shoes. Then the mutiny in May occurred. The Connecticut regiment that mutinied and almost took others with it was a litmus that the winter of

Morristown was not over yet. There were still other trials to come, and the biggest one was the battle of Morristown, where the British finally came on and Washington had to use his personal bodyguards to fight the enemy because his other troops were not ready nor even aware.

The army and Washington were at the breaking point, and it was only through the colossal bad decisions by British commanding officers that the bloodbath of Morristown did not occur. But maybe it was not luck, but the fact that the American army had survived this long and this put the British off balance. British regiments were decimated by men who popped up behind trees and the entire army vanished overnight. Even the Hessian mercenaries had no answer for the guerrilla-style fighting of the Americans, meant to wear out an occupying force.

And it had dragged on and on. And so came the knee-jerk decisions, the half-baked ideas that would have been rejected in the beginning of the war by men like General Howe who still believed in the invincibility of the British military, that is, until Henry Knox brought sixty tons of cannons to Boston and fairly blew the British out of their beds. That left the manic-depressive Clinton to inherit a mess he did not want and one he would have gladly left with one goal: destroy Washington and his pesky army as quickly as possible and go back home.

So, while the Americans slowly withered and persevered and froze, the British bungled. Morristown more than ever demonstrated the folly of trying to occupy a large country with military force and not winning the minds and hearts of the populace. The British did the opposite when they finally did attack, bringing local militias out of the morning fog that would harass them, shoot them, and ultimately drive them back. The British would concede that their style of fighting was not successful by 1779, but they had yet to replace it with something that would work against the Americans, and so the chicanery of kidnappings, collusion with treasonous officers, and not following through on a proven military plan was given precedent, and these of course were destined to fail.

But in the end, Lieutenant Colonel Simcoe and Captain Beckwith, who planned Washington's kidnapping and believed that without Washington the Revolution and the war might just die, were probably right. George Washington, half deity and half flesh and blood, half crusader and half miraculous leader if not savior, was the man they had to kill, kidnap, or at least defeat. And while this man from Virginia dealt with his own unhappiness with the war, his own declining fortunes, while pleading for food, arms, and shoes, he also set the tone that he never deviated from, one of unyielding resolve. How could this be?

He was being plotted against from every corner and had everything against him. Even when told of the kidnapping plot and its failed attempt, he did not cower but instead made some changes, and we see that he could not give real fear any credence as others would see that as wavering. And even when he was astounded with Benedict Arnold's treason, he merely reinforced West Point and pushed on and quickly hung André, his coconspirator. All this after keeping his dying army together through a brutal winter that in tone seemed to be continuing through the summer. George Washington was the Revolution, the war, the country. The British in that sense were right to take a shot at the prize.

So in the end, Morristown, this strange interlude where it seemed the American Revolution was unraveling from really nothing more than neglect from a people who were not sure they were in it for the long haul, proved that in fact the soldiers, Washington, and then finally the militiamen who melted out of the woods at the crucial moments would suffer and persevere for the still-unseen country based on the principles of freedom, justice, and liberty for all. But Morristown should be remembered for the blood, suffering, and sacrifice such lofty ideals required on the part of soldiers and civilians in the winter of 1779–1780. It is well we remember that bad weather always comes back . . . and the postman always rings twice.

Epilogue

George Washington never returned to Morristown except for occasional visits. In the winter of 1781, General Wayne led 2,500 Pennsylvanian troops to Jockey Hollow for the winter. In an eerie repeat of the winter of 1780, food was short, uniforms nonexistent, and pay not to be had. The winter itself was mild, but the Pennsylvanians had had enough and in January mutinied by leaving their huts and marching out of camp, In the process several officers were wounded, and Captain Adam Betting was shot and died later. The mutineers marched all the way to Princeton, where negotiations took place, and by January 11 it was all over. Two British spies who had tried to get the Americans to join the British army were later hanged. It was by far the worst mutiny in the history of the American army. Morristown just seemed to be a catalyst of misery for the men who stayed there.

After the Pennsylvanians left the huts in Jockey Hollow that had seen so much suffering in the winter of 1779–1780, the huts lay deserted with the roofs caving in and the doors now open to the snows that would follow. The Ford Mansion became a home again. The great victory at Yorktown for the Americans was but a year later, on October 17, 1781. The American Revolution would not officially end until April 19, 1783. Nine years of struggle had produced a new nation, and in the middle of that struggle was the winter in Morristown.

Benedict Arnold and Peggy lived in England the rest of their lives. Arnold later became a consultant on American policy to the Crown and died in 1801, with Peggy following three years later. Their four sons pursued careers in the British army. For all their efforts for fame and riches, the couple ended up in unmarked graves in a rundown part of London.

Lieutenant Colonel Simcoe would later participate in a raid with Benedict Arnold on Richmond, Virginia. He was wounded at Yorktown and returned to England and wrote a book, *A Journal of the Operations of the Queen's Rangers, from the End of the Year 1777, to the Conclusion of the Late American War*. He was the only participant in the kidnapping raid of 1780 to write about the attempt to abduct George Washington. He entered politics in 1790 and later became lieutenant governor of Upper Canada. Captain Beckwith never wrote about the kidnapping attempt and was later appointed governor and commander in chief in Bermuda. One possible reason the kidnapping raid might not have been written about was that George Washington had become a world figure and it might have been seen as an embarrassment to the British.

A National Historical Park in Morristown was created on March 1, 1933. Two hundred to three hundred thousand people come every year to Morristown and to visit the nearby encampment at Jockey Hollow and hear from park rangers the still little-known story of how men suffered through the worst winter of the century and how the American Revolution almost was lost.

Endnotes

Prologue
1. Jared Sparks, *The Writings of George Washington*, Vol. II (Boston: American Stationers Company, 1834), 262.
2. John Fitzpatrick, *The Writings of George Washington* (Washington: Government Printing Office, 1939), 293.
3. Ibid.
4. Ibid., 125.
5. Ibid., 217.
6. James Thacher, *A Military Journal during the American Revolutionary War* (Boston: Cottons and Barnard, 1827), 181.
7. Joseph Martin, *Ordinary Courage: The Revolutionary War Adventures of Joseph Plumb Martin* (West Sussex, United Kingdom: John Wiley, 2013), 113.
8. Ibid., 121.

Chapter 1. On the Frozen Hudson River
1. Christian McBurney, *Abductions in the American Revolution: Attempts to Kidnap George Washington, Benedict Arnold and Other Military and Civilian Leaders* (Jefferson, NC: McFarland and Company, 2016), 89.
2. Ibid.
3. Ibid.
4. Ibid., 83.

Chapter 2. General in Winter
1. George Washington, *The Writings of George Washington*, Vol. 12, 1790–1794, ed. Worthington Chauncey Ford (New York: G. P. Putnam's Sons, 1889), 399.
2. George Washington, *The Papers of George Washington*, Vol 14, ed. William Ferraro (Minneapolis: University of Minnesota, 1985), 497.
3. Louis Duncan, *Medical Men in the American Revolution 1775–1783* (Carlisle Barracks, PA: Medical Field Service School, 1931), 306.
4. Samuel Smith, *Winter at Morristown 1779–1780: The Darkest Hour* (Charlottesville, VA: Freneau's Press, 1979), 5.
5. Ibid.
6. Ibid.
7. Ibid.
8. Fitzpatrick, *Writings of George Washington*, 111.

9. Ibid., 101.

10. Ibid., 206.

11. George Washington, *The Papers of George Washington* (University of California, 1985), 336.

12. McBurney, *Abductions*, 86.

13. Ibid., 8.

14. Washington, *Writings*, Vol. 6, 1777–1778, 409.

15. Nathaniel Philbrick, *Valiant Ambition: George Washington, Benedict Arnold, and the Fate of the American Revolution* (New York: Viking, 2016), 68.

16. Washington Irving, *Life of George Washington*, Vol. 1 (University of Virginia, 1955), 234.

17. Paul K. Longmore, *The Invention of George Washington* (Charlottesville: University of Virginia Press, 1999), 182.

18. Robert F. Dalzell and Lee Baldwin Dalzell, *George Washington's Mount Vernon: At Home in Revolutionary America* (New York: Oxford University Press, 2000), 108.

19. David McCullough, *1776* (New York: Simon and Schuster, 2005), 45.

20. William Martin, *Citizen Washington* (New York: Tom Dougherty Associates, 2011), 472.

21. Washington, *The Writings of George Washington* (Boston: 1837), 229.

22. James Tyson, *An Outline of the Political and Social Life of George Washington* (Charlottesville: University of Virginia, 1895), 97.

23. Ibid.

24. Ibid.

25. Richard Steward, *American Military History* (Washington: Government Printing Office, 2006), 57.

26. Ron Chernow, *Alexander Hamilton* (New York: Penguin, 2005), 127.

27. Zoe Lowery, *The American Revolution* (New York: Britannica Educational Publishing, 2015), 126.

28. David Burg, *The American Revolution* (Boston: Facts on File, 2009), 287.

29. James R. Gaines, *For Liberty and Glory: Washington, Lafayette, and Their Revolutions* (New York: Norton, 2008), 131.

30. Washington, *The Writings of George Washington*, Part II (National Library, Washington, 1840), 151.

Chapter 3. General Simcoe's Affront

1. David Read, *The Life and Times of Gen. John Graves Simcoe* (Toronto: George Virtue, 1890), 57.

2. Ibid., 42.

3. Ibid., 40.

4. Ibid., 115.

5. Duncan Scott, *John Graves Simcoe* (Toronto: Morang and Company, 1906), 31.

6. John Simcoe, *Simcoe's Military Journal* (Boston: Bartlett and Wellford, 1844), 264.

7. Ibid., 277.

8. Ibid., 271.

9. Ibid., 283.

Chapter 4. Scott and Zelda
1. Philbrick, *Valiant Ambition,* 59.
2. Ibid., 221.
3. Ibid., 224.

Chapter 5. Log House City
1. Thacher, *Military Journal,* 215.
2. Ibid., 158.
3. Harold L. Peterson, *The Book of the Continental Soldier* (Ann Arbor, MI: Promontory Press, 1968), 227.
4. Thacher, *Military Journal,* 216.
5. Samuel Hazard, *Hazard's Register of Pennsylvania,* Vol. 4 (Philadelphia: Wm F. Geddes, 1829), 199.
6. Thacher, *Military Journal,* 189.
7. Ibid.
8. Ibid., 171.
9. John Nagy, *Rebellion in the Ranks: Mutinies of the American Revolution* (Yardley, PA: Westholme Publishing, 2007), 330.
10. Thacher, *Military Journal,* 186.
11. Ibid., 215.
12. Joseph Martin, *Memoir of a Revolutionary Soldier: The Narrative of Joseph Plum Martin* (Mineola, NY: Dover Publications, 2012), 94.
13. Ibid.
14. Ibid., 95.
15. Ray Raphael, *Founding Myths: Stories That Hide Our Patriotic Past* (Boston: New Press, 2014), 108.
16. Johann Conrad Döhla, *A Hessian Diary of the American Revolution* (Norman: University of Oklahoma Press, 1993), 119.
17. Robert Sullivan, *My American Revolution: A Modern Expedition through History's Forgotten Battlegrounds* (New York: Farrar, Straus, 2012), 204.
18. Thacher, *Military Journal,* 185.
19. Döhla, *Hessian Diary,* 119.
20. Thacher, *Military Journal,* 181.
21. Bruce Chadwick, *General and Mrs. Washington: The Untold Story of a Marriage and a Revolution* (Naperville, IL: Sourcebooks, 2007), 235.
22. Thacher, *Military Journal,* 181.
23. Ibid., 196.

Chapter 6. The Plot
1. Read, *Gen. John Graves Simcoe,* 10.
2. Ibid., 13.
3. Mary Fryer, *John Graves Simcoe, 1752–1806: A Biography* (Toronto: Dundurn Press, 1998), 40.

4. Read, *Gen. John Graves Simcoe,* 17.
5. Ibid., 67.
6. Simcoe, *Simcoe's Military Journal,* 130.
7. McBurney, *Abductions,* 83.
8. Simcoe, *Simcoe's Military Journal,* 33.
9. McBurney, *Abductions,* 85.
10. Ibid., 85.

Chapter 7. Sacricide
1. Brad Meltzer, *The First Conspiracy* (New York: Flatiron Books, 2019), 132.
2. Ibid., 192.
3. Ibid., 74.
4. Ibid., 75.
5. Sparks, *Writings of George Washington,* 358.
6. Fitzpatrick, *Writings of George Washington,* 422.
7. Washington, *Writings,* Vol. 3, 1775–1776, 466.
8. Meltzer, *The First Conspiracy,* 94.
9. Ibid., 135.
10. New York Department of State, Calendar of Historical Manuscripts (New York: Weed, Parsons and Company, 1868), 338.
11. George Washington, *Writings Being His Correspondence* (Chicago: University of Chicago, 1834), 415.
12. Meltzer, *The First Conspiracy,* 265.
13. Ibid., 265.
14. Ibid., 267.
15. Ibid., 297.
16. Washington, *Writings,* Vol. 4, 1776, 188.
17. George Washington, *Official Letters to the American Congress* (London: Caldwell Junior and Davies, 1796), 165.
18. Washington, George, *Official Letters to the Honorable American Congress* (Cambridge University Press, 2011), 174.
19. John Andrew, *The New England Historical and Genealogical Register,* Vol. 22 (Oxford, United Kingdom: Oxford University Press, 1869), 208.
20. James C. Rees, *George Washington's Leadership Lessons: What the Father of Our Country Can Teach Us About Effective Leadership and Character* (New York: Wiley, 2011), 42.
21. Wayne Whipple, *The Story-Life of Washington: A Life-History in 500 True Stories* (New York: John Winston, 1911), 272.
22. Andrew, *Historical and Geological Register,* 208.

Chapter 8. The Pent-Up General
1. Chernow, *Alexander Hamilton,* 126.
2. Ibid.
3. Ibid., 130.

4. Charles A. Conant, *Alexander Hamilton: A Biography* (New York: LuLu, 2016), 67.

5. George Washington, *The Papers of George Washington* (Charlottesville: University of Virginia, 1985), 508.

6. Sullivan, *My American Revolution,* 205.

7. McBurney, *Abductions,* 86.

8. James Thacher, *An Army Doctor's American Revolution Journal* (Mineola, NY: Dover Publications, 2019), 179.

9. Martin, Joseph, *The Revolutionary War Adventures* (Brandywine Press, University of Michigan, 1993), 104.

10. Army Medical Service, *Medical Men in American Revolution* (Washington DC, 1980), 68.

11. Thacher, *Military Journal,* 189.

12. Martin, Joseph, *Ordinary Courage,* Chapter 7, 104.

Chapter 9. The Hail Mary General

1. Fitzpatrick, *Writings of George Washington,* 473.

2. Washington, *The Writings of George Washington* (University of Michigan, 1834), 311.

3. Martin, *Ordinary Courage,* 43.

4. Michael Specter, *Denialism: How Irrational Thinking Harms the Planet and Threatens Our Lives* (New York: Penguin, 2009), 165.

5. Ashbel Green, *Historical Magazine* (Minneapolis: University of Minnesota, 1871), 361.

6. Fitzpatrick, *Writings of George Washington,* 29.

7. Jared Sparks, *Correspondence and Miscellaneous Papers* (University of California, 1847), 305.

8. Washington, *The Writings of George Washington* (University of Michigan, 1931), 14.

9. Thacher, *Military Journal,* 76.

Chapter 10. James Benedict Bond

1. Philbrick, *Valiant Ambition,* 243.

2. Ibid.

3. Ibid.

4. Ibid.

5. Ibid., 244.

6. Lauran Paine, *Benedict Arnold: Hero and Traitor* (New York: R. Hales, 1965), 145.

7. Philbrick, *Valiant Ambition,* 245.

8. Ibid.

9. Paine, *Benedict Arnold,* 145.

10. Ibid.

11. Ibid., 246

12. Ibid.

13. Ibid., 249.

14. Ibid.

15. Ibid.

16. Ibid., 250.

Chapter 11. The Most Daring Exploit
1. McBurney, *Abductions*, 86.
2. Ibid.
3. Ibid.
4. Ibid.
5. Ibid., 87.
6. Ibid.
7. Ibid., 89.

Chapter 12. The Seeds of Mutiny
1. Martin, *Ordinary Courage*, 100.
2. Sullivan, *My American Revolution*, 205.
3. Martin, *Ordinary Courage*, 97.
4. Ibid., 98.
5. Ibid., 109.
6. Ibid., 99.
7. Ibid.
8. John Barber, *Historical Collections of the State of New Jersey* (Boston: Harvard University, 1846), 387.
9. Bruce Lancaster, *From Lexington to Liberty: The Story of the American Revolution* (New York: Doubleday, 1955), 365.
10. Martin, *Ordinary Courage*, 125.

Chapter 13. The Trial of Benedict Arnold
1. James Kirby Martin, *Benedict Arnold, Revolutionary Hero: An American Warrior Reconsidered* (New York: NYU Press, 2000), 324.
2. George Dreher, *Longer Than Expected* (New York: Iron Horse Free Press, 1995), 111.
3. Fitzpatrick, *Writings of George Washington*, 363.
4. Philbrick, *Valiant Ambition*, 205.
5. Ibid., 233.
6. Ibid., 257.
7. Isaac N. Arnold, *The Life of Benedict Arnold: His Patriotism and His Treason* (Chicago: Jansen McClurg, 1905), 252.

Chapter 14. Valley Forge
1. Martin, *Ordinary Courage*, 68.
2. Bob Drury and Tom Clavin, *Valley Forge* (New York: Simon and Schuster, 2019), 238.
3. Daughters of the American Revolution, *The American Monthly Magazine*, Vol. 66 (Madison: University of Wisconsin, 1912), 599.
4. Philbrick, *Valiant Ambition*, 185.
5. Joseph Martin, *A Narrative of Some of the Adventures, Dangers and Sufferings of a Revolutionary Soldier* (New York: Glazier, Masters & Company, 1830), 75.
6. Henry Steele Commager and Richard B. Morris, *The Spirit of Seventy-six: The Story of the American Revolution as Told by Participants* (New York: Harper and Row, 1975), 638.
7. Drury and Clavin, *Valley Forge*, 166.

8. Ibid., 245.
9. Ibid., 252.
10. Ibid.
11. Ibid., 267.
12. Ibid., 268.
13. Ibid.
14. Ibid., 269.
15. Ibid.
16. Ibid., 270.
17. Ibid.
18. Gerald M. Carbone, *Nathanael Greene: A Biography of the American Revolution* (New York: St. Martin's, 2010), 91.
19. Drury and Clavin, *Valley Forge,* 266.
20. Ibid., 252.

Chapter 15. The Manic-Depressive

1. Christopher Hibbert, *Redcoats and Rebels: The American Revolutions through British Eyes* (Barnsley, South Yorkshire, United Kingdom: Pen and Sword Books, 2008), 250.
2. Stanley Weintraub, *Iron Tears: America's Battle for Freedom, Britain's Quagmire, 1775–1783* (New York: Free Press, 2005), 95.
3. James Paulding, *Paulding's Works* (Ann Arbor: University of Michigan, 1835), 178.
4. Chernow, *Alexander Hamilton,* 112.
5. Benton Rain Patterson, *Washington and Cornwallis: The Battle for America, 1775–1783* (New York: Taylor Trade, 2004), 192.

Chapter 16. Preparing to Kidnap George Washington

1. McBurney, *Abductions,* 87.
2. Ibid., 88.
3. Ibid., 89.
4. Ibid.
5. William P. Cumming, *The Fate of a Nation: The American Revolution through Contemporary Eyes* (Ann Arbor: University of Michigan Press, 1975), 234.
6. McBurney, *Abductions,* 90.

Chapter 17. Mr. Moore's Unspeakable Treason

1. Michael E. Newton, *Alexander Hamilton: The Formative Years* (New York: Eleftheria Publishing, 2015), 323.
2. Arnold, *Life of Benedict Arnold,* 252.
3. Ibid., 254.
4. Ibid.

Chapter 18. He Was but a Man

1. McBurney, *Abductions,* 90.
2. Fitzpatrick, *Writings of George Washington,* 470.

3. McBurney, *Abductions*, 85.
4. John W. Rae, *Morristown: A Military Headquarters of the American Revolution* (Charleston, SC: Arcadia Publishing, 2002), 31.
5. Ibid.
6. *The Pennsylvania Magazine of History and Biography* (Charlottesville: University of Virginia, 1920), 207.
7. Ibid.
8. Washington Irving, *Life of Washington* (University of Virginia, 1881), 438.
9. Ibid.

Chapter 19. The Diversion
1. McBurney, *Abductions*, 91.
2. Ibid.
3. Ibid.
4. Ibid., 92.
5. Ibid.
6. Nathan Hale, *Yale Alumni Weekly*, Vol. 15 (New Haven, CT: Yale University Press, 1906), 865.

Chapter 20. Desperate Measures
1. Washington, *Writings*, Vol. 8, 1779–1780, 160.
2. Ibid., 366.
3. Benson John Lossing, *Washington and the American Republic*, Vol. 2 (New York: Virtue and Yorsten, 1870), 666.

Chapter 21. The Coldest Night
1. Fitzpatrick, *Writings of George Washington*, 470.
2. Benjamin Huggins, "Raid across the Ice: The British Operation to Capture Washington," *Journal of the American Revolution*, December 17, 2013.

Chapter 22. The Indispensable Man
1. McCullough, *1776*, 79.
2. Washington Irving, *The Life of George Washington*, 2005, 63.
3. McCullough, *1776*, 130.
4. Ibid., 83.
5. Ibid.
6. *Proceedings of New York State Historical Society* (Boston: Harvard University, 1934), 128.
7. Bernard A. Drew, *Henry Knox and the Revolutionary War Trail in Western Massachusetts* (New York: McFarland, 2012), 156.
8. American Archives Documentary History of the United States, United States Congress, 1843, 295.
9. McCullough, *1776*, 84.
10. George Washington, *The Papers of George Washington* (University of Virginia, 1985) 29.

11. William Hazelgrove, *Henry Knox's Noble Train: The Story of a Boston Bookseller's Heroic Expedition That Saved the American Revolution* (Lanham, MD: Prometheus Books, 2020), 134.

12. Ibid., 116.

13. Charles Henry Jones, *History of the Campaign for the Conquest of Canada in 1776: From the Death of Montgomery to the Retreat of the British Army under Sir Guy Carleton* (Oxford, United Kingdom: Oxford University, 1882), 124.

14. McCullough, *1776*, 85.

15. Fitzpatrick, *Writings of George Washington*, 355.

16. Thacher, *Military Journal*, 39.

17. David McCullough, *John Adams* (New York: Simon and Schuster, 2001), 76.

18. Hazelgrove, *Henry Knox's Noble Train*, 202.

19. Ibid., 204.

20. Thacher, *Military Journal*, 49.

21. Washington, *The Writings of George Washington* (Oxford, 1833), 340.

22. Don Higginbotham, *George Washington and the American Military Tradition* (Athens: University of Georgia Press, 1987), 69.

23. Washington, *The Writings of George Washington* (The British Library, 1834), 543.

24. Roland Usher, *The Rise of the American People* (Boston: Harvard University, 1913), 137.

25. McCullough, *1776*, 273.

26. Thacher, James, *Journal of the Revolution* (Harvard, 1862), 70.

27. Cumming, *The Fate of a Nation*, 136.

28. William S. Stryker, *The Battles of Trenton and Princeton* (New York: Farrar, Straus, 2012), 217.

29. Hezekiah Niles, *Continental Offering: Republication of the Principles and Acts of the Revolution in America* (Cambridge, MA: Harvard University, 1876), 249.

30. David Hackett Fischer, *Washington's Crossing* (New York: Oxford University Press, 2006), 228.

31. Stuart Murray, *Washington's Farewell: The Final Parting with His Officers after Victory in the Revolution* (Mooresville: Indiana University, 1999), 99.

32. Isaac Newton Phillips, *George Washington* (Penn State University, 1903), 33.

33. Thacher, *Military Journal*, 71.

34. McCullough, *1776*, 280.

35. Philbrick, *Valiant Ambition*, 76.

36. Thacher, *Military Journal*, 64.

Chapter 23. The Black Hussars

1. McBurney, *Abductions*, 88.

Chapter 24. The Insomniac General

1. Fitzpatrick, *Writings of George Washington*, 432.

2. Ibid., 239.

3. Robert L. O'Connell, *Revolutionary: George Washington at War* (New York: Random House, 2019), 228.

4. Gaines, *For Liberty and Glory*, 131.
5. John Miller, *Triumph of Freedom* (New York: Little, Brown, 1948), 483.
6. Sparks, *Writings of George Washington*, 67.
7. John Marshall, *The Life of George Washington* (Columbus: Ohio State University, 1845), 37.
8. Washington Madison Papers Collected, 1892, 10.
9. George Bancroft, *History of the United States* (Boston: Little, Brown, 1848), 443.
10. Chadwick, *General and Mrs. Washington*, 245.

Chapter 25. The Second Diversion
1. McBurney, *Abductions*, 92.
2. Ibid.

Chapter 27. George Washington's Fate
1. McBurney, *Abductions*, 93.
2. Christian McBurney, *The Plot to Kidnap Washington*, History.net.
3. McBurney, *Abductions*, 93.

Chapter 28. The Circumspect General
1. McBurney, *Abductions*, 94.
2. Ibid.
3. Ibid.
4. Ibid.
5. McBurney, *The Plot to Kidnap Washington*.
6. McBurney, *Abductions*, 95.
7. Ibid.
8. Ibid.
9. Ibid.

Chapter 29. The Stressed-Out Family Man
1. Clare Brandt, *The Man in the Mirror: A Life of Benedict Arnold* (New York: Random House, 1994), 190.
2. Philbrick, *Valiant Ambition*, 261.
3. *Omnibook Magazine*, New York, Omnibook, 1941, 14.
4. Arnold, *Life of Benedict Arnold*, 262.
5. Philbrick, *Valiant Ambition*, 263.

Chapter 30. Some Violent Convulsion
1. Fitzpatrick, *Writings of George Washington*, 512.
2. Washington, *The Writings of George Washington* (University of Michigan, 1889), 147.
3. Thacher, *Military Journal*, 231.
4. Ibid., 233.
5. Ibid., 197.

6. *Journal of the American Congress* (Washington: United States Congress, Government Printing Office, 1823), 448.

7. *Journals of the Continental Congress, 1774–1789* (Washington: United States Congress, Government Printing Office, 1910), 356.

8. James R. Arnold and Roberta Weiner, eds., *Understanding U.S. Military Conflicts through Primary Sources* (Santa Barbara, CA: ABC-CLIO, 2016), 144.

9. Washington, *The Writings of George Washington* (University of Michigan, 1931), 394.

10. Paul Smith, *Letters of Delegates to Congress, 1774–1789* (Washington: Library of Congress, Government Printing Office, 1976), 106.

Chapter 31. The Volcano Explodes

1. Gary B. Nash, *The Unknown American Revolution: The Unruly Birth of Democracy and the Struggle to Create America* (New York: Penguin, 2006), 357.

2. Washington Irving, *The Life of George Washington*, 2005, 19.

3. Gaines, *For Liberty and Glory*, 133.

4. Philbrick, *Valiant Ambition*, 266.

5. Ibid., 267.

6. Ibid.

7. O'Connell, *Revolutionary*, 228.

8. Ibid.

9. Thacher, *Military Journal*, 197.

10. Ibid., 236.

11. Martin, *Ordinary Courage*, 121.

12. Ibid., 105.

13. Ibid., 122.

14. Ibid., 135.

15. Ibid., 122.

16. Ibid., 106.

17. Sparks, *Writings of George Washington*, 57.

Chapter 32. Bonnie and Clyde

1. Philbrick, *Valiant Ambition*, 268.

2. Ibid., 269.

3. Ibid.

4. Ibid.

5. Jack Edward Shay, *The Dock of Broken Dreams: Benedict Arnold, John André, and the Women Who Loved Them* (Bloomington, IN: Xlibris, 1999), 339.

6. Philbrick, *Valiant Ambition*, 270.

Chapter 33. The Darkest Hour

1. Washington, *The Writings of George Washington* (Michigan State University, 1780), 461.

2. Philbrick, *Valiant Ambition*, 266.

Chapter 34. The French Component
1. Philbrick, *Valiant Ambition*, 198.
2. Ibid., 216.
3. Ibid., 271.

Chapter 35. Americans Fight Like Bulldogs
1. Matthew H. Spring, *With Zeal and Bayonets Only: The British Army on Campaign in North America, 1775–1783* (Norman: University of Oklahoma Press, 2012), 133.
2. Paul Smith, *Letters of Delegates*, 291.

Chapter 36. The Neurotic Returns
1. Samuel Smith, *Winter at Morristown*, 40.
2. Ibid.
3. Ibid.
4. Ibid.
5. Ibid.
6. Thomas Fleming, *The Battle of Springfield* (Newark: New Jersey Historical Society, 1975), 18.
7. James Thomas Flexner, *The Traitor and the Spy* (Syracuse, NY: Syracuse University Press, 1991), 310.
8. Thacher, *Military Journal*, 240.
9. Ibid.
10. Ashbel Green, *The Life of Ashbel Green, V.D.M.* (New York: Robert Carter and Brothers, 1849), 121.

Chapter 37. Benedict Arnold's Final Play
1. Washington, *Writings*, Vol. 8, 1779–1780, 364.
2. Dave R. Palmer, *George Washington and Benedict Arnold: A Tale of Two Patriots* (Washington: Regnery, 2006), 326.
3. Cornel Lengyel, *I, Benedict Arnold: The Anatomy of Treason* (New York: Doubleday, 1960), 26.
4. Philbrick, *Valiant Ambition*, 273.
5. Richard Rush, *Washington in Domestic Life: From Original Letters and Manuscripts* (New York: Lippincott, 1857), 80.
6. Ibid.
7. Philbrick, *Valiant Ambition*, 274.
8. Flexner, *The Traitor and the Spy*, 317.
9. Philbrick, *Valiant Ambition*, 285.
10. Ibid., 290.
11. Ibid.
12. Ibid., 291.
13. Ibid., 294.

14. Joshua Smith, *An Authentic Narrative of the Causes* (Ann Arbor: University of Michigan, 1809), 25.

15. Ibid.

16. Ibid., 27.

17. Philbrick, *Valiant Ambition,* 299.

18. Treman, *The History of the Treman,* 1901, 844.

19. *Chambers's Edinburgh Journal,* Vols. 5 and 6 (Austin: University of Texas, 1837), 355.

20. Willard Steele Randall, *George Washington* (New York: Henry Holt, 1998), 380.

21. Ibid.

22. Fitzpatrick, *Writings of George Washington,* 95.

23. Rod Gragg, *By the Hand of Providence* (New York: Howard Books, 2012), 164.

24. Thacher, *Military Journal,* 215.

25. William Johnson, *Sketches of Life and Correspondence* (Boston: Harvard University, 1822), 208.

26. Albert Hart, *American History Told by Contemporaries* (Charlottesville: University of Virginia, 1908), 516.

27. Johnson, *Sketches,* 200.

28. Arnold, *Life of Benedict Arnold,* 300.

29. Winthrop Sargent, *The Life and Career of Major John André, Adjutant-General of the British Army in America* (Boston: Ticknor and Fields, 1861), 384.

30. John Anderson, *The United States Reader* (1876), 204.

31. Newton, *Alexander Hamilton,* 347.

32. Thacher, *Military Journal,* 225.

33. Ibid., 225.

34. Ibid.

35. Ibid.

36. Philbrick, *Valiant Ambition,* 318.

37. Ibid.

38. Thacher, James, *The American Revolution* (Hurlbut, 1860), 215.

Bibliography

American Archives Documentary History of the United States, United States Congress, Washington, 1843.

Andrew, John. *The New England Historical and Genealogical Register*. Vol. 22. Oxford, United Kingdom: Oxford University Press, 1869.

Arnold, Isaac N. *The Life of Benedict Arnold: His Patriotism and His Treason*. Chicago: Jansen McClurg, 1905.

Arnold, James R., and Roberta Wiener, eds. *Understanding U.S. Military Conflicts through Primary Sources*. Santa Barbara, CA: ABC-CLIO, 2016.

Bancroft, George. *History of the United States*. Boston: Little, Brown, 1848.

Barber, John. *Historical Collections of the State of New Jersey*. Boston: Harvard University, 1846.

Brandt, Clare. *The Man in the Mirror: A Life of Benedict Arnold*. New York: Random House, 1994.

Burg, David. *The American Revolution*. Boston: Facts on File, 2009.

Carbone, Gerald M. *Nathanael Greene: A Biography of the American Revolution*. New York: St. Martin's, 2010.

Chadwick, Bruce. *General and Mrs. Washington: The Untold Story of a Marriage and a Revolution*. Naperville, IL: Sourcebooks, 2007.

Chambers's Edinburgh Journal. Vol. 5 and 6. Austin: University of Texas, 1837.

Chernow, Ron. *Alexander Hamilton*. New York: Penguin, 2005.

Commager, Henry Steele, and Richard B. Morris. *The Spirit of Seventy-six: The Story of the American Revolution as Told by Participants*. New York: Harper and Row, 1975.

Conant, Charles A. *Alexander Hamilton: A Biography*. New York: LuLu, 2016.

Cumming, William P. *The Fate of a Nation: The American Revolution through Contemporary Eyes*. Ann Arbor: University of Michigan Press, 1975.

Dalzell, Robert F., and Lee Baldwin Dalzell. *George Washington's Mount Vernon: At Home in Revolutionary America*. New York: Oxford University Press, 2000.

Daughters of the American Revolution. *The American Monthly Magazine*. Vol. 66. Madison: University of Wisconsin, 1912.

Döhla, Johann Conrad. *A Hessian Diary of the American Revolution*. Norman: University of Oklahoma Press, 1993.

Dreher, George Kelsey. *Longer Than Expected*. New York: Iron Horse Free Press, 1995.

Drew, Bernard A. *Henry Knox and the Revolutionary War Trail in Western Massachusetts*. New York: McFarland, 2012.

Drury, Bob, and Tom Clavin. *Valley Forge*. New York: Simon and Schuster, 2019.

Duncan, Louis. *Medical Men in the American Revolution 1775–1783*. Carlisle Barracks, PA: Medical Field Service School, 1931.

Fischer, David Hackett. *Washington's Crossing*. New York: Oxford University Press, 2006.

Fitzpatrick, John. *The Writings of George Washington*. Washington: Government Printing Office, 1939.

Fleming, Thomas. *The Battle of Springfield*. Newark: New Jersey Historical Society, 1975.

Flexner, James Thomas. *The Traitor and the Spy*. Syracuse, NY: Syracuse University Press, 1991.

Fryer, Mary. *John Graves Simcoe, 1752–1806: A Biography*. Toronto: Dundurn Press, 1998.

Gaines, James R. *For Liberty and Glory: Washington, Lafayette, and Their Revolutions*. New York: Norton, 2008.

Gragg, Rod. *By the Hand of Providence*. New York: Howard Books, 2012.

Green, Ashbel. *Historical Magazine*. Minneapolis: University of Minnesota, 1871.

Green, Ashbel. *The Life of Ashbel Green, V.D.M.* New York: Robert Carter and Brothers, 1849.

Hale, Nathan. *Yale Alumni Weekly*. Vol. 15. New Haven, CT: Yale University Press, 1906.

Hart, Albert. *American History Told by Contemporaries*. Charlottesville: University of Virginia, 1908.

Hazard, Samuel. *Hazard's Register of Pennsylvania*. Vol. 4. Philadelphia: Wm F. Geddes, 1829.

Hazelgrove, William. *Henry Knox's Noble Train: The Story of a Boston Bookseller's Heroic Expedition That Saved the American Revolution*. Lanham, MD: Prometheus Books, 2020.

Heffner, Richard, and Alexander Heffner. *A Documentary History of the United States*. 10th ed. New York: Signet, 2018.

Hibbert, Christopher. *Redcoats and Rebels: The American Revolutions through British Eyes*. Barnsley, South Yorkshire, United Kingdom: Pen and Sword Books, 2008.

Higginbotham, Don. *George Washington and the American Military Tradition*. Athens: University of Georgia Press, 1987.

Huggins, Benjamin. "Raid across the Ice: The British Operation to Capture Washington." *Journal of the American Revolution*. December 17, 2013.

Irving, Washington. *Life of George Washington*. 5 vols. New York: Putnam, 1869.

Johnson, William. *Sketches of Life and Correspondence*. Boston: Harvard University, 1822.

Jones, Charles Henry. *History of the Campaign for the Conquest of Canada in 1776: From the Death of Montgomery to the Retreat of the British Army under Sir Guy Carleton*. Oxford, United Kingdom: Oxford University, 1882.

Journal of the American Congress. Washington: United States Congress, Government Printing Office, 1823.

Journals of the Continental Congress. 1774–1789. Washington: United States Congress, Government Printing Office, 1910.

Lancaster, Bruce. *From Lexington to Liberty: The Story of the American Revolution*. New York: Doubleday, 1955.

Lengyel, Cornel. *I, Benedict Arnold: The Anatomy of Treason*. New York: Doubleday, 1960.

Longmore, Paul K. *The Invention of George Washington*. Charlottesville: University of Virginia Press, 1999.

Lossing, Benson John. *Washington and the American Republic*. Vol. 2. New York: Virtue and Yorsten, 1870.

Lowery, Zoe. *The American Revolution*. New York: Britannica Educational Publishing, 2015.

Marshall, John. *The Life of George Washington*. Columbus: Ohio State University, 1845.

Martin, James Kirby. *Benedict Arnold, Revolutionary Hero: An American Warrior Reconsidered*. New York: NYU Press, 2000.

Martin, Joseph. *Memoir of a Revolutionary Soldier: The Narrative of Joseph Plumb Martin*. Mineola, NY: Dover Publications, 2012.

Martin, Joseph. *A Narrative of Some of the Adventures, Dangers and Sufferings of a Revolutionary Soldier*. New York: Glazier, Masters & Company, 1830.

Martin, Joseph. *Ordinary Courage: The Revolutionary War Adventures of Joseph Plumb Martin*. West Sussex, United Kingdom: John Wiley, 2013.

Martin, Joseph. *The Revolutionary War of George Washington*. Minneapolis: University of Minnesota, 1985.

Martin, William. *Citizen Washington*. New York: Tom Dougherty Associates, 2011.

McBurney, Christian. *Abductions in the American Revolution: Attempts to Kidnap George Washington, Benedict Arnold and Other Military and Civilian Leaders*. Jefferson, NC: McFarland and Company, 2016.

McBurney, Christian, *The Plot to Kidnap Washington*, historynet.com.

McCullough, David. *John Adams*. New York: Simon and Schuster, 2001.

McCullough, David. *1776*. New York: Simon and Schuster, 2005.

Meltzer, Brad. *The First Conspiracy*. New York: Flatiron Books, 2019.

Miller, John. *Triumph of Freedom*. New York: Little, Brown, 1948.

Murray, Stuart. *Washington's Farewell: The Final Parting with His Officers after Victory in the Revolution*. Mooresville: Indiana University, 1999.

Nagy, John A. *Rebellion in the Ranks: Mutinies of the American Revolution*. Yardley, PA: Westholme Publishing, 2007.

Nash, Gary B. *The Unknown American Revolution: The Unruly Birth of Democracy and the Struggle to Create America*. New York: Penguin, 2006.

New York Department of State. Calendar of Historical Manuscripts. New York: Weed, Parsons and Company, 1868.

Newton, Michael E. *Alexander Hamilton: The Formative Years*. New York: Eleftheria Publishing, 2015.

Niles, Hezekiah. *Continental Offering: Republication of the Principles and Acts of the Revolution in America*. Cambridge, MA: Harvard University, 1876.

O'Connell, Robert L. *Revolutionary: George Washington at War*. New York: Random House, 2019.

Paine, Lauran. *Benedict Arnold: Hero and Traitor*. New York: R. Hales, 1965.

Palmer, Dave R. *George Washington and Benedict Arnold: A Tale of Two Patriots*. Washington: Regnery, 2006.

Patterson, Benton Rain. *Washington and Cornwallis: The Battle for America, 1775–1783*. New York: Taylor Trade, 2004.

Paulding, James. *Paulding's Works*. Ann Arbor: University of Michigan, 1835.

The Pennsylvania Magazine of History and Biography. Charlottesville: University of Virginia, 1920.

Peterson, Harold L. *The Book of the Continental Soldier*. Ann Arbor, MI: Promontory Press, 1968.

Philbrick, Nathaniel. *Valiant Ambition: George Washington, Benedict Arnold, and the Fate of the American Revolution*. New York: Viking, 2016.

Phillips, Isaac Newton. *George Washington: An Address*. Penn State University, 1903

Proceedings of New York State Historical Society. Boston: Harvard University, 1934.

Rae, John W. *Morristown: A Military Headquarters of the American Revolution*. Charleston, SC: Arcadia Publishing, 2002.

Randall, Willard Steele. *George Washington*. New York: Henry Holt, 1998.

Raphael, Ray. *Founding Myths: Stories That Hide Our Patriotic Past*. Boston: New Press, 2014.

Read, David. *The Life and Times of Gen. John Graves Simcoe*. Toronto: George Virtue, 1890.

Rees, James C. *George Washington's Leadership Lessons: What the Father of Our Country Can Teach Us About Effective Leadership and Character*. New York: Wiley, 2011.

Rush, Richard. *Washington in Domestic Life: From Original Letters and Manuscripts*. New York: Lippincott, 1857.

Sargent, Winthrop. *The Life and Career of Major John André, Adjutant-General of the British Army in America*. Boston: Ticknor and Fields, 1861.

Scott, Duncan. *John Graves Simcoe*. Toronto: Morang and Company, 1906.

Shay, Jack Edward. *The Dock of Broken Dreams: Benedict Arnold, John André, and the Women Who Loved Them*. Bloomington, IN: Xlibris, 1999.

Simcoe, John. *Simcoe's Military Journal*. Boston: Bartlett and Wellford, 1844.

Smith, Joshua. *An Authentic Narrative of the Causes*. Ann Arbor: University of Michigan, 1809.

Smith, Paul. *Letters of Delegates to Congress, 1774–1789*. Washington: Library of Congress, Government Printing Office, 1976.

Smith, Samuel. *Winter at Morristown 1779–1780: The Darkest Hour*. Charlottesville, VA: Freneau's Press, 1979.

Sparks, Jared. *The Writings of George Washington*. Boston: American Stationers Company, 1834.

Specter, Michael. *Denialism: How Irrational Thinking Harms the Planet and Threatens Our Lives*. New York: Penguin, 2009.

Spring, Matthew H. *With Zeal and Bayonets Only: The British Army on Campaign in North America, 1775–1783*. Norman: University of Oklahoma Press, 2012.

Steward, Richard. *American Military History*. Washington: Government Printing Office, 2006.

Stryker, William S. *The Battles of Trenton and Princeton*. New York: Farrar, Straus, 2012.

Sullivan, Robert. *My American Revolution: A Modern Expedition through History's Forgotten Battlegrounds*. New York: Farrar, Straus, 2012.

Thacher, James. *A Military Journal during the American Revolutionary War*. Boston: Cottons and Barnard, 1827.

Thacher, James. *An Army Doctor's American Revolution Journal*. Mineola, NY: Dover Publications, 2019.

Treman, *The History of the Treman*. Ithaca, NY: Press of the *Ithaca Democrat*, 1901.

Tyson, James. *An Outline of the Political and Social Life of George Washington*. Charlottesville: University of Virginia, 1895.

Usher, Roland. *The Rise of the American People*. Boston: Harvard University, 1913.

Washington, George. *Official Letters to the American Congress*. London: Caldwell Junior and Davies, 1796.

Washington, George. *Writings Being His Correspondence*. Chicago: University of Chicago, 1834.

Washington Madison Papers Collected, Harvard University, Boston, 1892.

Washington, George. *The Writings of George Washington*. 14 vols. Ed. Worthington Chauncey Ford. New York: G. P. Putnam's Sons, 1889.

Weintraub, Stanley. *Iron Tears: America's Battle for Freedom, Britain's Quagmire, 1775–1783*. New York: Free Press, 2005.

Whipple, Wayne. *The Story-Life of Washington: A Life-History in 500 True Stories*. New York: John Winston, 1911.

Index

Note: Upper case **bold letters** indicate photo/illustration plates.